Life and Jazz Stories

a

jazz musician's
memoir

JAY THOMAS

Life and Jazz Stories

a

jazz musician's memoir

MCVOUTY PUBLISHING

CONTACT INFORMATION

JAY THOMAS

(206) 399-6800

www.jaythomasjazz.com

jaythomasjazz@aol.com

McVouty Publishing
(541) 388-0285

The critics say...

From the Vault: Seattle's Jay Thomas Tells His Story

Book Review, July 2021 By Paul de Barros

Veteran Seattle musician Jay Thomas' dazzling new autobiography, **Life and Jazz Stories**, bristles with the color, humor and detail of a picaresque novel while at the same time serving as a mini-history of local jazz from the 1960s to the present. It is a blow-by-blow account of one artist's musical development and a humble confession of recovery from a heroin addiction. On the page, Thomas comes across much as he does in person — witty, hip, eager, curious, vulnerable, and slightly amused by the craziness of it all. Refreshingly, he often sounds as excited about other players as himself. His stories about where and when he suddenly gained new musical insights are as priceless as they are rare in first-person jazz works. His musical descriptions such as, Tony Williams playing a "flibbertygibbet with a trap door hidden in it"are the very substance of good jazz writing. Thomas shares a plethora of hilarious insider stories, like the night he cold-called Thelonious Monk to complain that he couldn't find any good jazz in New York or when he dissed an arrogant Roy Hargrove at a jam session whispering in his ear, "You sound beautiful, man…we used to sound that way in the '60s." Sometimes the narrative is a bit dizzying (Thomas is not one for citing dates; however, he does offer 127 extensive endnotes about various people and institutions). Likewise, the book could definitely use a chronology and an index, but in a way that's all part of its conversational charm.

Thomas has become an integral part of pivotal Seattle area endeavors such as the Jim Knapp Orchestra, the Seattle

Repertory Jazz Orchestra, the Port Townsend Jazz Festival faculty and band, and the circus-style European theatre project Teatro ZinZanni. As a sidelight, Thomas also became an obsessive seeker (and trader) of instrumental gear, a pursuit that helped endear him to a cadre of Japanese musicians with whom he has been seriously working and recording since he first toured Japan in 1985.

For perhaps obvious reasons, given the temptations that once snared him on the road, Thomas did not return to New York where his talents certainly would have been more widely amplified. Thomas never directly addresses his decision to stay in the Pacific Northwest, but makes it clear he knows the score when he writes, "As far as jazz magazines and critics are concerned, Seattle is pretty far off the beaten trail" and when he refers to other local players as being in the "wrong town" if they want to get famous. Ultimately, it doesn't matter–at least for Seattle fans. Thomas figured out a way to produce great music and survive, immensely enriching the Seattle scene as both a player and teacher and passing on the tradition to a new generation. Indeed, Thomas is a bridge figure of sorts between the embers of Seattle's golden Jackson Street era and its modern era. For decades, we have had the music. Now we have the stories, too. Bravo.

To read the entire Earshot Jazz review:
https://www.earshot.org/project/2021-07-from-the-vault-seattles-jay-thomas-tells-his-story/

More ... **The Critics Say ....**

Although the trumpet is his main instrument, Mr. Thomas's full, sensual sound on tenor is equally compelling and personal. On all his instruments, there is constant spontaneity. And on ballads, Mr. Thomas exemplifies Quincy Jones's observation:' the melody is the most powerful thing there is Melody does something electrical to your soul."
Nat Hentoff ... The Wall Street Journal, April 19, 2000

"this CD demonstrates beyond doubt what a talented musician he is. He has a superb full sound, wonderful time, a delightfully relaxed a confident approach that stems from a superb technique, and is full of fresh ideas. He reminds me a little of both Clifford Brown and Kenny Dorham, but only a little. Mainly he is his own man. I shall be surprised if this is not one of my albums of the year".
Mike Shera ... International Jazz Journal, London, England

"A perfect example is Seattle trumpeter Jay Thomas' new album, "360 Degrees", on the Scottish Hep Jazz label. Thomas, who plays trumpet, flugelhorn, alto sax, tenor sax, alto flute and even adds a wordless vocal part at one point, would attract attention if only for his versatility. He also has a great ear for tunes...". **Bob Blumenthal ... Boston Globe**

It's hard to name a musician who might more aptly fill the role of "artist in residence" at this year's Earshot Jazz Festival than multi-instrumentalist Jay Thomas. One of the few remaining links between our city's storied jazz past and its promising present, the 69-year-old trumpet and reed player

has enjoyed a mostly local career that spans six decades.
Paul deBarros ... Earshot, September 2019

"Earshot Jazz bestowed Jay Thomas the honor of serving as the Artist in Residence for the 2019 Earshot Jazz Festival -- now it's the Jazz Journalists Association's turn to celebrate his heroism. At nearly 71 years of age, he's playing better than ever, thoughtfully, patiently and with welcome for all. For 50 years he has embodied the spirit of Seattle jazz. His sublime creativity and ability to express it on a variety of instruments has lifted Thomas to an important place in the history of west coast jazz. May he continue to do so, expanding on his legacy and that of the city which raised this Jazz Hero.
Paul Rauch, 2019

"I Want to Talk About You." When he finished the Eckstine song, Thomas told the crowd that when he first heard John Coltrane's recording, "my hair stood up and I got chills." His own playing on the piece generated a similar sensation. On trumpet, Thomas' lyricism and harmonic inventions make him one of today's most interesting soloist on the instrument
Doug Ramsey, January 2013

"Jay Thomas, a Walton protégé from Seattle, is a protean performer. A fluent soloist on trumpet and flugelhorn, he switches to flute and, to top it off, the amazing Thomas plays tenor sax. If fame reaches him now, it won't come a moment too soon".
Leonard Feather ... Five stars Los Angeles Times

DEDICATION

I dedicate this book to my father, Marvin, "the river that runs through this," and the women in my life; Marilyn, Jules, Becca, and most importantly, my mother Joanne, who always kept the door open for me.

TABLE OF CONTENTS

ACKNOWLEDGEMENTS

Cover Painting:
Dave Coleman, Sr.

Cover Design:
Marvin Thomas
UltraKahn

Photographs:
Daniel Sheehan
Dan Marcus
Lisa Glynn
Harold Rosencrans
Many, many in Japan

Formatting:
Christiann Thomas
MarvinThomas

Proofreading:
Alisha Thomas
Dan Marcus
Becca Duran
Jim Wilke
Marvin Thomas
Paul deBarros

Jazz Journalists Articles
Paul Rauch
Paul de Barros
Doug Ramsey

FORWARD

Legacy is a fleeting notion. It is incomprehensible in real-time when a career hits high points when certain doors open to quantitative opportunity. Jay Thomas can tell you a thing or two about that, based on his own personal experience as a jazz artist over half a century. His story includes playing on the Seattle scene as a teenager, and a career leading to opportunities hampered by, among other things, drug addiction. It is as well a story of overcoming those obstacles and producing an impressive legacy of recording and performance credits.

Now approaching 71 years of age, Thomas is one of the rare musicians that can play both trumpet and saxophone with virtuosity. At last, several recent recordings will provide the opportunity for his music to orbit around the jazz universe, outside of the Pacific Northwest, where he has attained legendary status.

Thomas grew up in the middle of the fertile jazz scene of the sixties in Seattle. Still a high school junior, Thomas began to gain a reputation as a formidable player, with a deep connection to the blues expressed through a style often described as melodic and lyrical. His probing style on trumpet began to reflect the progressive changes in jazz largely due to saxophonists like John Coltrane.

Thomas' teenage years were accentuated by recognition from Downbeat Magazine and Leonard Feather, resulting in a one-year scholarship at the Berklee School of Music in Boston. In 1968, he moved to New York, landing a notable gig in Machito's Latin Band, and recorded with James Moody as well. He was just twenty years old and now had one of his original compositions on a major jazz release. Moody recorded "The New Spirit" on his 1970 release, The Teachers (Perception, 1970).

Thomas was living the jazz life in New York City, dodging, and at times, falling into the many social distractions along the way. Still, while living in the now-iconic Albert Hotel, he discovered the tenor saxophone, and in the process, his musical and creative identity.

Thomas moved back to Seattle in 1978 and began to frequent Parnell's Jazz Club in the Pioneer Square neighborhood. Thomas performed at Parnell's with such notables as George Cables, Bill Mays, Zoot Sims, Harold Land, and Slim Gaillard, and made friends with jazz legends such as Sims, Chet Baker, and Sal Nistico.

In 1982, after another venture into the New York musical scene, Thomas returned to Seattle for good to address his illness, which had by this time completely dominated his life. His fate seemed to be tied to that which had taken so many of the greats that preceded him. He knew the stability of the family and familiar surroundings were important factors in finally staring his addiction down and placing it firmly in his past.

"That was the end of the line where I went into a treatment facility to get that part of my life handled," he recalls with a sigh. He would spend the next three years fighting this battle until completely free of drugs in 1985. November 1, 1985, to be exact.

He found himself focused and energetic, anxious to move forward with a career that, in a real sense, had been severely curtailed for some fifteen years. "I was this walking ball of energy and didn't know which way to go. I was an emotional wreck but busy trying to be employed all the time. At that point, things really changed," says Thomas. His dad Marvin arranged an opportunity to perform with Cedar Walton, David Williams, and Billy Higgins that eventually led to his first record, Easy Does It (Discovery Records), 1989.

Thomas was featured in a full-page article in the Wall Street Journal by Nat Hentoff in April of 2000. It appeared that finally, the jazz world would become fully cognizant of this master of the realm, sequestered in the great northwest.

Today Thomas is a member of one of Japan's leading big bands, CUG (Continued in the Underground Jazz Orchestra), and co-leads a sextet with Kohama Yasuhiro and Atsushi Ikeda. He records and performs in Japan several times a year. His efforts have built a bridge between Seattle and Japan's fertile and enthusiastic jazz scene.

Most jazz talent arises from academia these days, with most young players graduating from schools like Berklee and the Manhattan School of Music. Thomas provides mentorship in the oral tradition, much like his experiences as a teenage phenom in Seattle. Those fortunate enough to study privately with him are treated to an individual approach that places an emphasis on ear training. Thomas has never forgotten the sage advice he received from his elders on the Seattle scene.

In the age of digital media, the music of this jazz warrior will perhaps take its place among the top jazz artists of his era. It should call attention to the lyrical prose that is his signature, to the broad and pure sound that is his identity, that which we have known in Seattle for 50 years.

Paul Rauch

PROLOGUE

2020 and Covid-19

Today is November 9th, 2020. For the last seven months, the entire world has changed due to the pandemic of COVID-19 (novel coronavirus 2019). We started to hear about this sickness in January, but it seemed far away and was made light of by many. At first, it was just a Chinese problem, and then, through little news clips here and there, we heard some cruise ship passengers were infected. All the while, our government, led by Trump, was saying, "We got this" no cause for alarm.

Then, in March, a nursing home in Seattle was infected with COVID-19, and the fatalities just skyrocketed. New York City got it next, and thousands started to die in Manhattan, all the while, Trump kept saying, "We got it, don't worry."

Before this happened, I had traveled to Japan twice a year for the last 23 years to tour with Yasuhiro Kohama. Usually, I go in the spring and the fall. I had already purchased my ticket and everything. The tour had 19 confirmed dates in different clubs in Japan. Once again, I was stoked to go and do some serious playing and hanging with my Japanese pals.

The bookings in Japan were starting to fall away; my friend Kohama thought they were making way too much out of it! At the last minute, I canceled my ticket, without a penalty from the airlines, and decided to stay home. Shortly after, our Governor of Washington, Jay Inslee, instituted a policy of sheltering at home. The 5th Avenue Theater and Benaroya Hall, and Kirkland Performance Center, all places I play, closed their doors to live concerts and shows. Everything stopped in the whole world as far as live music was concerned.

Some clubs will survive, but many will be out of business. No telling what the scene will look like when we pull out of this; the estimate is that it will be a year or so at least before people start getting brave enough to go to restaurants and clubs. Places that serve alcohol and where there is intimate seating are all affected at this point.

+++++

I just turned 71 the other day but have no intention of stopping any of my playing or practicing. I immediately started in on a new practice routine. The chops have responded nicely with this daily practice time (strong high G).

I have done a few recordings where we all played our parts separately, and then we put them together later. That is kind of cool. We work from a metronome so we can sync up the parts. We use cameras or cell phones as well as mics to make the recordings. I did this with my friends in Japan on an arrangement of Jimmy Rowles's Peacocks and we played together long distance.

I have done a few outdoor gigs, one for a wedding and another for a New Orleans-style funeral parade. That is the tough thing about this time; memorials and church services and those sorts of things are out.

I am getting together twice a week and playing with an organist Scott Lytle and guitar player Milo Petersen. We are working on new material and various things together in a workshop format. Our Quintet with Mike Van Bebber has been cautiously getting together at a close-by school where we rent a large rehearsal space.

I still play with the jam band Pink Farm on Wednesday evenings; we practice social distancing.

Played an album release party at a club called the Royal Room and a few streaming gigs from Boxley's. We do live streaming on the internet. The musicians are stationed 6 feet apart, at least.

I played a *Birth of the Cool* concert at Benaroya Hall with the Seattle Repertory Jazz Orchestra (SRJO). The *Birth of the Cool* was the nonet recording featuring Miles that was released in 1957. It is not particularly high for trumpet players; still, it can be rough on the chops because there is a lot of "horn on the face" in the charts. But the concert went rather well due to all my trumpet routines. That was streamed through the SRJO website. Also, we did another SRJO small group at a performance center called Seasons in Yakima. We played the music of Monk and Miles. That was also super fun.

Curt Berg, transplanted arranger, and composer from LA has been writing for a sextet. At Curt's house, we individually put our parts on the songs, and Curt puts them together. These have been turning out very well, considering.

The worst thing about the pandemic for me is not being able to continue my tours in Japan. Usually, I am in Japan on US election night. I loved Obama, and he had lots of jazz musicians at the White House and was a big fan of John Coltrane. Unfortunately, we have moved pretty far away from that. This year I was home and watched the election unfold with my wife, Becca. Biden won. Now, we can only hope for the best.

Yesterday 11/19/2020 and we lost over 1000 people due to Covid in the USA. In January 2021, 3,000 to 4,000 a day!

I got some Covid blues for sure.

I imagine that we will come out of this with many new players regarding club owners and entrepreneurs. The musicians I know are mostly into practicing and improving. The creative process has always been more focused in times of strife.

I feel we have been in an enforced introspection, and I don't think it will hurt any of the arts. People are working away like mad on the things that give meaning to our existence. In my case, jazz music.

Now digital media is the way most young people get their music, so computers do not even have CD players anymore. I have two CDs coming out this year during the pandemic. I guess that is an example of being a jazz musician in the first place, bucking the trend!

During this COVID-19 epidemic, it is a particularly good time to decide what is important and what, by contrast, is not. Becca and I have certainly simplified our lives. We are becoming more aware of what things and values constitute good living. Food, music, friendship, good health are at the top of the list so far.

I look forward to seeing you all on the other side of this!
Jay Thomas January 20, 2021

BOOK ONE

1964 – 1981

It was to my family, probably like a slow-moving train wreck. I've often wondered why nobody made any serious attempt to stop this move on my part. But I always have to remember; it set in motion a chain of events that got me here today.

Jay Thomas

CHAPTER ONE

In the Beginning - Music in the Air

When I was growing up, there was music everywhere, so I was not aware of any particular music style. I loved the radio; Jerry Lee Lewis, Chuck Berry, Sinatra, Ray Charles, novelty songs, whatever. My dad had a stereo and many record LPs (Gil Evans/ Miles, *Porgy and Bess, Sketches of Spain* and later, Bill Potts, *Soul of Porgy and Bess,* and even *Ornette Coleman,* etc.). The music was also something that created an emotional feeling in me, my dad home from work, fooling with his music.

My dad was a gigging musician on the weekends, and he would often practice a Maggio routine he would do on trumpet. He also had a lot of charts and sheet music floating around the house. I also dug his band jacket he wore for some of his band gigs. It was red and green and would change from one color to the other if you turned it around! Cool stuff.

When I was in fourth or fifth grade, we were introduced to instruments at school and asked to pick one. I chose the trumpet because of my dad. There was never a question of whether I would be in a band or not. My dad had me take lessons from Don Anderson, a local trumpet player who used to

1

work in the studios in Los Angeles. Don was a proponent of the Maggio system.

I would travel once a week from our suburban neighborhood with my neighbor Mike Burdick to the Arthur Murray Building in downtown Seattle, where we would each take a half-hour lesson. I can't remember much except I was impressed with Don's autographed pictures in his studio. I think the first week, I was blasting away on the first lesson - C to G and back down, over and over!

About a year later, my dad switched me to a teacher who had a reputation for getting good results from kids. His name was Jim Weaver, and he was the second trumpet in the Seattle Symphony. With Jim, I slowly worked my way forward, mainly through the Arbans book.

I was not into practicing, but my parents made me practice for one hour a day. That was sometimes a pain because my friends would have to wait for me to put in my hour before heading to the movies or other stuff. It was slow going, but before I knew it, I was playing OK.

In my early school years, I was not a good student, and having one thing I could do well, in retrospect, was a boon to my esteem. I was probably a non-diagnosed ADD kid. I would do stuff like take the whip out of the Mexican exhibit at school when the teacher was not around. I often got into scuffles on the playground and was out of my seat, disruptive, and probably a drag in the classes. So, music was a good thing. It helped me be disciplined in at least that one area.

I remember somewhere in the sixth grade playing *Bugler's Holiday* with a nice sound, clean double-tongue, etc. At this time, Jim Weaver got me interested in the solo ensemble contest at the University of Washington. I practiced and memorized a three-part trumpet solo with a piano accompanist. When the competition came, I went to the U of W and received a rating of 1, which was high. I felt on top of it until I heard Rolf Smedvig[1], who was a finalist! Ouch, he was a monster player even as a young teenager.

+++++

About this time, I also met my dad's friends, Ronnie Pierce, Don Glenn, Rollo Strand, and Dick Thorlakson. Dick was a trombone player who was helped out by my dad many times. I remember the first time riding with my dad when we picked Dick up and brought him out to the house. We picked him up on Capitol Hill at a house that had two Lion statues on the porch. Dick came from a very musical family, with musicians on both sides of his family going back several generations. Dick was to become my best friend. He was an absolute blast for a kid to be around because he paid attention and asked questions and had a way of burrowing into my psyche. It's funny because Dick had spent time at Western State Hospital. Rollo was my other surrogate uncle. He started showing up at the house also.

When I got into Junior High, it was more of the same. Sometime in Junior High, I discovered the connection to the music I dug on the radio and jazz. One day, I heard Joe Newman playing on one of my dad's records, and something went "click." It had all the funky blues feeling but was so much deeper than most of the radio's stuff.

+++++

I can remember to this day when I decided to become a musician and specifically a jazz musician. I was in the back of a station wagon, and Dick was in the front seat. My mom had run into a store; it was a typical Seattle fall day, overcast, and gray. And boom, the thought came to me big time. Jazz musician, that would be cool.

I was already playing in a swing band at my Junior High run by a math teacher named Irwin Adler. Mr. Adler played baritone sax and had traveled to New York in a band with my dad when they were still teenagers during WWII.

Anyway, I got it into my head that I wanted to be a "blower," or, as we now say, improviser. I remember, when a solo would come up, there would be all these chord symbols on the page. Well, that meant absolutely nothing to me, so I would think of a few measures of phrases along the lines of the melody and hope that would carry me forward in the solo. Ha! No such luck. I would usually butcher my opening ideas, and it would get worse from there.

Soon it was summer, and I would be going into 10th grade at Shoreline High School the next fall. Shoreline had a band of mostly seniors, and they were excellent. I definitely wanted to get on that band. In those days, there were not two bands. If you did not make the "stage band" (that's what they called the big jazz bands in those days), you had to wait another year to audition.

+++++

That summer, I got a blues lesson from Dick Thorlakson and his friend Bob McDermitt, at The Vault, a dance club on Second Avenue owned by Ronnie Pierce, another friend of my dad's. They could both play some piano, and they were going to show me the blues. One guy would play blues changes on the piano, and I would play along, while the other would be shouting and commenting about my playing. They proceeded to get drunk while showing me how to play the blues. They would scowl at me and get kind of aggressive. Then they told me to keep practicing while they left to get some more "juice," Dick's slang for alcohol. They locked the gate at the front of the club. When they returned, they were shouting and pleading for me to hurry up and let them in. That mortified me because I did not have the key, and they even became threatening! It turns out it was a lark and part of the "blues lesson." Dick and McDermit would often dance and sing a song they made up from their days in the Coast Guard. It was: "Keep your C and B." At the time, I didn't know what C and B was! It stood for "Cock and Balls." They would usually do this

4

dance when they were drunk and singing their little song. It featured little can-can kicks while turning from left to right. I suppose I peripherally learned about blues that day.

Dick and I would sometimes play at my house. He would play "Lover Man," "Centerpiece," or other blues on the piano. Slow walking bass with attitude, and if I started to get it, he would shout in a serious, senatorial tone of voice, "That's that soul sound." I had a Bobby Timmons' tune, "Moanin" in my ear, and Timmons' style of blues-based minor pentatonic playing was what would occasionally come out of me.

That summer, I also went to a Stan Kenton stage band camp in Reno. That first camp was an eye-opener. I got into the best big band because I could read pretty well. It was a crash course.

CHAPTER TWO

Teenage Jazz Prodigy :>)

When I got to Shoreline HS, it turns out I did get in the band and played some solos, too. Fletch Wiley[2] was the lead trumpet, and he was cool because he knew how to swing and could play pretty high. That year the band played at the biggest stage band festival at that time, at Olympic Junior College in Bremerton. The festival's director was Ralph Mutchler,[3] an early powerhouse for getting jazz bands into public schools and community colleges' music programs. That Olympic Festival had judges like Leonard Feather there and, one year, Quincy Jones was there. Anyway, I got an award for my soloing.

I had started studying with Floyd Standifer[4] in Seattle. He was a young, clean machine freshly off Quincy Jones' band in Europe. Floyd helped me identify the keys that songs went through. He also pointed out stuff on recordings such as thematic playing versus just "licks." He was really helpful in my early musical development.

Also, at this time, my dad helped organize a band of young kids from teachers' referrals all over the city. He asked Milt Kleeb to loan us the big band music he had arranged for four saxes, one trumpet, and rhythm, and we had a band! We were called the Playboys, and we soon got bookings all over from an agent who booked military clubs. Officer's Clubs and NCO military clubs hired bands in our area, Paine Field in Tacoma and at Madigan and Fort Lewis.

So, I had a bunch of opportunities besides those at school to get it going better. I got into a habit of running my scales and patterns every day. I started to hear key centers a little better even though there was much functional harmony I did not understand.

+++++

Around this time, I remember a jazz experience when Freddy Greenwell[5] came through town. Freddy Greenwell deserves several books of his own. Freddy is in Bill Crow's[6] biographical accounts of Bill's start as a bass player. Anyway, my dad was very excited about Freddy coming to town. It turns out Freddy was everyone's favorite tenor saxophonist. Freddy was playing in Seattle at the 410 Supper Club with Johnny "Scat" Davis, and there was a session organized for Freddy at Walt Tianon's house after the gig. Walt lived in a big old house right next door to Chuck Metcalf's place in the Madrona District. That same weekend Harold Land was at the Penthouse.

I went to Walt's with my dad, and then it was all about waiting because gigs went late in those days. I got so sleepy waiting; I fell asleep. When I woke up, a virtual "who's who" of the Seattle jazz scene was there; Jerry Gray, Dave Coleman, Chuck Metcalf, Neil Friel (drove from Tacoma), Don Glenn, and others. Freddy showed up around the time that Hampton Hawes[7] showed, after his gig with Harold at the Penthouse. Freddy was a friend of Hawes from the LA Central Avenue scene in the late '40s and '50s.

I was like a bug on the wall, watching and listening. People had gathered around Hampton Hawes, so I knew there was something special about him. I overheard Hampton talking to some people, and he mentioned that Kennedy had pardoned him. Later, I looked it up, and yes, Kennedy had pardoned him from Federal prison where he was in for narcotics.

That session at Walt's house was way cool. I remember Freddy just started playing, no what shall we play or counting tempo or anything like that. He started in on: *"Is It True What They Say About Dixie."* Hampton Hawes looked like some stallion or purebred show-horse, the way he perked up and got right into it. And then Dave Coleman started playing brushes on a phone book!

I had big eyes and ears. After an hour or so, I had an epiphany. I realized it was about the swing and the articulation and inflections. It was a language, and it was talking to me! First time for that. It was great to hear fine, advanced players hanging out and playing for fun, just for the joy of it.

Freddy spent some time at our house, off and on. I think he had eyes for my mom.

+++++

Some of the musicians in the Playboys were older and a little more experienced than me. Some were playing in R& B and rock bands and smoking and having sex with girls. I was the greenhorn, and I looked up to these guys. The Playboys also had added Dick Thorlakson on trombone. Try as we might to get him to get us beer, he would have none of it! Rollo Strand was on sax. So, I had minders and direct eyes on me that reported back to central headquarters, i.e., my dad, Marvin.

My dad took me over to Jabo Ward's[8] house one day, and he pulled my coat to the fact that the guys that I thought were so cool were not playing very well in the key centers. We made a tape at Jabo's house, he went over some of the places, and he said, "See there, Thomas, you're playing the changes." Then, when one of the other players came in, he would say, "that guy is just playing 'stuff,' he's not really in the changes."

CHAPTER THREE

Jam Sessions at the Queequeg and the Llahngaelhyn

Sometime that year, I heard about some musicians referred to as: "those cats" who were playing excellent jazz. Dick was at our house again, trying to "straighten his wig," and my mom had him doing little chores and projects. Dick had a way of talking to himself and mumbling that would always get my attention. Then I would have to cross-examine him to get the gist of what he was saying. Dick kept mumbling about "those cats," kind of like he was upset or impressed. I managed to find out that those cats were Sarge West and Mark Doubleday.

The place he heard them at was a club called "The Queequeg." The Queequeg[9] was a jazz coffee house on 41st Street and University Ave in the University District. They had music most nights. Jerry Heldman started the club, and many guys would play there (such as Larry Coryell). Sometimes musicians would come in from touring bands. Jerry was up for playing any time, day or night. That club closed, then Jerry Heldman started the Llahngaelhyn,[10] another coffee house/jazz club by the University Bridge. Jerry practically lived there. He led a very ascetic lifestyle: bass, coffee, gallons of it, scalding hot. Maybe white "crisscrosses" or pep pills, as he once referred to them. Jerry was an ex-GI military police guy and a drummer. My dad said he had a great feel on drums, but now he was playing bass, and Bill Evans with Scott Lafaro was his ideal.

At this time, The Penthouse[11] was going strong, and there were name players always coming through Seattle. The Penthouse had sessions on Saturday or Sunday afternoon, so the Llahngaelhyn also had sessions on Sunday afternoon. The word was getting out that they were good sessions. When I first went there, I don't think I brought my horn; it is hazy. I do remember Mike Mandel[12] arriving at the same time as I did. Mike stepped out of the cab and proceeded to try to light his cigarette, and the whole book of matches went up in flame; "whoops," I thought to myself, "he must be very stoned." It turns out Mike was blind.

The Llahngaelhyn was happenin'. Sometimes very late, after regular jobs, Doubleday would show up. I saw him once there late at night, and he sounded so great with a Soulful, Blue Note style, an energized sound very much like Nicolas Payton. Mark had a great ear and was always funky with perfect time. Sarge West was also great on trumpet. Larry Coryell[13] would go there sometimes because Larry was just totally into playing all the time. Often, I would see Joe Brazil[14] (from Detroit) there. Joe Brazil was playing on a Friday evening when Rollo took me there, and I got up enough nerve to ask to sit in. Joe said, "Sure, what would you like to play?" I said, "Straight No Chaser," a Monk blues I had under my belt. Joe counted it off, and I safely got through the head and played a few choruses and didn't hurt myself too badly. Joe gave me the nod, like, "You did OK."

So that is how it all started, being able to hang.

I started going to the Sunday jam sessions regularly and memorizing standard tunes and jazz standards to call them at the session. There was no reading of fake books or changes on cell phones like today.

There was a caveat to this idyllic scene. Fred Harris was his name. Fred was a piano player from Chicago and had some job in research at the University of Washington. I owe Fred a lot of thanks because he did not give me the usual condescending, "Look at this young musician playing jazz, ain't it wonderful" routine. No, Fred expected everyone to be on the same page at these sessions. I was seriously lacking and did not know the changes the same way that a bass player or piano player needed to know them. I had the horn players' disease of using my ear to avoid most pitfalls riding on top happily playing, blithely unaware of many changes and possibilities. Fred would give me the dourest look and sighs and all kinds of histrionics when I would come up to play. Fred was, without realizing it, one of the guardians of the gate. He was standing there like an angel with a flaming sword, fiercely defending the craft and language of jazz from what he considered defilement.

+++++

Later that summer, my dad got me hooked up for lessons with Mike Mandel, the great piano/organ player who was gigging all over town. When I showed up at Mike's studio apartment in the Studio Fisher building downtown, I came into his apartment and took out my horn as Mike got behind the piano. Mike was a funny guy, and cheerfully he said, "Donald Byrd, page one!" He proceeded to play a pattern on the piano over a chord, then quickly told me he wanted me to learn it and practice it. A great lesson because, once again, we wrote nothing down. He played it slow enough for me to get it, and I soon got it. Mike also played many recordings for me. It was a great situation.

Dick Thorlackson worked around the corner at the 211 Pine Cafe as a dishwasher. Mike and I would sometimes eat at the 211 Pine Cafe. Mike had a thing about running as fast as he could, up and down the stairs. We would stop off in the alley,

11

bang on the door, and Dick would come out. Dick was like a message board, and he had little scraps of paper with messages for different people. And those days, we were innocent as a society about pep pills. Dick was involved in that, as were many others, including Mike.

+++++

From playing at the Llahngaelhyn, I started to get to know many of the players that were around. I met and became friends with a saxophone player named Jordan Ruwe. Jordan was a very intense tenor player who had been in the Navy. He was way into practicing and playing and would often be at the Llahngaelhyn. He would also hit the Penthouse session. Jordan taught me some tunes, and we had a nice little trumpet/tenor thing going at that time.

As I got into my playing more, there was another big piece of the puzzle in the form of R&B bands. At that time, the Dynamics were famous around Seattle. Mark Doubleday played trumpet with them, and guitarist Larry Coryell and Peter Borg and Ron Woods. They were very cool. They played at Parker's Ballroom and all the dance places around town. I was coming home from a football game when I first heard them. I was still in Junior High at the time. Because the High School was right across the street from where I lived, I would go to any event where other teenagers went, even though I didn't give a damn about football. It's a fall night, and I'm walking across the dark parking lot, probably smoking a cigarette, when the gym door opened, and the post-game dance band sounds spilled out into the parking lot. I was a snob at the time, even though I was just a jazz novice. I thought, "Rock, this is nothing" ha, was I wrong. They were playing a ballad, and the trumpet solo was beautiful. I went up to the door and looked in, and Doubleday was killing it on "Misty." Larry Coryell was on guitar.

CHAPTER FOUR

The Deacons, Jazz Festivals, and Leonard Feather

Now, it is 1966, and a lot of things were percolating for me. There were so many things happening that year that I could easily get hung up in this time slot. I was starting to get approached to play trumpet in some dance bands. I rehearsed with one band called the Counts, and then I got a call from a guy in a band called The Deacons. The Deacons were a band of young cats smitten by black R&B. They had a black tenor player from South Carolina named John Bush and a Japanese piano player. Actually, he might have played a Farfisa organ! We had various singers who were always African American front men.

We ended up getting a manager who was an ex-football star and worked for KYAC, the black radio station in Seattle. We wore clerical outfits. The Deacons! Man, it was great for a young guy like me. We started to get gigs at various dances in the greater Seattle area. We played a dance one time, and I went to have food in a restaurant with some of the guys. They were all University students except the singer and me. Anyway, I ordered wine, and because of the collar, they served me. I got drunk and was not 100% on top of that gig.

In my 11th grade, my junior year in high school and I still played some of the Playboy gigs, but I was increasingly drawn into other playing arenas.

+++++

The R&B scene was cool because when we played a long dance, the songs could go on for a while, and soloing over them was fun because the chords were a little easier than standards. More like hard bop or boogaloo with a longer time spent in a key center. That year most of the Shoreline players had graduated and were either at Ivy League colleges or music schools back East. Fletch was at North Texas State. Anyway, the Shoreline band was just so, so.

But this year was big for me at the band competition. In those years, Downbeat Magazine would sometimes have charts printed so small you needed a magnifying glass to copy them. Benny Golson's big band chart of "I Remember Clifford" was in the Downbeat, and my dad (the river that runs through it) had copied the chart. My dad was also very fond of Art Farmer. After I was bit by the jazz bug, I also was a huge fan of Art. Really, what's not to like? Art was very clear with his lines and played in a range I could handle on trumpet, not too high. My dad had transcribed Art's solo on "I Remember Clifford" from the *Jazztet* Album, so I knew large parts of it by heart. When our band played at the festival that year, I played it and got way into it, cadenza on the end, the whole shebang.

Well, Leonard Feather[15], the famous critic, was there as a judge. I knew he was there because I had seen him the previous year at the Reno Kenton clinic. We were both at a little private jam session that Charlie Mariano was having where I heard Toshiko and Marv Stamm as well. Leonard and I were part of a small group watching the session. So, my face might have been in his mind, subconsciously. When I played "I Remember Clifford," he probably did not know I was playing a lot of Art Farmer that day. Hmmm, or maybe he did?

Leonard was bowled over and put me in the Downbeat Magazine[16] Critic's Poll that year as "Talent Deserving of Wider Recognition." At that festival, I was also approached about joining the famous service band, *Airmen of Note*.

+++++

In 1966 I was in the University District a lot. Anyone who knows American history will remember that the counterculture movement was starting to come on strong, with the anti-war demonstrations and the beginnings of what became the hippie movement. Anyway, from being on the bandstand with the University cats and older players like Jordan Ruwe, I was introduced to "Grass." So, at the band competition, I was high when I played "I Remember Clifford."

I had read *Really the Blues* by Mezz Mezzrow.[17] That was a book all jazz players read, which featured grass pretty prominently. Louis Armstrong and many others were devout weed smokers. If someone had compiled a "who's who" of the top players, they probably would have netted many weed smokers. In certain circles, people did not think pot was a drug. One thing for sure in '66 and '67: weed was very quickly becoming the drug of choice for the young in America. I get a kick out of the current 2018 rehabilitation of grass, as seen by naming the new listening club in New York "Mezzrow's!"

CHAPTER FIVE

Berklee Summer School

That year, I sent a recording to Downbeat magazine as part of a scholarship contest. My dad helped me, and it probably was his idea. I used Mike Mandel and other pro players on the recording. I won a scholarship to Berklee School of Music in Boston[18] for the summer between my junior and senior years in high school. Berklee was a blast. The first day was an eye-opener. I had an arranging class that started right off, arranging standards in open and closed 5-piece voicings! Plus, dictation classes and Herb Pomeroy's big band. It was exhilarating. I was also pretty much transcribing all the time and playing as much as I could.

I met other like-minded souls who were a lot like me and some better! One guy who was way better than me mentioned the critic's poll. He asked, "Is that you?" I said, "No!"

My roommate was David Berger.[19]

I met an excellent drummer from San Francisco named Bill Weikert, and we hung and played. Somehow my name got out in the community. I also started working with a bebop baritone player, I don't remember his name, but Calvin Hill was on bass. I remember this guy (bari player) was kind of crazy and super enthusiastic and a real pot smoker!

I got the chance to play a lot. One day, I went with a piano player from Switzerland over to Steve Ellington's house. Steve Ellington is a drummer who plays some with Hal Galper and would sometimes gig with Roland Kirk and others. I remember, even though I was adept at smoking weed, sometimes the stuff was not very strong. This afternoon at Ellington's, they passed the pipe around and said, "You want some?" I said, "Sure," and smoked the pipe with them. Next thing, I was so high that I felt like a caterpillar, because every time I took a breath, I could feel all the hairs on my stomach brush my shirt!

But what got me was the music on the turntable. It was so complex and soulful and completely blew me away. I said, "What music is this?" They said, *Love Supreme!* Ah, that was a big moment. I had already received *Love Supreme* for my birthday and truthfully could not make much out of it. That day it all changed!

I was hooked on the Trane Quartet.[20] The hippie thing was going to town. I scored weed from the bari player and was happily ensconced in my little world of practicing and listening to music and doing assignments at Berklee. There was a book lying around called, The *Psychedelic Experience* by Tim Leary in the dorm. I read it, and it just so happened I was interested in Eastern religions at this time, so I put that on my bucket list of things I would like to do. The psychedelic experience was a good primer because it laid out that acid was not a recreational drug. It was quite strong for that.

CHAPTER SIX

Senior H.S., Black & Tan, The HOE, and Randy Brecker

Now, back to Seattle and my senior year in high school. I was busy doing gigs with the Deacons, and I also joined a band put together by Jimmy Ogilvy, who had the stage name, Jimmy Hanna.[21] Jimmy Hanna sang and fronted the Dynamics. Anyway, Jimmy wanted to get his jazz thing together as well as have a big band.

We rehearsed in the basement of his house every Saturday afternoon. It was almost all head arrangements, and that made it a lot of fun. It was also cool because it had a wide range of age differences and was racially mixed. There are some recordings of this band.

That band ended up backing Motown[22] acts that came through Seattle. Man, that was a blast for a young cat to be sitting back playing with the original Temptations, and Martha and the Vandellas, The Four Tops and Smokey Robinson, etc.

The other trumpet player in that band was Ron Soderstrom. Ron was a great player. He played with organist Ronnie Buford (those familiar with the book, *Jackson Street After Hours*[23] will recognize the name. He was the son of legendary sax player Pops Buford.) Soderstrom often played at the HOE (short for "House of Entertainment.") Ron was offered a gig with a good commercial dance band, so he passed the HOE gig on to me. Next thing, I was working at the House of Entertainment with Jimmy Pipkins and the Boss Five. That club only sold coffee, tea, and soft drinks. It stayed open until 4:00 in the morning. Our gig was 11:30 PM to 3:30 AM Thursday thru Saturday.

Anyway, any semblance of typical high school life for me crumbled at that time.

+++++

Around that same time, a young Randy Brecker[24] showed up in Seattle. I saw him at all the sessions at the Llahngaelhyn; plus, he had gigs with Ronnie Buford and was all over the place. Randy followed a girl out from Indiana, where he was going to school. Randy already sounded like Clifford to my ears, just a great all-around player. That summer in Seattle, he also liked to sit in at the Embers in West Seattle, where Sarge had a gig on the organ. Randy was friendly to me, and once at a session, I was playing a little diminished lick over a dominant chord on a blues. He looked down at me and said, "diminished scale," with a rising tone of voice, denoting approval and offering encouragement. Remember, I mentioned Sarge was a great trumpet player. He certainly was, but he could also play smokin' organ. The band was Larry Coryell, Dean Hodges, and Sarge West. Randy went there often and played. Later, when I was still in high school, the first *Blood Sweat and Tears* album came out with Randy soloing.

+++++

One morning, I got up after the HOE gig, and the coat I was wearing was not there. This was a problem because it was my dad's leather coat! I was alarmed because I had a pocket full of grass! I walked into the kitchen where my parents had the pot on the table, and they stared at me with eyes hard as stone. I was at a loss for words. They assured me that "things were gonna change around here, and I could forget playing that gig at the HOE" After the dust settled, I staked out my autonomy. I said that was not going to happen, and if they insisted, I would have to take up residence elsewhere. I was 17 and baby-faced but already identifying with the new wave of young people out there. I had experienced acid and been back to the primordial swamp, floating around like a single cell amoeba, and made it back to human form to play jazz! So, their threats were not enough to dissuade me from my course. They caved, and I went back to life as it was- playing gigs and barely getting through school.

+++++

I should mention that in my senior year, I changed to Mount-lake Terrace High School. They did not have the same course requirements to graduate, and I was shy of one requirement at Shoreline High School. When I went to Mountlake Terrace High School, I tried to better my academic situation. I had been labeled a behavior problem since middle school and was in some classes with kids who were not very bright, along with "problem kids" like myself. I told the administration at Mountlake Terrace that I did not feel this was fair because I was ahead in many areas. They agreed and put me in with advanced kids. The school was way better after that; not dull, no endless assignments, more discussions, and civilized behavior.

At this time, I was tight with John Carmody (guitarist at the HOE) and with Jimmy Hanna. My best buddies were drummer Dave Johnson and Joe Brazil (a young saxophonist, not to be confused with the older, Detroit-based Joe Brazil.) I met Joe at the Stan Kenton clinic, and he was utterly soulful and way ahead of most of us with his sound and ear.

I was pretty much careening along, but transcribing, playing at the Llahngaelhyn, and learning about jazz from my peers, Jordan Ruwe, Lee Parker, and older musicians, Mike Mandel, Butch Nordal, Bob Nixon, and even Dick Thorlakson.

+++++

Once, Floyd Standifer could not make a gig with Chuck Metcalf's septet, and it ended up in my lap. Chuck was an excellent arranger and writer. I remember "Love in a Taxi" and many other cool tunes Chuck had written. Chuck knew a ton of standards and jazz tunes and was a real "Monkophile." He was also aware of and dug the Beatles and other contemporary pop bands of this time. Later, Chuck was a member of Dexter Gordon's touring band.

That gig I did for Floyd had some of the best players in Seattle. I thought Sarge and Doubleday were both better players, but those guys were not available. They both played a lot of gigs, and Chuck's music required a rehearsal as well as the gig. Plus, both Doubleday and Sarge were known as opiate users. In bands, it is often the case where "comrades at arms" is an essential factor. Usually, for non-users, opiate addiction is seen as a problem better to sidestep.

The rehearsal went pretty well. Bob Winn was on alto, Jordan Ruwe on tenor, Dave Tuttle on bone, Chuck on bass, hmmm, I think Bill Richardson was on drums, piano, not sure. Chuck had a very cool arrangement for *Black Diamond* by Roland Kirk that was kind of tricky.

I did not drive till I was in my twenties, so I got a ride from "the old guys." Now that Pot is legal in our state, and the consciousness-raising is well underway regarding Cannabis, I don't think I'm letting any state secrets out here when I say most of these guys were old potheads. On the drive to the gig, out came the weed pipe. I sat staring straight ahead, but soon it was: "Like some of this?" I eagerly took a few tokes. The effects were immediate, and the song with the hook, "one toke over the line," could have been written for me! I was pretty stoned on the gig, and everything was going well until we hit "Black Diamond". They probably were saying to themselves: "What did we do to this kid? He's coming unraveled."

+++++

I realize this is some *Really the Blues* Mezz Mezzrow stuff here. I am also aware that, at this time, it is somewhat politically incorrect to connect drug use with jazz, but there it is. Or, in my case, WAS. You see, to be completely honest, my pals and I were little hipsters. We loved to hang and listen to jazz together, and part of that was occasionally a little reefer. We were not into booze. As an aside, most people are not aware of Mezz Mezzrow's book, *Really the Blues,* but Smalls' owner in New York certainly knows the book. He started another small jazz club and named it, Mezzrow's. Mezz was a clarinet player from New Orleans who, like Louis Armstrong, championed the smoking of Mary Jane, Pot, Weed, Cannabis. *Really the Blues* was a must-read for all the jazz musicians in my generation, and even my father's. Mezz was the first "white" hipster. Mezz was married to an African American lady when that was fairly advanced. Mezz lived in France later in his life and fancied himself a jazz critic.

I was already ensconced in a musician's life.

+++++

I should also mention the Black and Tan[25] here. When I got into Jimmy Pipkins's band and met Ron Soderstrom, I learned about the Black and Tan. Mike Mandel and many people I knew played there. The Black and Tan was on 11th, and Jackson and was a basement bottle club. A bottle club is where they don't sell drinks; they only sell mixers. The customers brought their booze and paid quite a bit for the mixer! I remember going to a Sunday afternoon jam session there and first hearing and understanding "Parker blues changes" when Ronnie Buford played the organ. Ron Buford was funky and could play changes like crazy. He was like Jack McDuff when McDuff had George Benson and Red Hollaway.

+++++

I could only get in as far as the coat racks at the Penthouse, but I could still see the musicians play. I saw Cannonball's band there and experienced the way that his band swung. I got into the Penthouse when Miles showed up with his "Herbie-Ron-Tony" band with Wayne Shorter. It was like watching a family unit at work. They were playing "Dolores," and Wayne was to come in after Miles' solo. They were kind of vamping a four-bar cycle for him to enter at will. Anyway, each time Wayne tried to enter, Tony would do an unpredictable and disruptive fill. Wayne calmly passed and waited to come in. The same thing happened the next time around; Tony did a flibertygibbet with a trap door hidden in it. Wayne passed again. Miles walked up and stood in front of Tony and said in a raspy whisper, "Don't play. If you're going to do that shit, don't play." Tony stopped, and Wayne entered and played for a while, and then Tony entered again, full steam ahead, later downstream. When Miles' band played, it was like being privileged to watch and hear musical conversations.

CHAPTER SEVEN

Jerry Gray, Steve Haas, Mike Mandel

It's 1966, and I started lessons from Jerry Gray.[26] Jerry Gray is a legendary NW piano player and teacher. Jerry is the stuff of legends, and there was a firm reality behind all of them. My dad hired him to come to our house and teach me. My sister remembers my father and mother told the kids to be quiet, so she knew that Jerry Gray was serious business. Jerry had taught Mike Mandel, Jordan Ruwe, and so many others.

Jerry came to the house and sat down and said, "Let's play." We started in on a blues, and immediately I was aware something had changed. Jerry recognized everything I instinctively played and knew how to make it entirely right. He was the first guy I had ever played with that could do that. Like, if I hit the minor third and fourth on a dominant chord, it will sound wrong to some people, but it sounded like a million bucks with Jerry.

We played, and here's the sick thing: the first thing I thought was, "Damn, I'm good!" That's what happens (and has happened through the years) when I get pulled in by the gravity of a very superior jazz musician.

He fixed me with a penetrating gaze and said, "too bad you weren't born 20 years earlier." He essentially told me I was twenty years too late, but he went on to teach me.

He was really into using one's mind to concentrate and learn and retain information. He showed me that changes on standards had many similarities and told me that he often already knows the changes when he hears a new song. If not, it is because there may be some minor moves that deviate from the typical progressions. So, he expected me to memorize songs and be able to play them in twelve keys. And he also pointed out, the same way Floyd had done earlier, the way to use thematic playing to not run out of things to say when improvising. Jerry was fond of Sonny Rollins in this regard.

I think, on the third or fourth lesson, I was fired as his student. As much as I wanted to jump on the Jerry bandwagon, I was busy playing R&B and had recently made a huge life change. I had fallen in love for the first time. Never one to half step it was intense, so playing "Jeepers Creepers" in twelve keys had to wait a while. But I will always be thankful to Jerry for his example of how one can do amazing things when one puts your MIND to work. Jerry (or Jerome, as we call him now) planted a lot of seeds. It just took many years of wandering before they fully germinated.

+++++

That year, I also met and started playing with a great drummer from New York named Steve Haas. Steve had been in the army and discharged at Fort Lewis. He fell for an artist named Betty Cheney and stuck around in Seattle to be with her. Steve and Betty had a house on the hill in Rainier Valley just off Genesee Street. Jordan Ruwe lived next door, and there were always sessions at Steve's.

I went out there with bassist Dave Press when I was still in high school. The playing was so much fun. A little about Dave Press: Dave was a very talented guy who knew a lot about jazz. He had been in Vegas, playing with a young Monty Alexander, and had it going for himself. But, alas, Dave fell in with a crowd of cats who were into speed, and Dave took too much. From lack of sleep and other factors, he got into a speed-induced paranoia. Legend has it that he was hanging out with friends and somehow got out in front of the 4th of July parade and thought the Red Chinese were coming through Canada to get him. Dave ended up at Western State Hospital, Dick Thorlackson's old alma mater, and they gave him shock treatments. For many, that works out OK, but in Dave's case, it kind of goofed him up, according to people that knew him before. But he was still fun to play with, knew a lot about jazz harmony, and knew a ton of tunes.

Back to Steve -

Steve was a great drummer and ended up working all the time at the Checkmate with Mike Mandel. Betty was a real intellectual counter-culture person with a master's degree and was friends with Richard Alpert and other psychedelic pioneers. Sometimes, there would be blowout sessions at their place that would last all night. After one of these all-night sessions (Chuck Metcalf was there), it was dawn, and we were still high. Chuck whispered to me, "I got it all figured out, and I wrote it down." I was probably speechless, but he handed me a little folded slip of paper. When I opened it up, it read, "Well, whaddya know."

+++++

I was tight with a group of young guys in Seattle. We could boogaloo our asses off on tunes like the "Sidewinder", and "Cantaloupe Woman", and "Freedom Jazz Dance", "Eighty-one", "Dolphin Dance", and some Miles' songs and things we liked. We were not wed to the standard tunes the older musicians wanted to play, that was for sure.

I remember playing at a party at Jerry Carasco's house in Seattle. Jerry was a Mexican American guy who was friends with many jazz players. He had a big party every year when Cal Tjader[27] came to town. Jerry just loved that band. Well, we young guys were playing and having a ball. And at the party, a slightly drunk Cal comes up and says, "Gee, you guys sound great. Can I sit in?" We said, "Sure." He called "Just Friends"; we looked at him like he was from Mars and said, "Let's do something else." We played and had fun, but we did not feel an obligation to play "Just Friends." We were full of ourselves, but hey, that's life. We were trying to make our own   way.

CHAPTER EIGHT

San Francisco and The Summer of Love

I graduated from high school in 1967. I had turned 17 last October. For all you history buffs, that was also the "*Summer of Love*" when hippies burst on the scene. The Monterey Pop Festival and Jimi Hendricks, and so much was happening with changes in the society. My friend from Berklee, Bill Weikert, invited me to come to San Francisco and stay at his apartment. He was going to be staying at his girlfriend's place.

As soon as school got out, I took off for San Francisco. What a scene. My friend Joe Brazil drove down from Seattle and brought Marilyn, my love, with him. That was a young man's dream! Bill Weikert got me on a band with some excellent San Francisco cats: Jim Dukey (alto player and arranger) and Charlie McCarthy (on tenor.) The piano player ran it-damn can't remember his name, but they had won a big festival back East. They were called the San Francisco Jazz Sextet (not sure, but it might have been a quintet before I got there).

I rehearsed with them, and then we went to a gig at a place called The Straight Theater in the Haight Ashbury District. The place was packed. The equipment was already set up, but

I remember the piano player had to ask how to turn on the keyboard. The guy who told him how looked like a very funky biker.

Anyway, we played our jazz music for them. The last song was a great arrangement of "Dolphin Dance" by Herbie Hancock. I remember thinking with the arrogance and naivete of youth: "Follow this!" When I was walking across the large dance floor with people sprawled all about, they dimmed the lights, and a chord blasted from the new band that almost took my breath away. It was so loud it was like an explosion. The listeners literally kicked any furniture aside and started to dance with insane 'dog joy' everywhere! Girls with pigtails and patrol boots and a lot of Farmer John one-piece outfits. The band that followed us was the *Grateful Dead*! All I can say, the people were at least patient and polite when we played.

+++++

Later, Joe and I went to a jam session at a club packed with good players. Being young certainly has its perks. I was like a kid in a candy store when I heard anyone that could play well, and I would get excited by the differences in people's playing. The bass player seemed very fine. There was something a little off about him, though. He was wearing a sweater he might have worn for months, and his whole demeanor was a little rigid, and his eyes showed the whites around the eye. It was Henry Grimes.[28] Henry Grimes was one of the baddest bass players of all time. This is probably right before he disappeared from view due to mental illness.

CHAPTER NINE

Berklee for a Minute

Marilyn, my girlfriend, was probably the instigator of a very weird move I made that summer. I was going to Boston in the fall on a full-year scholarship to the Berklee School of Music. Marilyn and I, of course, were going to be together forever. A combination of youthful idealism and lust was still fueling the relationship. Somehow, marriage came up. I think she was trying to get away from her parents and launch herself toward an exciting new life! She wanted to come with me to Boston.

I remember she asked me after we got back to Seattle, "Did you talk to your parents?" I got a small, funny feeling and decided to override it and said, "No," or maybe I lied and said, "Yes." But whatever, I was married at the end of the summer! I remember the wedding was wild. We had been up all night at Steve and Betty's and were still high on acid at the wedding. Needless to say, the parents on both sides were not thrilled with the wedding or our condition. It was to my family, probably like a slow-moving train wreck. I've often wondered why nobody made any serious attempt to stop this

30

move on my part. But I always have to remember; it set in motion a chain of events that got me to today.

+++++

Soon Marilyn and I were in Boston looking for an apartment. We ended up getting a place on Hancock Street. It was a small studio-style apartment. When we received the keys and went to look at the apartment, we tried out the bed for good measure.

Then I was at Berklee. The next part is a little surreal. I'm there going around to classes, and I remember going to take a lesson with their trumpet instructor. He and I did not get along at all; I was too young and full of myself, and he was a dick to me. I was holding the trumpet wrong etc. Next, I'm in an indoctrination lecture for the incoming class. The instructor came out in an ugly brown suit, had a bad haircut, and started to make jokes that I found stupid and not funny. Everyone looked so young and unhip around me. They were all laughing at the swill this guy was slinging. Then he switched gears and said, "You people will need to listen," as if this would be a chore. He mentioned Terry Gibbs band, a band that was not even remotely interesting to me. I was already busy transcribing stuff from a Wayne Shorter album with "Yes and No" on it and "JuJu", etc.

Then I made a completely selfish and impulsive move. I decided right then I needed to get out of there.

I had to come up with a whopper of a story, so I went and talked to the Dean. He could see right through me, but to his credit, he said, "You know you are right; you can do it on your own; it will just be a lot harder." Prophetic words.

We stayed in Boston for a little while. Marilyn got a job at a jewelry store called Shreve, Crump, and Lowe. We decided to move to a larger place in Malden. We owed money at the little apartment on Hancock Street. I told the landlord just to hold on, and I would get the money. As we got in the cab to leave, she came running after us, and I just told the cab driver to keep driving. We had part of a house in Malden, but the man who rented to us was a peeping Tom and spying on Marilyn, so we moved again to Revere Beach. Not much was going on except practicing on my end. I got a job at Shreve Crump and Lowe during the holidays. However, Marilyn was much more mature and was taking care of business.

+++++

In the early spring, we moved back to Seattle and quickly were in a house with many other musicians: Dave Johnson, Joe Brazil, and Bob Thrasher. Then Marilyn and I rented a house out in Rainier Valley, where rent was cheap. The house was quite funky. Soon, a place became available on the hill above Genesee Street next to Steve, Betty, and Jordy. The house rent was 40 dollars a month!

CHAPTER TEN

New York

I was practicing a lot and playing quite a bit with Steve. One day, Steve said, "I'm going back to New York; do you want to come?" I did not hesitate and said, "Yes." Before this, I had a job at Boeing for a few months through a Dick Thorlackson connection. Dick knew a guy who hired for Boeing. This guy hung out drinking at the 211 Pine Street Cafe, where the bar was essentially a waiting room for a treatment center.

+++++

In the fall of '68, Marilyn and I and Steve and Betty took off to New York in Steve and Betty's old Volvo. We had adventures on the trip and camped out on the way. We camped in Yellowstone, and we camped outside of Chicago. At one campsite, we woke up in the morning in Iowa, surrounded by what we thought was pot. It was hemp. Same thing, but no THC content and won't get you high!

We slowly made our way across the country. We did stop off in Nebraska to visit my great-grandmother in St Edwards, Nebraska. Her home was in the center of town. She asked if my father still played trumpet. My father's dad died during the depression, in Olympia Washington, and my dad went to stay with his grandparents, who bought him a trumpet when he was a kid.

+++++

We pulled into New York late at night, and we were trying to find Steve's old buddy's pad in the East Village. His buddy was a good tenor player named Terry Pippos. We tried to find his address when we saw a guy walking down the sidewalk with a horn case. I asked if he knew Terry Pippos. He said he did and pointed out the address. I asked him his name, and he said, "Rene McLean." I said, "Any relation to Jackie?" He said, "I'm his son." Since I have always been a huge fan of Jackie McLean, that was like arriving in the Promised Land.

Terry Pippos' apartment was close to Slug's Saloon[29], and right after we were there, we went to Slug's. Unfortunately, the first time we went, a jazz bagpipe player named Rufus Harley was performing. We wanted to get hooked up with jazz as soon as possible. Shortly after arriving, we were on the street and heard jazz playing loudly. The sound came from a tall, young African American cat walking down the sidewalk with a boom box blasting jazz. He was also carrying a trombone. I ran to catch him. His strides were huge, and it took me several blocks to run him down. I caught up with him, and we chatted. Betty charmed him, and we smoked some grass and just hung out. He told us about a session, and we said we would like to go. That night, he took us to Musart, a club in a basement on Spring Street in Greenwich Village. When we walked in, it was way more sophisticated than the places in Seattle. There was a scale model of the solar system as we entered. We walked down a hall and entered the club's center section. There was a little raised bandstand, a lot of low furniture, some pillows, hanging rattan chairs, and lots of people. A mostly black crowd, but not entirely.

That night the music sounded so great. There were cats there that I recognized from albums, Albert Dailey, Beaver Harris, Dizzy Reese, and others.

George Braith[30] had me come up after a bit, and he asked me, "What do you want to play?" I answered, "Forest Flower." Not a good move! He looked a little disgusted and said, "A standard," so I said, "Getting Sentimental Over You." I knew that tune from the Monk, *San Francisco Holiday* album and had transcribed Joe Gordon's trumpet solo and was pretty good with that. When we got through, he gave me the OK sign, so I guessed I passed the competency test. Nobody was jumping up or down or excited, but I did well enough to hang. When we left the club, the sky was just starting to lighten. At another jam session, I asked the bass player Gene Perla about diminished and half-diminished chords. I was unhappy with the way I was playing diminished shapes. Gene understood what I was saying immediately and, regarding half-diminished chords, told me to learn Bill Evans' "Gloria Step". For diminished, he said to throw in the interval of a fourth.

+++++

The four of us rented a storefront on Thompson Street in the Village right down from the Village Gate. It was small, but we built a sleeping loft to provide more room. We put a piano in the little place, and we started to settle in. Marilyn got a job quickly. I would go down to George Braith's club, Musart, and play. Steve got to be the main drummer there.

One day, hanging at the pad, it was Betty and me. I was looking in the phone book, and I looked up Miles Davis-whoa, there is his number! Wow! I told Betty, and she said to call him. She was like the caterpillar with the hooka, and I was like Alice. I said OK, dialed, and lucky for me, no answer. She's into it now and says excitedly, "Who can we call?" Meaning, of course, who can you call. I looked more and said, "Whoa, here is Thelonious Monk's number." She said, "Call him." Boom, a deep voice came on the line, "Hello," I covered up the phone quickly and said (in an urgent whisper,) "What shall I say?" Betty is squinting at the canvas she is working on, dabs on some paint pauses, and says, "Tell him you're going to commit suicide." Ha! It went from there with Betty having a conversation with Monk through me. Monk, "Why are you going to commit suicide?" Me, "Because I came all the way here from Seattle to hear jazz, and I haven't heard the kind my soul hungers for yet." Soon, he was laughing, and we had a pretty good time. Hung up after a while and said bye cordially.

+++++

When I was first in New York, I had to find some work. My first job was as a Fleet Messenger out of the Life and Time Bldg, right across from Radio City Music Hall. I would deliver packages by hand all over Manhattan. It was an excellent way to get the layout of the city. Manhattan is laid out in a predictable grid and not that tough to navigate. From lack of discipline and lack of sleep, sometimes I would get a load of packages and just think, "Jesus, how can I catch a couple of winks?" One way was to go into a phone booth and prop my head upon a package and go to sleep. I had some angry people bang on the phone booth a few times.

There was an older black guy on the job who played guitar. He did gigs and stuff, and I asked him if he knew Freddy Greenwell? He said, "Of course." Our storefront rental turned out to be too small for two couples, and it got tense. Especially with Marilyn and Betty, so Marilyn and I got a place of our own in Spanish Harlem right on the edge of the projects, on the sixth floor of a walk-up.

+++++

I started going to a big band rehearsal at Lynn Oliver Studios,[31] a pay-to-play situation, $15 bucks a pop. But no sweat; I was getting my feet wet and meeting people. I was also going to other sessions — Port of Call and others.

I got hired for a weird little club date, some kind of Ukrainian dance. I was working my ass off trying to project on the trumpet, and the other trumpet player was not even breaking a sweat and had a beautiful full sound. The guy took pity on me and told me to see Carmine Caruso.[32] I took his advice and started taking lessons from Carmine. He had me doing his six magic notes and gave me different stuff to do each time I took a lesson from him. It really started to work. I would practice the Carmine stuff in my apartment. Some people in the building heard me, and the next thing, I was playing in a neighborhood Puerto Rican band (the leader was in Vietnam). They had real pro charts, and we rehearsed and played at the YMCA in Harlem. Then I got a tip at one of the Lynn Oliver sessions to join another big band and not be charged. That was the Harry Shields' rehearsal big band. There were a couple of very good trumpet players in that band. Tony Cafrizi was one of them.

+++++

Around this time, Marilyn and I were coming to the end of the line. Even though I was laissez-faire about the marriage in the beginning, I was devastated. But it was out of my hands.

Jay with the PLAYBOYS

Chapter 1 & 2

Dick Thorlakson

Type here
Jay and Dick

Jabo Ward

Bob Nixon

Floyd Standifer

Ronnie Pierce

Freddie with Bird

Fred Greenwell

Chapters 3 thru 7

Joe Brazil

Mike Mandel

Joe Brazil Quartet

Sarge West

Don Rizzo and Jay

Larry Coryell   Sarge West   Dean Hodges

House Of Entertainment

Featuring the finest live musical entertainment.

Jazz - Latin - Blues - Calypso
Easy Listening - Good Dancing
Serving fine Tea-Coffee-Food
Open Thurs.-Sat. 11 pm-4 am
plus SUNDAY 7 to 12 P. M.

OCCIDENTAL & WASHINGTON

Jazz-Music Spot Still Open

The House of Entertainment, Skid Road jazz-music spot at 204 Occidental Av. S. has not been affected by the collapse of a wall Monday at the rear of the building in which it is situated, Robert L. Marshall, manager, said today.

Marshall said the business is open as usual, despite the collapse of the wall and erection of a sidewalk barricade.

Jerry Heidman

Jordan Ruwe and Jay

Chapter 24 to 26
Bay Area

Chuck Sher

Chuck Metcalf

Jessica Williams

Cathy Casamo

Merry Prankster's bus
"FURTHUR"

Cathlene Marie Casamo

Michael Aragon, drummer at the
No Name Bar weekly for 38 years

CHAPTER ELEVEN

A Bad Move

*T*hen *I had an experience that was to dog me for some time.*
One night right after Marilyn left, a Puerto Rican named
Johnny Cruz, who played trombone and lived in the building,
came by with a slightly older cat. They knocked on my door,
and they were soaking wet from the rain. They came into my
pad and informed me they were going to get me high. I always thought I was a counter-culture guy, totally down on
booze, and thought heroin was entirely out of the question.
My face must have been doing a double and triple take, but
they assured me that it would only relax me, no big deal,
right? So much for my ability to set barriers or personal
boundaries. They skinned me. That's skin popped. Not into a
vein, but like a muscle shot you get at the doctor's office. I got
really high and was scratching and sick and trying to play this
piccolo that I had while they played cowbell and drums and
sang. They were laughing their asses off. They asked me if I
was high, I said, "No." Wrong answer.

I had to give up the apartment shortly after, but I did have
a new, straight job at the Kennel Club office where I filed dog
names all day long.

+++++

The topper in that period came in the form of a draft notice. It turns out I missed the first one. This one was serious. I had a date to go downtown to the Whitehall Street Draft Board. They said, "Bring toiletries and be ready to leave!" So, I decided my strategy was to pretend to be a junkie and tell them I was gay for good measure. I thought, "Gay drug addict." They'll probably let me alone after that. So, I asked Johnny to get me some stuff. It was all over the place, deuce bags that came in little Visine envelopes that were only two dollars a bag. I got high a few times, and sure enough, they did not take me when I went to the draft board. I was pretty high and "on the nod." In fact, I rode all the way downtown, and the train turned around and went back uptown before I woke up enough to navigate back down to Whitehall Street.

I was going through the inspections like the hearing test, etc. when it got to the disrobe part, and the probing was to begin. I said, "I can't do this." The examiner asked why, and I said I was gay. He could see I was high as hell also, so they sent me upstairs for a psychiatrist to give me the once over. I went upstairs and was sitting there waiting and fell asleep again. The guy finally came out and said to come in, obviously irritated at the sight of me. I went in, and he said in a disbelieving tone of voice, "OK, what makes you think you're gay?" I replied, "I just can't perform sexually without a man in bed." A little clinical, but it certainly got the job done. It turns out the Weathermen blew the hell out of the Whitehall Street Draft Station. I wonder if my record was still there or what happened to it? Believe me, the Army didn't need me anyway.

CHAPTER TWELVE

Machito

I was still rehearsing with the Harry Shields Big band when trumpeter Tony Cafrizi got me hooked up with a gig for the summer in the Catskills. It was with the legendary Cuban bandleader, Machito! I was not quite hip to who Machito was at the time; I would have been freaking out if I had known.

Machito's[33] band was an "on-the-job" opportunity for me to learn. I was supposed to share a room with the alto player. I did not care for him and switched right away to room with Warren Fitzgerald,[34] an excellent jazz player, ten years my senior. He used to play with Bird and was very good. Warren was like Jerry Gray; he could hear the changes to just about anything quickly and accurately. He was the trumpet player on Bob Dorough's first album, *Devil May Care*. Warren was also friends with Freddy Greenwell and used to play at a well-known, famous photographer's loft where many musicians hung and played. The photographer was W. Eugene Smith, and he had over 4,000 hours of reel-to-reel tape. Warren and Freddy used to play there and Bill Crow, Phil Woods, Paul Bley, Bob Brookmeyer, Zoot Sims, etc. He told me a lot of Freddy's stories. Freddy really got around.

The gig with Machito was at the Concord Hotel in the Catskills and consisted of two long dance sets each night. After the two sets, we were free. We ate in a separate area and went through a line to load up our tray with all kinds of good food. We could use the pool during the day; life was easy.

The first week we had an ace lead player. I think it was Victor Paz. I know he said, "God Bless Carmine Caruso!" It was smooth sailing that week. Then he had to leave, and his replacement was a guy named Danny Little. Danny Little was an older trumpet player who used to play with Art Dietrick. Charts by Art Dietrick were everywhere when I first started and were very easy and not fun to play. Danny was very white and older, with stiffness in his phrasing that was at odds with what Mario Bauza wanted to hear. Danny was a complete idiot. He would get excited sometimes and work his elbows rapidly like a chicken on speed and yell, "Heba-hoba heba-hoba heba-hoba." It turns out he had just been on a cruise ship and had been confined to the boiler room for fighting and creating havoc.

With Danny Little, the Machito gig took a turn for the worse, and Mario Bauza was bummed with Danny. Mario Bauza looked at me with a sour, doleful expression that said, "Why can't you play the lead trumpet part?" Oh boy! Anyway, just a little way into the gig, when he realized I could not handle the lead trumpet chair, he fired me. I kept on that week. Then, because I could contribute by standing up and playing during the medleys that went non-stop over either cha-cha or rhumba, Mario had a change of heart. He talked to me and said if I did not have another gig, I could continue. Also, I was playing my parts strong.

At that point, I got a smaller bore trumpet. I had an Xtra large-bore Benge that I wished someone would have talked me out of before I bought it. I was young when I bought it and thought a big bore horn was better. For someone like myself, who is not a "powerful" player, that could be a big problem with range and endurance, especially on longer gigs in large rooms. My dad sent me the old medium-large Benge I grew up playing that I shared with him. Later, I got a horn at Manny's Music, a Martin Committee model, 460 bore or medium-large. Also, some help was changing my mouthpiece. There was a salesman with a big briefcase full of jet-tone mouthpieces, traveling from one show band to another. I got one that worked better for me.

+++++

Mario Bauza[35] played alto on the band and got a beautiful sound. When he played "Besame Mucho", it was great; gorgeous, and not corny in the slightest! Later, I heard that Mario Bauza had learned the trumpet in a matter of weeks, though that might be a stretch. But the story went that Mario was fresh in New York from Cuba, where he had been a clarinet player at a symphonic level. He was very hungry for work, and someone told him about a job. Unfortunately, it was on trumpet. However, Mario said, "I can do it." He got a trumpet and basically "discovered" how it went as far as blowing, including high notes. When I say discovered, that is what happens a lot of the time, rather than day-to-day practicing at a snails' pace in micro increments. Yes, day-to-day practice is essential, but real progress often becomes more of a discovery than doing the same thing day after day in the same way. So, when I showed up blowing my jazz on a trumpet that was too big to play without a bright enough sound to project consistently, Mario probably saw red. I was occasionally getting loaded, and this certainly did not escape his all-seeing eye. He eventually warmed up to me, and Machito and Mario used to joke about me mercilessly. They would ask if I liked clams, and then they would laugh their asses off! I didn't mind. I was the kid.

On the last night of each week, many cats came from the other hotel bands and played our last set with us for fun. We had Chico O'Farrill charts that were fun to play.

I was the youngest guy in the band and kind of an odd duck. I did not drink and was looked at as "different," so to speak. My drug use was not at an addiction stage yet, but I did score one time from a Puerto Rican working in the kitchen. I brought stuff with me a few times and nodded on the bandstand. That could have been a not-so-good thing with Mario Bauza.

Danny Little once asked me if I would take him to an orgy! He assumed all young people like me were into communal free sex. He said he would not participate, only watch! Once when Warren was soloing, Danny started to yell and beat his foot, so the bandstand was shaking. Warren had a short fuse and told Danny never to do that again. Danny went to "the kid in the sandbox mode" and said in a real hurt tone of voice, "You kicked my case!" Warren said, "Shut up motherfucker, this isn't kindergarten." Mario Bauza turned around and, with his coke bottle lens glasses, put the stare on us. That stopped them immediately.

I was always trying to widen my repertoire of standards so I could solo during the medley sections. I was practicing piccolo at the time, and on my rather long breaks, I would find a room in the back and practice playing "Giant Steps" on piccolo. (I was like the kid that knew two songs, "Giant Steps" and "Happy Birthday"). I played piccolo a few times in front of the band, and they were digging me, but alas: one of the times, I was getting bugged trying to tune the damn thing, and I stopped playing during the song. That ended their promoting my piccolo soloing. My pic was super old with an older fingering system. But it was really fun to play.

CHAPTER THIRTEEN

WOODSTOCK

The Concord Hotel was in Monticello, New York, up-state, and was in the "Borscht Belt" of the Catskill Mountains, primarily where Jewish families vacationed., One day, during the Machito run, I noticed a helluva lot of traffic outside. Many of the cars were full of hippies. I asked one car creeping along what was up. They said there was a big music festival happening close by. I asked, "what are the hours?" and they said, "Nonstop for two whole days." It was Woodstock.[36]

That night, I said to the bass player and Warren, "Let's go to the festival." We left after Machito's last set and drove as close as we could get to the sounds of music and the lights over the trees. Soon we were walking on a dark path through the woods. We could hear branches breaking in the trees and were alarmed, thinking some stoned hippie would drop out of a tree on us! People on motorcycles were speeding down the path, oblivious to us. We had to leap out of the way every time. Warren, a very macho guy who had a motorcycle himself and was often "packing a pistol," said the next guy who does that, he would tear him off the bike. We said maybe not a good idea considering the pack-like nature of the biker gangs.

Anyway, we got there without any mishaps and watched bands into the evening. It was a revelation to Warren, the Jazz guy, and the Puerto Rican bass player. They were amazed at the sheer spectacle, as was I. The next night Warren and I and the bass player went there again, and I gave them a hit of acid! That was a hell of a night. When Jimi Hendrix played the Star-Spangled Banner, I was so high I thought it was just free playing or tuning up. It was early in the morning, and there were a lot fewer people when Jimi came on. As the sun started to rise, it was a bit much on our dilated pupils, and the hippie thing was wearing thin. When Sha Na Na came on, we literally ran out of there.

+++++

That afternoon, we played a pool session at the Concord, where Machito's band played for people who were drinking Pina Coladas and little drinks with umbrellas, etc. The customers would get a free dance lesson, and then we would play. I, the bass player, and Warren were totally wrecked from the Woodstock night. When the bass player had a hard time hooking up with Pete Escovedo, Mario Bauza just gave me the devil stare knowing it was my fault.

Not too much else was eventful that summer. The hotel had seven different bands, which was cool. Our bungalows were off to the side of the golf course, where some of the other bands played. I used to see Erskine Hawkins' band on my breaks when they were playing. Erskine Hawkins is famous for "Tuxedo Junction". Those cats were the real thing, a band of old black guys, so it sounded better than the standard society fare.

One afternoon, we played a little gig for a party up in the mountains. This one was for all Spanish speakers. It was looser than the hotel's gigs, and people were dancing and drinking and doing lots of blow. I was not into coke; I tried some when I was on that gig. I guess I was expecting something way different. I know coke appeals to many, but others don't have much of an affinity for it, like me.

I played the whole summer with Machito, and I'm grateful that Mario Bauza helped me rather than fire me.

+++++

One weird thing about Woodstock was I met up with the people who took over my six-flight walk-up apartment in Spanish Harlem. They had my record player, which I had left at the apartment. I liked that turntable, 'cuz I could put it on half speed for transcribing. Sometimes I even listened to music at half speed. Doing that, you can hear the inflections in pitch and vibrato. Jazz has pitch fluctuations and various forms of vibrato and articulation variations to make it come to life.

CHAPTER FOURTEEN

MUSART

After the Machito gig, I continued to go down to the Musart sessions. George knew everybody and would hire different people for the jam sessions. One time, he hired bassist, Wilbur Ware.[37] Wilbur Ware was a very bad junkie but played with a majestic sure-footed beat and was still one of the greats. Once, when I played with him at the session, I played along, and something changed. I turned around, and Wilbur was lighting up a cigarette. Wilbur could also sing quite well and knew the lyrics to all kinds of songs. There was an Armenian singer who hung around and "helped" George around the club. Wilbur was always flirting with her and grabbing harmony on anything she sang. They were even singing Hank Williams' tunes. It was strange to see and hear Wilbur Ware harmonizing on "Your Cheatin' Heart". Once the singer sat in, and the music was just burning. She only sang one phrase over and over, backward and every which way. The phrase was, "I found out." Of course, it was very cool on a variety of levels. She was a real beauty and sang that phrase with such passion, my imagination roamed. I imagine we were all wondering what she had found out!

Once I was playing and having a better than average time of it when George just walked up to me and said, "Flugel!" Anyway, I'm sitting there with a drummer named JC Moses[38]), who had some food George had prepared, and he was sharing it with me. Suddenly there was a commotion in the hallway that leads to where we were. It was Freddie Hubbard[39] with a whole entourage of people, kind of a mobile party in progress. George and Freddie had kind of a rivalry. George even went to the West Coast with Freddie playing bass, according to George.

Anyway, they had this kind of really high, soft voice sparring going on, and Freddie got his horn out and said one word, "Steps." Boom, they were off into "Giant Steps" and it was moving! Then they played "Afternoon in Paris", and I was just blown away by Freddie's crisp chops and vocabulary.

JC Moses started explaining to me that, in New York, you needed to take your vitamin pills. Then he proceeded to tell me I should get some gigs and hire him. I did not realize that that was the way to go forward: get a gig and hire the best people you can, even famous names. But, alas, I hadn't reached that stage of enlightenment.

One thing I had going for me (by the very virtue of my ignorance) was that I was not into a pecking order based on ability. Not quite as much as someone, for instance, coming up in New York and taking a number! I met a lot of good players that would have never considered even going to Musart and playing.

George often hired Albert Dailey[40] on piano. Albert was down there a lot. When I first arrived in New York with Steve and Betty, Albert would come over to our place and get high. He would go on the nod and talk, mainly about his life. Albert said he had an athletic scholarship to a university because he could pick up a basketball with one hand. He talked about all kinds of stuff. Albert wasn't doing well career-wise because of the smack.

George would hire some really good cats on the weekend, and one time I got to play with Jimmy Garrison[41]. I was like a bug on the wall at the end of the session. I would just hang there and listen to scuttlebutt and gossip about different players. It was quite an education.

CHAPTER FIFTEEN

The Albert Hotel, Howie Wyeth, The Albert Band

So now, I'm into the last of August '69 and staying with a lady named Faola who lived in a rent-controlled apartment next to Steve and Betty. Faola was a real tough cookie, but beautiful. Her boyfriend bartended at a jazz club. Faola used to hang with Jim Pepper, and she was a dabbler in narcotics. She also was not keen on my staying there. One evening she came into the apartment and said, "I'm not having you sit around here any longer. Here call this number!"

There was an ad in the Village Voice for a band needing a trumpet player. I had already called some of the bandleaders from Dick Thorlakson's New York contacts, and guess what? They were only interested in lead players. So, with that in mind, I called the number she gave me, and they said to come right over. The audition was going to be at the Albert Hotel.

The Albert Hotel[42] was between East and West Village and was a sister hotel to the Chelsea Hotel. When you came into the lobby, there were pictures of all the musicians who had stayed there, virtually everybody.

I went up to the suite and knocked on the door. The door opened, and I went into a big living room area. Hmmm, no band! Just three guys were standing there, and one guy says, "OK, play something." I took my trumpet out and played "Freedom Jazz Dance", a tricky head. Freedom Jazz Dance is an Eddie Harris head brought to people's attention by Miles on *Miles Smiles'* record. The "head" of "Freedom Jazz Dance" was popular among jazz/contemporary/boogaloo musicians who had some chops.

After I finished, they said, "We're leaving tomorrow morning. Can you come?" Oh boy, I was rescued. I said, "Sure, and by the way, I need a place to stay."

At that time, the band's name was *The Otis Elevator* because the frontman- bandleader was a huge African American singer named Otis Smith. The other guys were John Huston and Howie Wyeth.[43] Howie lived at The Albert Hotel in a suite with another guy. It was kind of small quarters, but they were tight from college. Howie was very personable and a little older than me. He played drums and organ. John Huston played trombone and tenor. Otis sang. Soon, we were headed upstate to Lake George to play at a dance club.

Before we left, though, I said I needed to get an advance to settle a few things. I got the money and headed uptown to Spanish Harlem to score. Not a wise move without Johnny Cruz and the fact that I no longer lived up there. I went to where the action was, and a guy said, "Come on with me; I'll fix you up."

We walked a few blocks and entered a building. We had been chatting nicely, but as soon as we got into the building, the guy had a gun at my temple and said, "All right, take off your clothes and give me all your money." I turned to jelly. I complied as quickly as I could. Then, I put my clothes on again, all the while talking about the Latin band I played with and Machito and my harmless nature "Just let me go!" etc.

Instead of ushering me out the front door, my big scare came when he motioned for me to climb down these stairs to a basement area. Whoa, that's where my life passed before my eyes. But luckily, there was a way out from down there, out the back of the building. As soon as I was out, I ran and flagged down a gypsy cab and had him take me to the Village and the Albert Hotel. I had no money to pay the guy, so he had to go inside to get paid. I have no idea what the band was thinking at this time. It must have been at least W-T-F!

The next day we were heading up to the gig by train. There was a guy kind of on the nod at Grand Central, and I sidled up to him (I had a few dollars left from paying the cabbie), and he rolled off a few bags for me.

The Lake George gig was cool, and I even had my own motel room. I was learning the book and found I had no problem playing with the band. Nonetheless, my ability to just hang on the breaks was nil. I had no social skills and was very uncomfortable when I was not playing. If it was not about music, I did not know what to do with myself.

I was playing my flute, as well as trumpet and flugelhorn. At the end of the week, I went back to the city and headed uptown again. This time I connected with Johnny Cruz. Johnny and I were just heading out to score when a pack of cats stopped Johnny to talk about me. I recognized one of the guys as a neighborhood bad guy named Manny, who once flashed a knife at me when I lived up there. After a short discussion with Johnny in Spanish, they took off, and Johnny informed me they wanted to take me down. But he told them I was his boy! Well, I was happy about that indeed.

After Johnny and I scored, he was walking me back, and I was going to get a cab to the Port of Authority to catch the bus up to Lake George. The pack of Johnny's friends re-appeared. This time Manny got in my face and said, "Give me some money." I said I did not have any, but the dope had me in a surly attitude, and when he asked what I was doing, I told him I was going to catch a cab. Johnny immediately said, "You blew it, man," and he kind of walked away at a distance. At that point, they were dragging me off the street and into a doorway. After the terror of the previous week, I shouted, "Not the doorway! "Ha!

They took my money, my new shirt I had just bought and my flute. That's where Johnny stepped in, and they gave me back my flute! Now I had to get myself to the bus station and then find the bus that would take me to Lake George.

+++++

After the hassle of getting back to the gig, the band would not let me go to the city anymore on my days off.

I settled into the gig, and I even managed to get a girlfriend! I can't remember her name, but her dad was a real gangster in Rochester, Soprano's style. The dad never married her mother and had houses of prostitution. She told me her dad put the kittens that were born from her cat in the freezer. Hmmm.

We played there for a while, and then we were back at the Albert Hotel. This time, the girl I was with, and her friend got a suite across the hall from Howie. By now, I had gotten into the musical fabric of this group of musicians. They added a player named Mike Gibson[44] , who was a helluva arranger in addition to playing trombone. He was great and later went on to write for Broadway. He wrote the score and music to Grease.

+++++

I was still going to Musart, and one night I was there when George had hired Roy Haynes[45] to play the jam session. It was unusual to have someone of Roy's stature be the jam session drummer. It was a semi-private jam session, not all the way open to the public. That night a tenor player was hanging around named Rocky Boyd. He had been down there before and even once borrowed George's tenor and played great. It turns out Rocky had a record out with Kenny Dorham and had played briefly with Miles Davis. This night, Rocky was on the piano playing some weird shit, and Roy said, "Rocky, play your horn." Rocky had no horn. Rocky proceeded to tell Roy the kinds of things he was playing on the piano as if the explanation would matter. Roy replied, "Rocky, it hasn't got any feeling." Roy said it sadly, so I could tell Rocky was, even though crazy, respected. He had a giant book and said, "Everything you need to know is in here." I looked in his book, and it was a car manual, car parts, etc. Whoa. It was a cold night, so I took him to The Albert to put him up for the night.

It was a little weird. Rocky took a shower and then started walking around naked!

+++++

The life I had going had more pitfalls related to that pesky narcotics thing starting to gain ground with me. I continued to go over to Musart and play and was still after it musically. I would go into the closet with all the coats to do my Caruso stuff, even though I was not taking lessons from him at this time.

CHAPTER SIXTEEN

New York to Seattle and Back to New York

Around Christmas, my folks sent me a plane ticket to come home for the holidays.

As soon as I got in Seattle, guess what? My friends Dave Johnson and Joe Brazil were farther along the dope path than me. Dave was playing with Sarge West and Rich Dangel and working all the time. Dave's drumming was on fire. Dave and Joe had a place by the dump on the edge of Fremont. Sarge and Rich used to go by and fix at their house. Dave and Joe both looked up to those guys because they were cool guys and great musicians as well as dopers. So, one time, Dave said he wanted to try it. Dave's rationalization was that, as part of the trio, he wanted to feel the "time" the same! Dave was already playing great, but it probably was a little lonely with Sarge and Rich doing their thing; anyway, that was his thinking. But nature took its course, and Dave was soon ensconced in the subculture. Joe, on the other hand, had a time with drugs way back in High School that nobody knew about, so Joe went from "straight" to "hope to die junkie" overnight, no midway point for him.

I spent Christmas with my family and started getting some gigs. Dave would pop by sometimes on the way to work and leave me a *cotton*. Even that small amount would knock me on my ass. I was back into hangin' with Joe. I loved Joe's playing and said, "Joe, let's go back to New York together; the band will love your playing." The only problem was Joe's horn was in hock at Joe's Music on 15th, which later became Joe's Guitar shop. I remember there was some real drama about getting his horn back. We got it and were soon on the plane back to New York together. Joe scored some dope with me and said he would give me my share on the plane. Ha! He did it all. He was a dog, but I loved him anyway.

When we landed in New York, it was a real cold spell. I was only wearing a sports jacket, and I was freezing. We first went to Steve and Betty's place where my girlfriend from Lake George and her friend were. I knocked on the door. She was with a guy, but she told him he had to split. Well, we did not last but two hot seconds. She said, "It's me or the drugs," so I moved into Howie's suite at the Albert and had a cot in the kitchen. Not sure where Joe slept!

Also, when we first got to New York, we discovered Joe had left his horn at the airport. We miraculously retrieved it with Al Pace's help, a piano player friend of my dad who lived in New Jersey. A little about Al: Al was doing transcribing work for Rahsaan Roland Kirk. I had also met Davey Schnitter at his place a year earlier. Al was originally from Seattle and helped me with theory and chords when I was first starting. Joe and I moved into the suite at the Albert, and, sure enough, the guys did dig Joe's playing. He was very funky.

Howie and John, and Michael Gibson were starting to write for the band. We had some rehearsals, and the music was cool and original. We were building a whole book for the Albert band, which, by the way, became just The Albert. I continued to go to Musart for my jazz hit when I could, and I was getting better, despite the chaos in my life

I slowed down a bit with my drug thing. A whole series of burns really affected me. There is nothing worse than spending money you don't have, going way out on a limb, and then getting burned or ripped off with nothing to show for it and no chemical relief.

Joe and I were practicing in the basement of the Albert Hotel at 3 or 4 in the morning, and he asked me, "Man, can I try your trumpet?" I handed him the trumpet and was holding his sax. He was blowing it, but the trumpet is not kind to novices. On the contrary, when I put his horn up to my lips, I already knew the fingerings from Flute. He had a great setup. I put some air in it and started with all my fingers down and lifted my fingers one by one, starting with my lower right hand. I went right up the scale. It was a hop, skip, and a jump 'til I was playing lines and stuff. At that moment, I knew I needed to get a saxophone soon.

Another tragedy happened that was just an added problem to the already mounting set of them around this time. One night, I took some acid and headed down into the basement to practice all night. As the acid was coming on, I went over to where, I swear, I had just seen my trumpet. I kept looking for my trumpet. The suite was not that big, and after kind of mentally leaving the room and looking in little drawers and stuff for my trumpet, someone finally came up and said, "Stop! Your trumpet is gone." I had a Martin Committee model I was getting comfortable with and a mouthpiece I liked, etc. Gone! In the kitchen, I looked out the window into the space between the buildings. There was a lot of junk down there. Someone piled it up to the window, hopped in, and snatched the horn, and went back out the window. Welcome to the big city, kid! I borrowed John Huston's cornet for a while before I got another trumpet.

+++++

Howie Wyeth, the band leader, was starting to get way into recording and various things. Howie was a young scion of the Wyeth family. Here, I had thought he was just some educated hippie! His grandfather was the famous illustrator, N.C. Wyeth; his uncle was Andrew Wyeth; his brother, Jamie Wyeth.

I remember going to Atlantic records with Howie and cutting some tracks. Howie was also tight with R&B songwriter Solomon Burke[46] and Don Covay.[47] When he was at the hotel, it was cool to watch Covay work writing songs. "Mercy Mercy" is his best-known song, not to be confused with the Joe Zawinul "Mercy Mercy" played by Cannonball.

Things were starting to happen about this time. Howie got us hooked with Perception Records to do a James Moody[48] CD. I must admit it is not my favorite Moody album, but James Moody was always great. We went in and did a whole album with him. I wrote a song, "The New Spirit", that we recorded. When I listen to it now, it sounds kind of strange, a real 1970 vibe! Later on, it sounded good when Joe Brazil played it. The album was called *The Teachers*. We also recorded all the music we had been rehearsing/playing for the past year at this session. The album was called *The Albert*. The Albert released two albums on Perception, both self-titled *The Albert*.[49] The one from 1970 I'm on, but I'm not on the one from 1971.

CHAPTER SEVENTEEN

The Inside Track Band

While we were waiting for the album to come out, I got a call to go on the road with a band called *The Inside Track,* run by legendary Texas tenor man *Billy Tillman.*[50]Dave Johnson was on the band, and Chris Peterson was singing. Chris was a great singer from Detroit. She was married to the bone player. It was a three-horn front line behind a rhythm section and vocalist. Bob Brenner on bass had been touring with Buddy Rich. Van Roblow, a very soulful guitar player and singer, was from Louisiana. I was taking Fletch Wiley's place. Fletch and I went to the same high school, and he had graduated from North Texas State. It was a burning band.

I flew into Lawton, Oklahoma, to join the band. They had sent me money for a plane ticket and enough for me to bring some dope. The band was all into smack, except Van, an alcoholic, barb head, and occasionally, speed. Chris Peterson was not a drug taker, but she would drink and get into big emotional jags and lash out at her husband and Billy Tillman. Billy was into speed and smack. The name of the band even had a double meaning: *Inside Track.*

I was not doing super well; my horn was in the pawnshop in New York. I borrowed a Conn Constellation from the bone player. Like an idiot, I did not have a decent mouthpiece either. It did not matter; the first night, I was great, picking up the charts fast. The next day when I was clean, whoops, I was in deep shit. Withdrawal is characterized by loss of energy and inability to focus. It took a bit of doing to get on top of that one. I was copying my friend Dave, who had substituted alcohol for dope.

We toured the South, playing in Texas and Florida, and ended up recording in Washington DC. I had the gig going pretty good by then. We were in the middle of a recording session in Washington, DC, and there was a chart that had a high and held repeated figure. I suggested (since we were at the beginning of the session) to play one, leave one out, play one, etc., come back and float them in later. Suddenly, the engineer got into producer mode and was talking to Tillman, "What the hell's wrong with that trumpet player?" I heard that and flipped out, said, "Fuck off," grabbed my suitcase, and headed to New York, hitchhiking!

After I left, they got Sal Marques[51] to play. Sal was a very gifted jazz trumpeter with excellent chops. Dave had his stepson and wife and their little dog, Tiger, on the road with him at this time. Dave said they were in close quarters, and Sal took to blowing double high Cs at Tiger, which did not help their situation! According to Dave, Sal said that when he played with Bill Chase, Bill would play a high G, and Sal said he would play Double high C and Shake it!

Sal ended up in LA right after that band and recorded with Frank Zappa on Hot Rats. Chris Petersen also was on that. (Even so, Sal was a great jazz trumpet player who later got the call to play with Branford's Tonight Show band backing Jay Leno.)

+++++

When I got back to New York, I immediately pulled my trumpet out of hock and headed up to the Lake George gig that The Albert was doing for the whole summer. I quickly found that Joe had been a bad boy when I was gone; he owed money to everyone on the band. I got my gig back, and the band was sounding great, but they were watching me closely after Joe had kind of fouled the nest.

I played well one night, but the second night was a disaster. The club owner, a rich hippie, had a pith helmet full of little candy wafers with acid. I took one and was playing the gig and started to drink. You won't find that winning combination in the Dale Carnegie book! At some point in the evening, I was singing my parts loudly into the microphone instead of playing them on the trumpet. Otis turned to Joe, of all people, and told him to control his friend! Joe flipped him off, and the music came to a stop. Otis and Joe got into it, Joe swinging John Huston's borrowed sax like a weapon. At one point, Otis was punching him, and every time Joe got punched, he said, "That's cool!"

I won't go too far into this, but the next morning when I opened my eyes, a friend and trumpet player, Richie Meisterman, came into my room and said, "You guys got way out last night." Then he brought the tenor in, and it looked like a pretzel. I had a bad feeling in the pit of my stomach when I saw the sax. I knew I would not weather this one.

CHAPTER EIGHTEEN

"They Mailed Me Back Home!"

We were escorted to a bus that afternoon. John Huston was super pissed. He said, "Get help; see someone about this." He had had enough. Howie was friendly and sad. Most of the old-time members saw Joe and me off. While traveling back to New York City, Joe got off the bus at one of the stops, and the bus left with Joe in the mountains. Boom, I was going into N.Y. with his bags and my own!

I kind of got adopted by the Rouda family, who lived next door to the suite I had shared with Howie and others in the Albert. I was clean and remorseful. There was even talk that they would probably take me back. I was in regular contact with Howie.

However, Joe was not doing well at all. It's getting hazy now, but, as I remember, Joe was using the fire escape to sneak into suites that did not have locked windows and sleeping. He was working on fruit trucks uptown and got beat up several times.

We sent for money to get him back to Tacoma. It was a load off everyone's mind when he sailed home. He could have died quickly in New York.

I could have persevered, but I was worn out, so I returned to Seattle instead.

As my old friend, Willie Thomas once said, "they just mailed me back home."

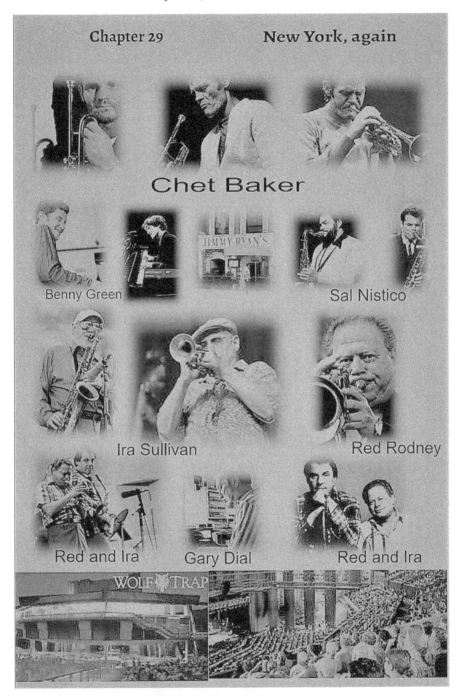

Chapter 29 New York, again

Chet Baker

Benny Green Sal Nistico

Ira Sullivan Red Rodney

Red and Ira Gary Dial Red and Ira

Kim Eggers et al

Peaceable Lane

Bullseye

Dave Lewis

Big Mama Thornton band

CHAPTER NINETEEN

The '70s were my 20's:

In the fall of 1970, I'm back in Seattle feeling like a washed-up, has- been, and I was only 21 years old.

The 1970s were some crazy years, and I'm glad I survived. I was 21 years old when I returned to Seattle in 1970, and I had absolutely no "self-propulsion." I went from one band to another, and my priority was far from any sensible self-improvement program. I was consumed with my drug life, and 1970 started with a very lonely Jay in the personal relations department: no girlfriends and only a few friends. Many people looked at me as washed up, and I had barely begun. Sometimes, I would go to a jam session and just nod out. Not exactly a way to win fans. But, in that decade, I made contacts in San Francisco and took up saxophone in a big way, so positive things were going on, despite my life's chaos.

When I returned from New York, I lived in the basement at my folk's house on 51st and 15th in the University District. It had been a boarding house my grandmother ran and rented to university students before my dad and mom moved the family in. I started to act up in this period because there was quite a dope scene on "The Ave" in the University District.

The summer of love was no longer so loving on parts of "The Ave," where speed and heroin were sold continuously.

I started playing with a band led by Kim Eggers and Mark Whitman, but that did not last a long time. I played with several R & B bands and worked out at the airport strip on a funk Top 40 type band with horns for a while.

At that time, I had moved into the Fischer Studio Building. Pat Gossan was the vocalist for a famous northwest band called *The Floating Bridge*, which featured Rich Dangel and Joe Johannson, both formidable guitarists. Pat said he knew someone with a tenor sax they wanted to sell so that I could score a Tenor sax at that time.

I went to Seattle's Central District (as it was called then) and went to a little house, and a black guy (named Speedball) answered the door. He showed me the horn. It was in a case and was virtually in pieces, wrapped in string. After checking to make sure it was a tenor and had all the parts, I bought it for 50 dollars. It was weird in Speedball's house because there was no furniture. Only a record album propped upright by the door; it was Bobby Bland's *Two Steps from the Blues*. I took the sax to Seattle's preeminent repairman, Given Lots, and he completely re-padded it and went through it for a ridiculously low amount of money by today's standards. It might have been 25 bucks! Oh, and I needed a mouthpiece, so my "uncle" Rollo Strand came by with a cigar box full of Otto Link Tenor mouthpieces -which he just gave me. All kinds of vintages. They would be worth thousands of dollars today.

+++++

I got on the Methadone[52] program. I was living with a girl and went utterly insane. Because of the drugs from the psychiatrist, as well as the methadone, I went nuts. Somebody gave me a bunch of Peruvian flake coke, and that was not helping either. I was practicing all the time on tenor; however, it was a precarious time for me.

At that time, Dave Johnson, his wife, Tammy, and their son came off the road with the Inside Track band. I will always be grateful to Dave. He literally saved my life when he moved me into his house out in Richmond Beach. I was around a family again with my buddy Dave Johnson. I moved next door into Dave Press' basement. Dave, Corky Ryan, Dave Press, Andy Duvall, Charlie Morgan, and I started a band. After a failure to find a steady source of income, the band floundered and broke up. We rehearsed a lot and were going for "The Dream." It was a good band.

Since I was on the methadone program, I got public assistance, so I was going slowly forward financially. Bassist Bob Brenner, from the Inside Track, showed up from Texas to play with Dave Johnson. They locked up so well; it was a special thing they had. Billy Tillman, the leader of the *Inside Track*, joined *Blood Sweat and Tears*. Brenner and I ended up getting a house way out north by Martha Lake. Because there was a severe lack of direction in the band, Corky Ryan had made some personnel changes. I knew I was probably next on the chopping block.

+++++

Andy Duval, a very soulful singer, and drummer who Corky had fired from the band showed up one night out at Martha Lake. He kind of surveyed the scene saw my condition, looked around, and sucked his teeth. He knew I had no car and was stuck way out there in a quasi-pit of my own making.

Andy had driven up in a bright red hearse that was his vehicle. He wore a pair of Levis that had a patch that said, "Please Fuck Me!" He was the real deal, an electric blue-eyed, soul man. We always got along. He was a little older and saw me as a throwback to the late fifties and early sixties when he played with Ron Holden. He loved Ray Charles and used to play the *Ray Charles Introduces Fathead* album all the time, so we communicated powerfully.

Anyway, Andy says, "Hey, c'mon down to Olympia and play with the band I have with Brady Anderson." I knew Brady because he played with the Dynamics and the Jimmy Hanna Big Band, so I knew it would be fun. I said to him, "Man, can I come tomorrow? I have to pick up my dose of Methadone." I had already been a day without, probably took more the day before, or sold my take-home dose, which I used to do.

Andy looked around, again surveying my scene, and looked straight at me and said, "You have to come now!" I did not hesitate that long. I thought, "What the hell," I grabbed my coat, saxophone, and trumpet and hopped into the red hearse. That was the first time I walked away from a methadone program.

I had a ball on the gig and met a girl who took care of my carnal needs. She gave me a pile of diet pills to try to speed my way out of withdrawal symptoms, and that kind of helped. I went back to Seattle but did not go to the house out north. Instead, I either stayed at Dick Thorlakson's apartment or my dope connection's pad. Then I would go back down to Olympia for "super fun." A whole community loved that band, so I was part of a social group again that was appreciative of my playing.

CHAPTER TWENTY

Olympia and Jules

After a couple gigs in Olympia, I met and fell for Brady's sister Jules, who I later married. Jules was a star in that community and was a striking, tall, red head. Jules and I hooked up, and I soon found that the "going back to Seattle during the week and that whole thing" would not work. Jules and I were both on the comeback trail, as it were. She had a history with speed and had cleaned up, and I was trying to change as well. I was a mess, but a healthy young mess! Jules was and is a very down-to-earth person, and I learned a lot from her. Hey, I learned a lot from Marilyn, as well!

I moved in with Jules in Maytown, a small town south of Olympia, where her mom put us to work with various projects.

+++++

About this time, I found a doctor. I heard good things about this doctor from one of the girls getting "diet pills" from him. I went to him one evening before the gig. His office had a nondescript waiting room right out of a Norman Rockwell painting from the 1950s. When I was in the cubicle, he asked me what the problem was. I made up a story that I worked at the laundry downtown and that getting the wet clothes out of the washer was killing my back. I told him that I had a history of back trouble, which was kind of true. When I was in Jr High and High School, I had a weird condition that was a back fungus called epithasitius. The doctor went to write me a script for muscle relaxants and a mild pain killer. I quickly shifted gears and said I was more interested in pain relief. He kind of stepped back and lifted his eyebrows and asked me if I had found anything that worked. I said my girlfriend had something for pain called "New Morphan"- slang name was blue morphine. He let out a little whistle and said he was not going to write for that. He calmly prescribed Dolophine. That saved me from going back to Seattle every week. Dolophine is the retail name for Methadone. I found that I could control my intake pretty well. I would not take it every day. Because the half-life in the system lasts a long time, I could make my pre-scription for 50 pills last one month. I had to walk a fine line and could never say I was an addict. I had to have a plausible reason for taking medicine because the doctor was a respected surgeon and a GP doctor in Olympia. I got a kick out of the movie about Bird, showing Red Rodney going to doctors and working them for pain meds.

+++++

After being with Jules for a few weeks, she said to me one night before a gig, "You drive yourself to the gig." I got in the car, and it was an automatic, so I just steered myself down to the club. This was when I finally became a "driver." I didn't crash or anything, and Jules gave me pointers along the way. But I can certainly say I'm a self-taught driver.

That Olympia band was a lot of fun. The music was funky; we did stuff by BB King and War and the Crusaders and The Allman Bros and just a whole hodge-podge of material.

Around this time, I met Chuck Stentz. Chuck ran a music store in Olympia, and he was a fine tenor player my dad's age, maybe a few years older. Anyway, I came into his store on a rainy winter evening right before closing time to get a reed. As I was waiting for him to finish up with a customer, I picked up a flugelhorn that was sitting in the window, and before he could stop me, I started to play. He freaked out and kept saying, "That's jazz, that's jazz." I guess he didn't expect a loaded hippie to show up at his store to buy a reed and start playing Art Farmer stuff on the flugelhorn. Later we became friends; he was like a Dutch uncle to me at times. He was not one to hold back about what he thought of my lifestyle.

After a while, I traded my Reynolds Supertone sax for a Selmer Mark VI. I bought the VI from Art Morgan, a friend of my dad, who was also my sister's flute teacher back when she was in high school. The VI was a Selmer Varitone with a pickup built into the neck to connect to an amplified speaker and play in octaves.

I ended up hooking a wa-wa pedal to it also, and it was a lot of fun. I could play, trading with the guitar, and it was like two guitars. I learned something at that time, and that is: Often, where your horn sound is sitting in the mix is essential. If your volume is under the accompaniment, you would have to be a genius to make an impact, and even then, it might not get anyone's attention. But if you are loud, then when you do a simple declarative statement or even one note, it works. When Miles plays just one note, it's not way down in the mix; it's very present. Same way with Miles' Harmon mute sound, Miles puts the Harmon right up to the mic; it gets over the band and has good volume.

I continued to play with that band with Andy and Brady. Jules and I remodeled a gas station in Maytown that Goldie, Jules's mother, owned. We made it into a truck stop with food and gas. I was not very good at that life. Waiting on truckers was not pleasant for me, and the truckers did not want to see me either!

CHAPTER TWENTY-ONE

Dave Lewis and More Bands

About this time, I got a call that Dave Lewis[53] was putting a band together to play at a new club opening up out on Martin Luther King Way called the Heritage House Club. Dave's band would play between national acts. Junior Heath and Joe Johanson were on guitars. Joe Johnson was on bass, Dave Johnson on drums, Don Rizzo on tenor, me on trumpet, and Dave Lewis on organ, vocals, and fronting the band. It was a pretty good-sounding band and did not take a lot of effort to get it off the ground. The Heritage House was a gravy gig that was not hard and paid well. We even got great Creole-style soul food at the gig, which was a big plus. That started a couple of years of my working with Dave Lewis.

I think it was 1971 now. I was angling to play tenor on that band, and after a bit of finessing, I got Ron Soderstrom on trumpet, and I played tenor. Musically, I was way happier. Later, we would do little gigs where I was the only horn. The Heritage House gig finished, and then the Dave Lewis band got a gig at the Fresh Air Avenue Tavern on Broadway. We were the house band. We played before and between the star acts, people like Flora Purim and Flo and Eddy, etc. We were also going to be the Paramount Theater's house band. It was to be The Dave Lewis Big Band. I remember my dad and Dick Thorlakson and Biggie Lewis and Jordan Ruwe and Leonard Rose were some of the band musicians. We only did one gig, though. It was opening for B.B King.

+++++

Then I joined a band that was led by Kim Eggers, and it was quite good. I had played on a band with Kim Eggers earlier, and even though that first band ended with some bad feelings, Kim did not hold onto them. Gene Argel was on Organ, and Danny Hoeffer was on guitar. Danny joined *Tower of Power* right after this band, and Gene moved permanently to Hawaii. The band was called *Bulls-Eye*. We rehearsed a lot but only played a few gigs.

I got a call around this time to join *Springfield Rifle*. I think Mark Whitman might have recommended me. They were a road band and were out most of the time. I rehearsed with them and was scheduled to play with them. Now that I think of it, I believe I did one gig in Salem, Oregon, with the Rifle. However, I had a referral to give a sax lesson to a guy from Tacoma. The guy showed up, and I gave him a lesson. He had a weird sound, probably due to inadequate equipment, unfocused air stream, and tight embouchure. I helped him out rather quickly. I said to him, "Keep practicing, and then you can start getting gigs." But to my chagrin, he was already working steadily! And then, he proceeded to tell me the band he worked with needed a trumpet player. I quickly said, "I'm your guy."

+++++

I drove down to the Back Forty, a dance club in Tacoma where they were playing. I sat in with them on a set, so they could hear me play. On the break, I went out with them and smoked and came back in. I sat down to drink and chat with a female patron in the club. A big, tall, muscular guy walked up to our table and said something unintelligible, and I said something flip to him and went back to my chat. The guy proceeds to punch me on the side of the head. I went down, and then he picked up the chair I had been sitting on and tried to finish me off with it. Luckily, the chair just deflected off my body.

I was probably too relaxed for it to hit any hard surface!

Anyway, the guys in the band, especially the bone player Charlie Foster, were way into Karate. Later, when we were on the road, our hotel always had lights kicked out and elevator buttons hanging. So, many people in the band ran up to my assailant and whapped him. When I pulled myself off the floor, the guy was standing sideways to me semi-stunned from the blows he had already received. I very quietly and sneakily and low to the ground saw my chance, and I ran up to him and gave him my best shot. Right before I hit him, I heard like a roar in slow motion: "Noooooooooooo," Anyway, he went down, and I went down, and there were many bodies in a wild melee at this point. I pulled my way out of a mass of bodies and ran back up by the bandstand. There I could quickly go over the side of the stand to a stairway going down to evade anyone following me. A band member came up to the bandstand and calmed me down.

I started playing with the band the next week. The band was ironically named *Peaceable Lane*. We worked at dance clubs in the greater Seattle area, Canada, Spokane, Bellingham, etc. We were a "Bill Stephan Agency" band. Bill Stephan headed up an agency that booked many dance clubs, and most bands that were interested in working full-time wanted to be one of his bands. (As far as working all the time as a jazz player, nobody (or I should say very few) could do that in Seattle. Frank Sugia had a band with Floyd Standifer or Bob Winn on horns and Gary Steel on bass. They worked and played standards, and there would be some soloing and a lot of jazz style, but not a "straight-ahead" jazz group.)

That Peaceable Lane gig was a mixed bag for me. I got to play a lot, and my chops were pretty good, so that part was good, and I would get a lot of solos on tunes. But I got into a routine of basically a schizophrenic lifestyle. I would get up and sometimes still be in my suit. Then I would have a long walk, hit the health food store, read inspirational literature and practice, etc. Every day, I would make a vow that I was on the comeback trail and no more of that "degenerate" alcoholic lifestyle. Sun would go down, and so would my resolve. I would start drinking, and during the gig, I had to keep running sobriety tests to make sure I could get through the night. Sometimes, they would torture me and call difficult tunes at the end of the night. Chicago's "Make Me Smile" was a bit of a problem if my tongue was not working fast enough. I guess I was experiencing what was often fatal for many addicts, and that was the "alcohol cure." This band worked for a while, but we had one problem. The band manager also worked for the Stephan Agency, and he was taking quite a cut. I tried to engineer a coup; it did not work, but it did terminate me.

+++++

I was still going to some places occasionally to sit in to play. At this time in my life, I still had very little emotional control or common sense. Once I played at the Bombay Bicycle Shop, and I felt I played poorly. Still, people thought otherwise and were clapping wildly. I gave them the finger from the bandstand. I would not recommend that as a career advancement move. Kind of like Mingus, though. Mingus was famous for telling the audience not to clap if he didn't think it was up to snuff. Sadly, I did not have the cachet of Mingus, and they had already started, so it was not a matter of "don't clap"- they were already doing it.

CHAPTER TWENTY-TWO

Steve Wolfe

Another time I went to the Bombay Bicycle Shop, and James Knapp was playing with Steve Wolfe.

Steve Wolfe is a legendary "operator and junky." You might be familiar with him from his recording with Nancy King and Ray Brown and Jack Sheldon and Nick Ceroli. (It was called *First Date* and got a lot of radio play. It featured great playing and spiffy arrangements by Steve and superb singing by Nancy.) Steve was a very smart guy and uniquely weird. Anyway, Steve liked my approach, and my chops were still good from all the Top Forty horn band stuff. So, we started playing together, and I joined forces with him.

Steve came to Seattle from endless work on the road and went to one Seattle Jazz Society meeting and somehow became president! He rented a space that had been a bowling alley on Broadway located on Capitol Hill and started a jazz center club. Steve had all kinds of plans for the place, all drug-free and community-oriented. He brought a piano in, began to have sessions, and even brought in Woody Shaw. Steve wanted my wife, Jules, to run the kitchen. He purchased kitchen equipment and was on the path to making this happen.

Meanwhile, Jules and I lived only a few blocks away on Harvard Street in an apartment where we were busy painting apartments for spending money.

Steve Wolfe was also one of the founders of a cult in Berkeley, California, called the *One World Family*. He gave me their book. It said that we needed to become vegetarian to re-enter the federation of planets. We Earthlings would not be able to kill ourselves with a bomb because the spacemen had us on their radar and would step in. Steve told me he used cosmic energy to accomplish things that seemed extraordinary to people. He said that flying saucers sometimes would do tricks for him and his friends.

So, we were going along when one day he came over to my apartment when I was in a quarrel with two exotic dancers from downstairs over some dope deal. One girl had taken the dope into the Walla Walla prison, and her boyfriend said it was no good. I said I would need the dope back before I would consider a refund. It turned out she did have some of it. Suddenly, Steve came to the rescue. He was Mr. Responsibility, just helping me out, and he bought it from her and sardonically said, "I don't know-- what am I going to do with this?" As an aside, I was never a dealer. However, the cost of narcotics and the difficulty of procurement meant that one way users had of keeping it going was to "score" for people and take some out for personal use.

Well, Steve obviously had a history, and when I was working at painting the next day, there was a tap-tap-tap on the window and, "Hey, it's Steve." He said only, "Can you cop?" I said, "yes." So, Steve gave me the money, and I'm off in my 67 Chevy Impala with the bad muffler telegraphing my journey about a mile away to my connection's apartment.

Steve was almost immediately way further along than I had ever been. That movie with Matt Dillon called *Drugstore Cowboy* was kind of where Steve was at with his drug use.

Pretty soon, he was selling his equipment from the club, and he was off and running, I mean: "On a run."

Later on, Steve showed back up in Seattle and was up to his ears in his old tricks. He was selling fish door to door. He would go to Pacific Fish (a wholesale outfit), where he had somehow acquired a legit business tax ID. Steve would buy nicely packed, high-grade frozen fish, lobster tails, and all kinds of high-end stuff. Then he would go into a bar on a Friday night and very politely ask the bartender, "Excuse me, do you mind if I show my friend some fish?" Who could say no? Immediately, the lobsters would fan out on the bar, and he would often sell hundreds of dollars' worth. He would go into a business and say he was delivering fish for the Land and Sea Seafood Company. He still had some inventory, and rather than going back with it: "Would you like to see some?"

He was going to doctors for prescriptions and paying them with fish! I tried working with him one day and could not sell one fish. He told me I needed to use "cosmic energy" to sell the fish. Steve also was a master of the art of shortchanging. That is a scam involving getting a hapless clerk totally confused in making change. Steve could really do it. But he was also very talented musically. Steve played piano as well as saxophone and knew many Horace Silver and other hard bop band arrangements.

Years later, Steve got me on a recording session with the great bassist, Ray Brown.

I could go on about Steve, but that would be a whole other book!

CHAPTER TWENTY-THREE

Getting Out of Dodge and Joining the Marines

The feeling that I should leave town was irresistible, so I decided I would take a "geographical" and head to LA.

My trumpet was in the pawnshop. I figured I would send for it later. It turns out that leaving was a good move. The band, Floating Bridge's drummer, Mike Marinelli's wife, got popped outside of Dave Lewis' pad, and so did Joe-Joe. They rolled on Dave, and that took Dave out of the game. Jules and I got our things together shortly before these events took place, and with a few hundred dollars in the pocket, took off for LA.

We ran out of funds in Vallejo, California, a dingy little Navy burg located in Northern California. Very nasty place, but Jules' dad and his second wife lived there, so we crashed in their trailer. They lived in a nice trailer park that had mainly older people retired or getting ready to retire. Jules's dad still worked at the shipyard.

Jules got a job in a restaurant right away. I managed to talk to a guy looking for an apartment manager with handyman skills. Well, I had no handyman skills, but my magic mouth just made the right sounds to convince him otherwise. The first thing the owner did was to show me all these water heaters under the building. He wanted me to take them upstairs to the apartments, my apartment first because we had no hot water. I took the water heater and hooked it up, but it sprang a leak and was spraying all over the place. I had to get Jules' father to come over and bring some tools. We got it sorted out. Meanwhile, I got a second job in a 7-11 as a night clerk.

I found a jam session and went to it and had fun on tenor. I had a 9 Florida Otto Link, and it put out a lot of sound. I was selling blood at the blood bank, and that certainly is very close to a bottom. I did discover, though, that if you had a hangover when they gave you back the saline, bam, no more hangover. Not that I would recommend that cure.

+++++

In the daily newspaper, almost on the front page, there was an advertisement for "Bandsmen Needed." It was an ad for the Marine Corps, and they needed trumpet players. Starting pay of $26,000 a year with a bonus after basic training. After mulling it over, I thought, "Sounds good to me." The government had recently made the switch from the draft to the all-volunteer armed services, so they worked to fill the ranks. I called home, and the family sent me my trumpet after getting it out of pawn.

At this time, I learned how pathetically impressionable I am. Just from being around the recruiting center a few times, I started to stand straighter. And as Dick Thorlakson and later Ronnie Pierce always said, "shoulders back, straight ahead and striving for tone." I started practicing and was thinking thoughts like, "we stopped 'em on the 33rd parallel," etc. Jay, the Marine, to the rescue.

The day came to go to the Marine induction center for my audition at Government Island in Oakland, California. A Marine came to pick me up in a Marine car. When I got in, he said in a southern accent, "Musician?" I said, "Yes," and then he proceeded to tell me that the greatest musician that ever lived was a Marine. I thought, "I didn't know Miles was a Marine." I said, "Who was that?" and he fixed me with a stare and said, "John Phillips Sousa." I was beginning to get a bad feeling about this. When I got to the audition, I played for a guy and told him I played the trumpet and told him I played tenor saxophone as well, sight-read some swing stuff, played a little jazz. I played a march, it was all good, but I started to think, why not Navy Band?

Anyway, they got to the physical part of this adventure. After having everyone bend over, checking for what I wasn't exactly sure, then it was the old cough while they checked you for a hernia. Then the new test was to hold out your arms, and the doctors walked up and down and checked everyone for tracks. After the amount of drug use in Vietnam, specifically narcotics, this was, of course, wise.

I had some tracks, not new, but easy to see. They said step out of line. I complied, and then it was down to see the doctor for a little interview. He asked about the marks, and I told him I was a professional blood donor. He arched his eyebrows and said, "Come back with some verification." Yeah, that was going to happen.

Probably just as well. Right about this time, a young guy died at Camp Pendleton going through basic training. And there was always the possibility of my Whitehall Street records coming back on me. Even though, as I said earlier, Whitehall Street was blown up by the Weathermen.

CHAPTER TWENTY-FOUR

San Francisco and the Bay Area

About this time, I got the idea to call my friend, bassist Chuck Sher[54] in San Francisco. Chuck, I knew briefly from when he stayed in Seattle in the early '70s. He and I used to jam quite often at his house with a good tenor player named John Reckovitch, who now lives in San Diego. Chuck played with Dave Johnson, Jack Brownlow, and myself at my sister's wedding. We had a lot of fun.

I called Chuck. He lived in and managed a big house full of musicians in San Anselmo, California, and there was a room just available. Quick as a wink, we were packed up and motored to San Anselmo. At the house, we all shared a kitchen and refrigerator, and bathroom. Chuck had sessions all the time, and immediately I heard about a band forming that needed a tenor player. After I auditioned for the tenor chair and got it, I whipped out the trumpet as well, and they were happy and surprised. It was a funk band with two tenors. The other tenor player was Mike Morris, who played a lot with Mark Levine[55] at the Reunion club.

+++++

A couple of guys I knew from Seattle were also living there, Joe Villa, a young guitar player, and Chuck Metcalf,[56] a bass player. Chuck had been a real mover and shaker on the Seattle scene for many years. I met and played with saxophonist Burt Wilson and pianist Jessica Williams[57] when I was down there. Michael Aragon lived right across the street. He is a beautiful cat and a great drummer and still has the No Name Bar gig in Sausalito (at least last I checked). I immediately became a member of the *River City Rats*. The club was called The Sleeping Lady, and it was in a beautiful little town in Marin County called Fairfax. Dick Conte, a famous DJ, was the piano player and ex-defacto band leader. Bob Maize and Chuck were the bass players, and they switched off if one was gigging. Bob sounded great to my ears, I asked him who he had played with, and he said he used to be a member of Philly Joe Jones band. Later, Bob became a mainstay for Concord Records. Bob also played with Horace Silver a lot; he was the bass player when I later auditioned for Horace.

+++++

I was also doing gigs with a band called *Bank of America*. We had a young piano player who was a Berklee School of Music grad and played great. His name was Bob Bower. I remember telling Bob about a dream I had where my sax turned into a boa constrictor and started to choke me before I woke up. Without missing a beat, Bob said, "Bank of America BOA"! Bob later became the main transcriber for Chuck Sher's Fake Books.

+++++

I used to play over at a place right by Golden Gate Park called the Omnibus, and the other horn player was Manny Boyd. Manny played a lot with Bobby Hutcherson. My advice to anyone who wants to up their game is to make sure you play a lot with players better than yourself. I also started playing with an R&B band called Madam Butterfly. In the band was Jack Shroer[58], a tenor player who also went to Berklee and arranged and played solos on Van Morrison recordings. I don't remember the other names now, but Michelle Hendricks and her sister, Jon Hendrix's daughters, both sang with the Madam Butterfly band. That was a strange band, Coke was starting to rear its ugly head, and sometimes, they had a pile of coke that was unbelievable on a table; just help yourself. I asked them if they were concerned about being ripped off. The band manager reached under the couch and pulled out what looked like a military weapon. They were in a different league than me and had me scared.

+++++

I also played with a guitarist named Mike Simon. Mike was another Berklee graduate. Mike was a good arranger, and he wrote for a sextet that I helped form. It had Jan Davis AKA Boogie on alto sax, Tom Donlinger on drums (brother of James Vincent), Jack Shroer tenor, Mike Simon on guitar, and maybe Chuck Sher or Marty Fuche bass. Mike wrote a beautiful chart on "Duke Ellington's Sound of Love", and I started to come up against a problem. The problem was, I did not have the music theory to understand by seeing it written, "what was what" on various kinds of dominant chords. I knew the sound of them but did not always know what to play unless I was very familiar with the tune. So, reading a G7flat 9 flat 13th versus a G13th #11. G7alt. G7 sus flat 9 was sometimes tricky business. For the amount of playing I had done, it was a little strange not to have this down as well as any piano player. It was a little later down the road when I got tired of this and taught myself functional jazz harmony in a more complete way. I'm still learning.

+++++

My trumpet chops got better around this time after taking some lessons from Johnny Coppola.[59] Johnny got me hooked up with a routine again and stretched my range, and my projection improved also. It had been many years since I had my lessons with Carmine. The kingpins down there who were playing all the time were: saxophonist Hadley Caliman and trumpeter Eddie Henderson.

+++++

I also played in a band called the *New Life Big Band*. We rehearsed at Delancey Street, which was a kind of "Synanon[60] light." At the time, Charlie Haden and Jessica Williams were on the band. Charlie Haden was a resident there and suggested a stay there could help me. We played a big fund-raiser at the Fairmont Hotel. Before that big fundraiser, things were a little shaky for me.; I was separated from Jules, just living with my dog Frodo and my scene was unraveling. My car and dog Frodo both overheated on the way to the rehearsal. While I was putting water in the car and waiting for it to cool, at this very same time, at the rehearsal, the latest directions were given about where to pick up our tuxedos that were provided for the Fairmont gig. Previously we had just to show up, and the tuxedos would be there. Now, we had to go to a certain place to pick them up on our own. When the big gig came around at the Fairmont, I arrived with no tux. I was patiently trying to explain to an angry band member what had happened. After my explanation, he fixed me with a pointed look and said, "But why does it always happen to you?" Yes, that would seem to be the $64,000 question, alright!

+++++

Other gigs that I did a few times were Chinese Funerals. We had our black suits and would march through China Town behind the Casket and play. I was wondering about the other musicians. "Who are these people?" I asked the guy next to me, "Who are you?" He answered, "Mark Isham." Mark Isham was playing with Art Lande's *Rubisa Patrol*, and later, Mark Isham went on to score a lot of movies.

+++++

Another playing situation for me was a bebop band put together by a little cab driver cat named Scotty Mack. The other horn players were Vince Wallace and Ed Neumeister. We played a few times and had a couple of gigs. Vince was an awesome player; you can hear him on YouTube "City by The Bay." Later, he was street busking and not sounding so good. It was odd, but Vince and I never said one word to each other. An example of how being a junkie can be lonely sometimes.

+++++

For a while, Chuck Sher and I shared a Dodge Dart that we got from a service station by our house on Michael Aragon's advice, who knew about cars. This car came in handy when we both used to drive down to play at a bar by the airport with a "psycho unit" named Joe Burton. Joe was out of his mind, liked to talk like a gangster. Joe got his kicks by humiliating us; he would just start playing tunes that neither Chuck nor I knew. Once, he paid the drummer with a bad check, and when the drummer brought it up to Joe, Joe said, "I warn you, I'm packing!" The Burton gig was also weird because not only was Joe abusive, but the bartender hated me. The bartender would polish glasses and just let me wait there to try to order a drink. He would call me a bum and other names periodically.

John Boucher was the drummer on that gig. Originally from England, he was a guy I met when I first arrived in the Bay Area. John was from Manchester and used to be the road manager for Maynard Ferguson's English musicians' band.

That band was essentially Ernie Garside's band. Maynard hired them once and then just co-opted the entire band. Ernie Garside was also a promoter of US jazz musicians in Europe. I met him later in this story.

Maynard had a gig at Town Hall in New York, and John was to bring the band's music from England. John liked to drink, and the night before the band was to leave for the states, he was in his cups. Because the charts were locked in the club, John was in a panic and had to take a later plane to New York, hoping to get the music there in time for the gig. Maynard's band did not have their music until moments before they had to start playing! John told me he lived thru the old musician's joke, "How do you get to Town Hall?" Ha! The recent immigrant cabbie John hailed had no idea where the Town Hall was.

Joe Burton, the psycho bandleader from San Francisco, heard about John's connection to Maynard and that John was going to see Maynard. Joe said, "Say hello to Maynard; he will remember me; I played on his band." Sure enough, Maynard remembered him all right. Joe Burton was playing bad changes on Maynard's band. When the bass player said something, a fight ensued where Joe practically pounded himself into a pulp. The bass player had rubber-soled shoes, and Joe was wearing patent leather-soled shoes. Every time Joe threw a punch, he went down on his face on the slippery dance floor.

CHAPTER TWENTY-FIVE

More Bay Area

I lived in four places in the Bay Area. First was San Anselmo. Then I moved to San Rafael with Jules when she got a job as a cook at a retirement home in Tiburon. Her boss had a property in San Rafael that she wanted to tear down but could not because it was on the historical registry. We stayed there for free to discourage squatters. We had to do certain things, like hook up the gas again and get some appliances. Later, when Jules and I split up, I moved into the city, briefly, living right off Haight Street on Post.

+++++

Next, I moved to Fairfax into a house that my new girlfriend rented. Her name was Katrina, but her real name was Cathryn Casamo.[61] She was one of the most beautiful women I had ever seen, and she was the girlfriend of the bandleader for Bank of America. When we got together, David, the bandleader, got his pink slip. She had been on the Ken Kesey[62] Merry Pranksters' "Furthur" bus and went by the handle, "Stark Naked." On the bus, they thought of her as their potential movie star.

They were in Texas, and everyone was on acid, and she got into a fight with Neal Cassidy and took off walking. She was Italian, and I guess she looked a little too Mexican to be walking around in the neighborhood they were in, so the police yelled at her to stop. She put her nose up in the air and walked, not paying any attention to the calls to stop. A policeman grabbed her, and a melee ensued. She turned into a hellfire, Tasmanian devil and started biting the policeman! Off to jail she went, where they deemed her crazy. Kesey and the gang hightailed it out of there. Kesey's friend, Larry McMurtry of "Lonesome Dove" fame, got her out.

+++++

Later Chuck Sher shared the house with his new bride, Abbey Greenwald (Marc Smason's sister). Bob Bower moved in downstairs. Katrina's daughter stayed downstairs when Bob was out of town. She read his diary and informed me that Bob, the young Christian Scientist, the straightest guy on the planet, was very gay. I chastised her for reading the diary, but I could not unlearn that.

Chuck Sher was the first to publish legal, legitimate fake books with transcriptions by Bob. That was an astute calculation by Chuck. When the band *Weather Report* put out *Heavy Weather*, I remember Chuck was talking to Bob about one of the new, dense pieces on that album, maybe "Teen Town". Bob transcribed it in nothing flat. Chuck being the smart and enterprising guy he is, probably heard a little bell go off in his head after Bob had done that so quickly. Chuck's first few New Real Books were all Bob Bower transcriptions. Later Bob changed his name to Sky Evergreen and was lost to gay cabarets, no more jazz gigs. He later died of aids.

+++++

Our band played on public TV one time; I think the studio was in Richmond. We played "Peggy's Blue Skylight" Orange Was the Color of Her Dress" by Mingus, and I am not sure what else. Hadley Caliman told me he saw it. I wish I had it. I had a bunch of Slant Signature hard rubber Otto Links, and I seem to remember the one I had really went well.

+++++

All in all, I had a lot of adventures, musical and personal, during my three years in the Bay Area. My San Francisco days are a little of "the best of and the worst of" as far as my experiences there. The thing was, I was young, and San Francisco is beautiful, and there was a lot of stuff going on that had a youthful vibe and a real bastion of the liberal elite, which is not such a bad thing when considering the opposite.

CHAPTER TWENTY-SIX

Back to Olympia and Seattle

Jules headed back to Olympia, and Boucher and another friend followed her North. I came back late in the summer of 1977. I headed back to Seattle with Mike Simon and his dog, Heproc, from the Slim Gaillard recording Heprock-o-recy. Oh, and I had my dog, Frodo. When we got back, I went to work for a minute doing labor for my dad. Pretty soon, Mike and I and Dave Johnson found a house to rent in West Seattle.

+++++

I went back and forth from Olympia to West Seattle with not many gigs, but I do remember one gig I had after getting back. It was at the Cirque Theater, a supper club hosted by Norm Bobrow.[63] Norm is known for managing singer Pat Suzuki. He was a very cultured, rich guy who had a radio show and put on jazz concerts back in the 1950s. He had a lot of stories, also. One is, he used to say, "I slept with Charlie Parker." He had put Parker up for a night, and they slept on the same bed. But he would get a lot of raised eyebrows with that line.

99

At the gig, the other horn player was a big, African American guy with a huge tenor sound named Art Foxall. Art used to be a railroad porter, and the rumor was he used to play for Lionel Hampton at one time. His favorite song was Flamingo that he played with a big husky tenor sound to good effect. Red Kelly,[64] the famous wit and bass player of so many bands, was on the gig and also pianist Barney McClure.[65]

There was one funny sequence where Norm Bobrow outdid himself on my introduction. "Ladies and gentlemen, tonight we are so lucky to have Jay Thomas with us, he is so busy, etc., etc." He starts veering off-road with, "his father was a pharmacist who was interested in jazz." Red Kelly pipes in immediately, "Hey, what about a bass player really interested in Pharmacy!" Red Kelly was a bass player who played with Kenton and Woody Herman and spent years playing with Harry James. Red was a big strong Irishman with forearms like hams, and he could really pump the bass over any ensemble and did so for years. Then, sometime in the 70s, he went to the "sit down bass," also known as the Electric bass. The concert was nothing too eventful, but when playing with Barney McClure, a very facile and gifted piano player from California, it really took off. Barney and I forged a friendship that lasted years and many CDs.

+++++

The Pioneer Square Tavern, or as we called it, the PST, had sessions, and I started to go there, and a place called Skippers Tavern right off Eastlake. Through these forays, I started getting work with dance bands in Pioneer Square. One band was Kathy Hart's band. We played quite a few gigs, and the band was pretty good. Nick Moore did some playing with her, and I think Larry Turner, and sometimes John Boucher, who had settled in the NW from the Bay Area. I got a chance to play R&B tenor, which I have always loved. For a while, we did a mixture of jazz and R&B.

+++++

Around this time, I got a call from Bill Sheehan, who had the Tuxedo Junction dance band. I got my tux and started working for him. Ronnie Pierce was in the band, a New York guy named Al Fields, and my hero Freddy Greenwell. Freddy had hung up all his craziness with drinking and drugs and ended up back in Seattle and was playing with Sheehan. Freddy still had a droll sense of humor and wicked timing.

Another guy in the band who was a significant influence on me was the bassist Buddy Catlett.[66] On one of the first gigs with Tuxedo Junction, I noticed the bass seemed pretty damn good. Buddy Catlett was a legend around Seattle. He left town with Horace Heidt, and later played with Louis Armstrong for years, Count Basie, Eddie"Lockjaw" Davis, Johnny Griffin, and so many more. He was in Europe with the Quincy Jones band as well. Dave Keim, who plays lead trombone with the Basie band, was also on Tuxedo Junction.

The band played a variety of big band stuff and was not really about jazz, but occasionally something would happen, and the magic from one of those guys would take place. I remember one Easter when we started in on Easter Parade, and Freddy Greenwell began playing a solo that had so much swing and history and sound that the band was stunned by the beauty of it. I swear nobody came in on their parts; they were so enraptured with Freddy's playing.

+++++

I was drinking quite a bit on these gigs, but functional. I had picked up a new narcotic source called Tussionex. That is a powerful cough suppressant, very popular among junkies because there were no fillers or anything, just a form of hydrocodone in a resin form. It was easy on the body because of the absence of all the stuff they usually put in those cough medicines. Usually, these medicines have antihistamines and expectorants and prodigious amounts of aspirin or Tylenol. Tussionex was just the straight narcotic. They called it house-wives' heroin in the Bay Area.

I made a career out of finding ways of procuring it. One day in West Seattle, Dave Johnson was mumbling that more people were named Dave Johnson than any other name in the Seattle phone book. Bingo, a light went off in my head. I had the brilliant idea of calling the doctors' offices and medical clinics and asking for a refill on my Tussionex. Of course, that would have been a little bold and obvious, so I devised ways of getting under the radar. I had a telephone line where I could have many people on hold. I started calling from the phonebook, plugged up my nose a bit, and said, "Hi, this is Dave Johnson." "Oh, hi Dave, let me get your chart…. Do you still live on such and such address?" Then I would tell them I was going out of town on business, and I needed something for this irritating cough. I had to have patience and let it play out naturally. I would say something like, "I tried a couple of brands last time, and one worked really good; wait for a sec-ond while I get the bottle. I would make a rather lame attempt at pronunciation, "oh yeah, here it is" slowly now, "Tussy- on -nex?" The hoped-for answer, "Ok, I will check with the doc-tor, please hold. Hello Dave, where would you like that called in?" If they did not know who I was, I just said, "Oh, I'm sor-ry, I must have dialed the wrong number," and then went to the next one down on the list. Since there are hundreds of doctors, this worked well for a while.

+++++

I did a lot of one-night gigs around that time. Once I got to play with Big Mama Thornton[67]. After accepting the job to play with Big Mama Thornton at the Buffalo Tavern, I had some logistical problems to address. My tenor was in the pawnshop, and my car was not working, so I had to get my horn out of the pawnshop and take the Greyhound bus to Seattle from Olympia.

I had Jules drive me to the pawnshop, but there was a fire in a business in the same building, and everywhere I looked, there were fire trucks and hoses, so I had to kiss that idea goodbye. I was in trouble because this was definitely a sax gig.

I had an old Nickel-Plated alto, so I hightailed it back to the house and dusted it off and blew some notes, and it sounded OK to me. It might have been a Conn; I'm not sure now what it was. I was way more comfortable on my tenor, but off to the gig, I went on the Greyhound.

These things always happen to junkies, so their lives sometimes are full of turns and twists that "straights" don't really understand and have little patience for that life! Like, when the guitar player in the Bay Area said to me, "But, why does it always happen to you?" The short answer, it just comes with the territory.

But I made the gig. What a kick. When she sang Hound Dog, it was way, way better than the watered-down Elvis crap. Super funky. I waited for her to show up before the gig and asked her if we would rehearse. She said, "Can you play?" I said, "Yes," she said, "That's our rehearsal," Bam. And she could also really comp on guitar.

+++++

I continued to practice. Mainly I was practicing various shapes and started trying to put them through keys. That's an excellent way to practice for any instrument.

There was a jazz club in Seattle called Parnell's, down in Pioneer Square owned and run by a guy named Roy Parnell. I got a call to play with Danny Ward there, with the legendary Dean Johnson on bass. Things were chugging along despite myself.

CHAPTER TWENTY-SEVEN

Parnell's

A round the end of '78, my father, who was now retired from pharmacy practice, saw an ad in the business opportunities section for a Pioneer Square nightclub. It turned out to be Parnell's Jazz Club.[68] Well, long story short, he bought the club from Roy Parnell. In the back of his mind, he thought it would be ideal for Jules and me to run the club. For me, this was a real learning experience musically and an opportunity to hear a lot of jazz. And the opportunity to watch the inner working of groups as they rehearsed and did their soundcheck.

Roy's formula was to book mostly LA musicians. My dad wanted more East Coast musicians. He booked touring bands such as the Heath Brothers, Cedar Walton, Freddie Hubbard, Mingus Dynasty, Red and Ira, Woody Shaw, Jackie McLean, Dizzy Gillespie, and Sonny Stitt. And we put in singles like Zoot Sims and Chet Baker and lesser-known musicians like Sal Nistico. We had Art Pepper when his book *Straight Life* came out. Sometimes the headliners were backed by local players. We always had a jam session, and I usually ran the sessions as well as being the daytime bartender.

+++++

Art Pepper [69] was a funny guy, he had the usual jazz crowd, but he also had many ex-felons! He was obsessed with prison, and he was incorrigible when it came to altering his consciousness. He could not seem to understand that we were not a hard liquor club. When his wife Laurie, who was also his handler, wasn't looking, he would quickly sidle up to the bar and try to order a whiskey or a scotch. Laurie would see him, and she would yell, "Aaart?" from across the room, and he would quickly step away. He even followed my dad into his office once, probably thinking every person in business had a bottle stashed in his desk like in the movies.

Art was promoting his book, *Straight Life* when I saw him play at the B. Dalton Book Store in Seattle. He was with a drummer, bass, and piano player, just doing a few standards. At one point, the drummer started to go into double time because Art was doubling up on a ballad. Oh man, Art turned into the devil and just snarled at the drummer and told him, NEVER do that again! They were playing along when the management told him that he needed to stop because Darth Vader was in the store. Star Wars had just come out. Anyway, Art thought it was his competition, and he said to his wife, Laurie, in a loud whisper, "who in the fuck is Darth Vader?"

+++++

I also worked a week with Harold Land.[70] Harold had a record out called *Mapenzi* that he did with Blue Mitchell. Blue had just died, so I played the trumpet parts. What a thrill to play with him. Years later, I recorded his song "Rapture". It was a real learning experience to hear how he could chromatisize and still stay in the key. Also, he was into a kind of Trane thing. He was working to find that zone he described as pure bliss or love, and he was always searching for a peaceful place. He was deep. I wish I would have had more snap. I would have picked his brain about Clifford.

+++++

Chet Baker[71] put a scare in us. Chet was booked for a week, and he informed us that he could not stay because he needed to get back to New York to "score." Chet had just played in Edmonton, Canada, at the Yardbird Suite. The methadone program paperwork for him to go from New York to Canada was a bit too much for Chesney to navigate. So, Chet had jumped off the methadone program when he played in Canada. Well, that was a job I could handle. I put him in my house and had him in such great shape for the gig that he was almost on the nod! Regardless, Chet sounded beautiful, he was doing Richie Beirach tunes like "Leaving", and he was also doing Wayne Shorter stuff like "ESP". Jules fed him cookies and milk and asked if she could wash his shirt. He said, "No, it's cool." Finally, she just said, "Chet, take your shirt off." He immediately complied, and she popped it into the washer.

Chet was a major talent, no matter his lifestyle. I'll never forget when Chet first played with the house band we had for him; Dave Peck, piano, Chuck Deardorf, bass, and Dean Hodges on drums. Chet called, "If I Should Lose You", but his count-off was so soft, the band was straining to hear him, and then he just held the second note in the pickup for a long time. Ha! The band was scrambling to find the tempo. Chet played the week and packed the house.

I did sit in with Chet on his last night at the club and had fun playing with a jazz icon. More about Chet later in the story.

+++++

When Zoot Sims[72] was at the club, he was a lot of fun to be with. I chauffeured him around, and he was full of stories.

Many of his stories featured his "using" days with hilarious stories about Stan Getz and others. On the road, what he liked to do was scope out the best restaurants. He was way past his "bad boy days" and just was enjoying life and playing.

I got to play with him a couple of times. Fred Greenwell came down and played with him also. Freddy knew Zoot from the loft sessions in New York. Zoot was totally relaxed and swinging. Freddy, Lanphere, and I all sat in on his last night. What a blast!

CHAPTER TWENTY-EIGHT

Bill Ramsay, Slim Gaillard, Bill Mays

At this time, I made a lifelong friend who helped me in several ways. Bill Ramsay[73] was a kingpin around the greater Seattle area. He did a lot of playing and contracting and was a first call on tenor or alto in the Northwest. Bill had established himself on name bands, with stints playing with Maynard's and Basie's bands back in the day; had toured with Buddy Morrow, and spent time in LA.

+++++

I had a gig at Parnell's on a Friday when we had no headliner, and I hired Bill Ramsay. Bill and I got along great personally, and most importantly, musically. I recall he brought some charts and a couple of Thad Jones things and a few standards he had arranged. He could see I could read, and I played both trumpet and tenor. He was impressed by my tenor sound and thought I had a real "jazz tenor" sound. Soon after that gig, Bill put together a four tenor and rhythm section library; the band was called *Tenor Dynasty*. It consisted of Bill, Chuck Stentz, my old friend and mentor from Olympia, Denny

Goodhew, Bill, and myself. We had some gigs at Parnell's, Jazz Alley, and, as I remember, Centrum Jazz Week. From a professional standpoint, it was great for me to get the nod ahead of some established players. Bill did not care about the rumors of my addiction swirling about in Seattle. Bill was old school and had been around many using musicians, so I was OK as long as I showed up, did the job, and kept my nose clean on the bandstand.

+++++

Bill would call on me to play when Pops Concerts and various shows came to town and even the Puyallup Fair. Bill is a very bluesy player and can tell a story on his horn. He could also tell a great story verbally. He has an incredibly fast wit and is one of the funniest guys I have ever met. My world shifted a bit when I was accepted and trusted by Bill. For that alone, I will forever be grateful to him. Around this time, Bill was playing with the Benny Goodman band on tenor. Later he played the baritone sax chair in the Count Basie band while Basie was still alive. He also recorded with the Frank Wess Big Band that had all the old-timers after Basie passed.

+++++

The guy we saw a lot of at Parnell's was Slim Gaillard.[74] Slim Gaillard was famous among jazz musicians for a duo he had with Slam Stewart and, for his novelty hits "Flat Foot Floogie" and "Cement Mixer, Puti Puti". Slim had a record he did with Charlie Parker and Dizzy Gillespie when they were in California in the late '40s. Slim Galliard was also in an early movie that featured African Americans called *Hellzapoppin*. He was very tight with Steve Allen and other big entertainers from his Hollywood days. Slim was on Steve Allen's *Hip Fables* recording along with Al "Jazzbo" Collins.

Slim was living in Tacoma. I am not sure how he ended up there. My Dad owned a motel out by the Sea-Tac Airport, so

Slim ensconced himself there after establishing himself as a fixture at Parnell's. He would come down to the club where he and I would entertain at brunch before Seahawks games. The Kingdome, where the Seahawks played, was only two blocks from the club. Slim could do it all; he played Latin percussion, piano, guitar, sang, and told jokes.

Having Slim around the club added a festive feeling. Slim had his own way of talking, and his own language, sort of similar to Lester Young's. He called it Vout. If he wanted you to repeat something, he would say, "Begyourpardi." Kids were called "Reen-i-mos." "McVouty" was a loose term for "that guy" or someone whose name he could not remember.

When the Sonics won the NBA championship, they asked Slim to sing the Star-Spangled Banner at the next game the Sonics played. Roy Parnell was the club owner at that time, and as the big gig got closer and closer, he asked Slim, "You know this, right?"

Slim assured him it would be cool. That was one of the most interesting versions of the Banner ever sang at a sporting event! It started OK, and then he got out of sync with the melody and the lyrics! Ha. He brazened his way through and started to go improv; the crowd was kind of stunned, and the announcer said something like, "That was different."

I had a lot of fun playing with Slim, just laughing and hanging out. My dad had fun with him too. They would go on little trips to Canada together, and Slim would try out all his languages because Vancouver, BC, is such an international city. Slim said he was a gourmet cook in seven different languages. Slim really got around.

Years later, when our band with Becca Duran, Boucher, and I were in Japan, we talked about Slim. And then, at the subway kiosk, as though we had summoned him or somehow conjured him up, we looked at a Japanese Times newspaper. Who should we see on the cover but a very prosperous and well-coiffed Slim Gaillard! Slim was modeling clothes at a big Japanese department store! It said London Jazz Drummer,

Slim Gaillard models for Parko Nagoya. But that kind of stuff always happened with Slim. He was like a character out of *Hitch Hikers Guide to the Galaxy*

+++++

Bands would sometimes come to the club, and they would have young cats, and I would invite them to the jam session and hang out with them. Mongo Santamaria had a real young horn section with a sax player named Sam Furnace and a trumpet player with marginal chops, but a pretty good player. That was always fun to play with those guys.

Sometimes the headliner guys would come down and jam. Steve Turre was with Woody Shaw, and he and Woody were down at the jam sessions. Turre was not very friendly to me, but Woody was a gas. I remember playing at the jam session, and Woody yells out, "There's that New York sound!" It made me feel really good. He was a sweet cat even though he looked forbidding. I had met him way back in Seattle with Steve Wolfe.

The days started to blend into each other, and it was a routine: play some gigs and do some bartending, usually in the day. Watch the bands play that came thru.

I was learning, but I was not pushing to improve my harmonic knowledge, and my transcribing was on hiatus.

+++++

Our head waitress and booking assistant was a beautiful girl named Bebee Salazar.

She and pianist Bill Mays[75] fell in love. Bill lived in LA and did a lot of studio work, and played on the game show, Name That Tune. Bill started to be semi-regular at the club. He was perfect for many acts. We became friends, and he was very encouraging to me. Bill was always writing material and was quite inspiring musically. He was a great example of working at something you love. He was after me to practice regularly again and organize my life.

Bill helped produce what would have been my first album. We had Bill on keys, Chuck Deardorf on bass, Dean Hodges on drums, and me on trumpet and tenor. Bill arranged some stuff, and he knew his way around a recording studio. It turned out very good, but I did not move on putting it out. I was too scattered and was thinking, of course, that it wasn't good enough.

We recorded a few of Bill's originals and "So Near So Far", from the Miles Davis CD. I did the George Coleman tenor part as an overdub that was something on the Miles record. When I finally pulled myself together, unfortunately, the master tape of the session got away. It's out in the ether somewhere, probably taped over! I had a cassette for a while and everyone that heard it freaked out because it was quite good.

I played one gig with Bill in Los Angeles at *Carmelo's By the Sea;* the drummer was Roy McCurdy, and the bass player was my old friend from Marin County, Bob Maize.

Bill also recommended me to Horace Silver. That never came to pass, but I did go to his audition, where four young trumpet players were in a small room at the LA musician's union. The trumpets were Mike Mossman, Brian Lynch, myself, and another guy I cannot remember. I had to get a ride with Horace after the audition, and my dad says that when I had Horace stop the car so I could run in and get a six-pack of beer, that probably did not help. Brian Lynch got the gig. Brian, I knew from New York, and he was serious and prepared.

Back to Parnell's. I loved when Cedar Walton's[76] band with Bob Berg would play the club, it was so swingin', and Bob Berg was just on fire. They would open up, and Bob had all kinds of room to move. The songs were catchy, and the arrangements were super hip. Cedar had been a mainstay with the Jazz Messengers and earlier with Kenny Dorham. It would get feeling so good that I would just break out laughing, happy to be alive. Music can do that sometimes. We had Cedar's band at least three times, twice with vocalist Abbey Lincoln.

+++++

I also got to play a week with altoist Charles McPherson.[77] It turned out we were both Albert Hotel people! Charles had a new recording with trumpeter Tom Harrell and some cool arrangements, so on the tunes with charts, it was way cool. He was very friendly to me. We had some glitches, though, with the happy camping factor of the band with McPherson. I remember McPherson counting off a tune, and he looked at Dean and said, "Man, you're already rushing, and I haven't finished the count!" He was also on Buddy Catlett's case. In the 70s, people were used to amplified basses, big old notes like giant medicine balls (thank God we're past that). Well, Buddy was old school, and his quarter notes were short. McPherson kept riding Buddy all week long, but Buddy being Buddy, just played the gig and didn't fight back.

The last night of the gig, Chick Corea was in the house, and McPherson called him to the bandstand to play. Chick was slightly reluctant but quickly got into it. He probably knew Buddy from the many years of Buddy's work in New York. Anyway, Chick sits down at the piano, and without asking anybody what they would like to play or counting the tune off, he goes right into a medium tempo "I Hear a Rhapsody", just channeling Monk big time. As great as Bill Mays was at that time, Chick was a whole other animal! After the first five notes of the melody, Dean and Buddy had it covered. Buddy, with his impeccable quarter notes and Dean with a great propelled light shuffle. Chick was staring right at Buddy and Dean and smiling. Charles was upset; he said, "Shit, I don't know this one!" I had fun playing, and Chick was complimentary after. Nice guy, Chick.

+++++

We had a doorman named Sarge, and he could fill the house if we had an act that people wanted to hear. Sarge would just cram in the people. We did well with very popular or legendary shows; then, we could turn the house or charge a separate cover for each set. Joe Williams and Dizzy Gillespie were two such acts. Everybody wanted to see Dizzy. In fact, we had someone that wanted to get into an already full house so badly that when Mark Solomon,[78] who was working at the club, said to the guy, "Please come outside so we can talk," the guy shot Mark and got away. I don't think he was ever caught. Mark had a very close call. Fortunately, he lived. Having a jazz club in the heart of the city was sometimes thrills and chills.

+++++

We had so many people come thru the club, and sometimes it was a real eye-opener for me. I remember how the Heath Brothers[79] were continually expanding their repertoire. I was bartending in the afternoon when they did a soundcheck /rehearsal. Jimmy Heath had a new chart, and he wanted a specific thing from the piano, and he walked over and played it. At the time, I thought that was just so hip. But now, I realize that Jimmy was just a complete musician. They did not just blow over changes; they had a unique band sound and cool arrangements that created an atmosphere.

+++++

We also had Red Rodney[80] and Ira Sullivan[81] , which was a thrill for me because I was a big fan of Ira. Freddy Greenwell was a friend of Ira, and he had turned my dad and me onto him. Ira played trumpet and tenor, both great. They had a young band; Garry Dial was on piano, Jeff Hirschfield on drums, and Jay Anderson on bass. They were fun to hang with, and they came to the sessions and were very friendly to me.

My Dad asked Ira what he should do about me. Maybe not directly, but Ira said it looked like I had too much time on my hands, kind of a cryptic remark!

Anyway, I sat in the last night. And it was kind of cool and set the stage for another chapter. I came up and was feeling no pain. Ira puts me in his sights and says, "Just Friends". It's usually played in F, but Ira started in the key of G. I didn't much care, but Red said in a flustered tone, "What the fuck key is this, Ira?" And then Ira turned it over to me. I logged on pretty hard, and Ira had to really work! Ira was trying to fuck with me also. He said, "Don't you like your sound?" I said, "Yeah, I like my sound!" It was kind of a classic of the pup up against the master.

Well, Red was impressed, and at the urging of Red, I went to New York again. Ira wanted to do less traveling on the road. I think for one hot second, Red might have had me in mind as a sub for Ira.

TWENTY-NINE

New York, Round Two

A nyway, I took off to New York again, but it was doomed from the start because I was still up to my old tricks. I stayed with a Dixieland piano player, a little older than me, named Dr. Roscoe. We used to play at Skippers Tavern and the PST together. He stayed in a brownstone his father owned in midtown Manhattan's Eastside. I think at the time, it was the most expensive real estate on the planet. His dad was on the original Atomic Commission and was quite a celebrated cartographer and a personal friend of Peewee Russell.

The first person I called when I got settled in was Sal Nistico.[82] I talked with Sal, and it was totally, "Hey man, how are you doing?" "Great" ... "Staying out of trouble?" "Uh uhuh sure." Back and forth. Finally, after saying how great it was to be clean, I said, "Sal, where's the shit?" He did not hesitate and said, "Rivington Street." I was hesitant to go by myself, and I begged Sal to come along. He just growled at me, "Go down there and watch first, and see what's going on, and you'll be fine." That's what I did, and it was a little scary; the area looked pretty much bombed out. Junkies would cue up in a line when word came out that the stuff was almost there. Then, kids would come out of a building with the drugs. There would be an adult who took the money and another standing there scanning for police and providing muscle if something got out of control. You had to be ready with your cash and orderly, and things moved quickly. Then the line would dissipate, and it would be over. They had the kids transport the drugs because they did very little or no time if they got popped.

I would go over to the Manhattan Plaza Artist Housing, where Garry Dial lived, and play jam sessions. Davey Schnitter lived in the same building, and he would also usually be there. I had a ball with the playing. I also went to a lot of sessions around town.

I played one out-of-town festival at Wolf Trap Park in Washington, DC, with Red and Ira. I got to see them up close, and they had a cool relationship, a little like the *Odd Couple*. Red was wrapped way tighter than Ira. Ira liked to smoke grass and was totally loose. He would try on every pair of sunglasses at the service station, while Red just wanted to get going. Ira did not read music, so, how Ira played the chart; that's the way they played it! They were also both Christians. Red had a kind of *Burning Bush* experience. Ira said he read the Bible straight through, and he thought, "It just made a lot of sense."

We played the gig, and I played, but as far as the playing went, it was not so memorable for me but watching them and soaking that up was priceless. We arrived back in New York in the morning with the sun just coming up. We let Ira out, and Ira said to Red, "Here, Red, take my horn to Sol," and off he went to catch a plane to Florida. Red immediately says, "What the fuck? I'm not his fucking valet; here, Dial, you take the horn to Sol!" I was with Garry Dial when we took the horn to Sol Fromkin, legendary saxophone repairman. I think Roberto's is now in Sol's old location.

Dial told me, on the road, Ira was a real live wire. He would want to see all the sites, wherever they were, and could tire people out; he had so much energy. Red is gone, but Ira is still with us, and he will always be able to play. *(Ira passed, September 2020)* If he is ambulatory and can hold a horn, he will be a force. They came to Seattle a few years later, and Burt Wilson cornered Ira and said, "Man, I love your bari playing." Ira says, "What?" and then when Burt names the record, a Johnny Griffin record, Ira told him that was the only time he EVER played bari. It turns out the horn was just at the studio. Then Burt started talking about a tune he had written, mentioning this cycle stuff with the chord changes. Ira was smiling and nodding his head the whole time. As this is happening, Dial whispered to me, "Ira doesn't know anything about what Burt is saying." Ira does not think much in technical terms about changes.

In New York one time, I was mumbling to Garry Dial about one particular scale and the altered scales, and I was doing it from the first degree of the root of a dominant chord. Garry pulled my coat and just said, "Oh, that's just a melodic minor scale up a half step from the root." Bingo, that was so simple, but I had not seen that before. It was something I had been playing for a while because early on, I was introduced to that sound by peeling some Kenny Dorham. The solo was on Blue Spring. Kenny was playing a G blues, but it seemed like sometimes he was in A flat minor. Dial's remark brought this into focus.

+++++

I did see Chet a lot when I was in New York, and I would see Sal Nistico a lot too, going to sessions with him and even a time busking on the street with him. Sal was playing with Chet. We would sometimes meet at Leo Mitchell's apartment right by Washington Square Park. Leo's wife was a nurse and had a good-paying job. Leo was a great drummer, and he played a lot with Chet. One time I tagged along with Sal to rehearse with Chet. It was at the loft that Dennis Irwin and Brian Lynch shared. Chet did not show, and we just played, and I had a ball playing with those guys.

Chet called me one time at Roscoe's house where I was staying. He was pretty cold and bold, and he asked me if I had any money. When I said, "No," the conversation was terse after that. I can't remember who told me, but Chet was peeved and said, "Who comes to New York with no money?"

Anyway, my phone number was lying around Chet's apartment, and his wife/girlfriend/co-dependent using partner called and says, "Is Chet there?" in a very raggedy-sounding voice. And I thought, how bizarre. Then she said, "If you see him tell him his good friend, Art Pepper, just died." I did see Chet down at Leo's place later that afternoon with Sal. It was always easy for me to fire up, but Chet was working hard to find a vein, spinning his arms, and doing all kinds of contortions to hit himself. I'm already feeling the rush, and I suddenly remember the call and message I'm supposed to deliver. I said to Chet right when he hit himself, "Your wife called and said Art Pepper died." Chet let out a big sigh before abruptly sitting down and said in a barely discernible voice, "I never cared for his playing; his lines were too short." Some cold shit there. Earlier, when we were hanging out in Seattle, my old friend, Joe Brazil (not Detroit Joe Brazil) called Chet, "Ghost Man".

That afternoon I had the thought, and it was that I was somehow stuck on a rung of Dante's Inferno; in other words, it was getting through to me that I was literally in Hell.

+++++

When I was in New York, I hooked up a few times with Carter Jefferson, who I had met in Seattle. I had played with him on a week-long gig at Parnell's with George Cables[83] right after *Cable Vision* came out. Carter was doing kind of poorly, and one night he wanted to sell me his soprano sax, not a good sign!

I did see Benny Green[84] at just about every session. I'm sure he does not remember, but he was very kind to me. I was maybe 31, or so, maybe 32, and Benny was 19. He was a big fan of Kenny Dorham, and at a session on 15th where Junior Cook played, he said I reminded him of Kenny. He probably heard me playing some Kenny, verbatim. At that time, Benny was fixated on Bud Powell. Every time he sat down on the piano it was Un Poco Loco! Benny was just learning that stuff but was great already. I was not surprised when he became famous; he was after it so strong.

I used to go by *Jimmy Ryan's* in New York and hang out because my buddy from Marin County, Boogie, Aka Jan Davis, lived upstairs from Jimmy Ryan's.[85]Boogie's brother Spanky had the gig there. Spanky could play good trad-style trumpet, had a real buttery sound, and could also play lead trumpet if pushed to do it. He played trumpet on the short-lived Tom Harrell/ Sam Jones big band. Also, he had played lead trumpet on Gerry Mulligan's big band. Roy Eldridge gave Spanky the gig at Jimmy Ryans. It was a cool scene; all kinds of players would sit in. Because of my relationship with Boogie and Spanky, I was also welcome.

That summer, 1980, Slim Gaillard went to the Kool Jazz Festival, so his fortunes improved again. As I said earlier, my dad was helping him around this time.

I was tempted to stay in New York and just try to find a niche, but, alas, I left to go back to Seattle, to Jules, my wife, and my young baby son Miles. I was in such bad shape that Roscoe had called my dad, telling him that he should pull me back home. As soon as I got back to Seattle, I got my "old jersey back" down at the methadone clinic.

CHAPTER THIRTY

Tour of England with Slim

I think we're now getting into the fall of '81, and my next musical adventure was a tour of Great Britain with Slim Gaillard. We were to play in England, Scotland, and Wales.

My dad had helped Slim because Slim needed a PR person, and my dad was doing that for him. As everyone knows, it's hard to call people and say, "Hire me, I'm great." Marv being the owner of Parnell's, one of the US's major clubs, gave Slim credibility.

The big day of departure was on us, and John Boucher, the guy from Marin County who used to be the road manager for Maynard's English band, came along as the drummer. Slim was also bringing an entire drum set with no heads! We were puzzled, but by this time realized, we were always in uncharted territory with Slim, so it just barely elicited a passing glance.

When we were at Heathrow airport, there was some hold-up with Slim. I'm not sure what that was all about. Slim had a hazy background. I think he was born in Detroit; however, there were rumors that he was born in Cuba! Whatever the case may be, soon we were on our way to London in TWO

London cabs. Slim's drums took a lot of space and forced us to get the extra cab.

John and I were deposited at the club where our digs were, upstairs from the club. It's hazy in my memory, but I think it was called the Red Onion. Slim was whisked off to an expensive hotel befitting his star status. Unfortunately, when Slim arrived at the hotel, "There was a mix up in the registration, sorry," they said. I think it was the fact that Slim showed up with AT&T bags full of cassette tapes hanging out that were unwound and broken. That got them nervous, so the club found him another up-scale hotel. Ernie Garside[86] set up the tour, and Alastair Roberts, who had Hep Records company, was also helping. The owner of the Pizza Express chain in England was also in the mix of promoters.

+++++

As for me, I had jumped off the methadone program and was counting on the more liberal narcotics policies of England to be able to procure what I needed. The first day I walked to the closest apothecary and talked with a pharmacist. I got on the phone and worked my way up various phone trees. With an unbelievable amount of stamina, I was finally talking to someone in the "Home Office," which was a feat. They referred me to a psychiatrist on Upper Wimpole Street. I managed to convey my desperation, and they set up an appointment right away. It was raining cats and dogs when I arrived at a mansion and sat down, waiting for the Dr. to finish with a patient. I was the last guy he saw. He loaded his pipe and got my full history, very patiently writing down details. He got on the phone and called the apothecary down the street and said to please stay open, that he was sending a patient. He loaned me an umbrella and sent me into the night. At the apothecary, they gave me a virtual jug of methadone. Enough for two weeks. Hey, I was swingin' again!

+++++

Cab to the club and opening night with Slim. The club was packed with Annie Ross and John Mayall and Ronnie Scott and a virtual "who's who" of jazz and R&B luminaries.

We hired a bass player to play the shows with us. There was a different bass player in every new club we played. Part of my job was to show the bass player the music. It was mainly novelty songs on "I Got Rhythm" changes and some blues, so that was hardly a job. Slim would also do his shtick, where he played Claire de Lune by Debussy on piano with the back of his hands. He would make a big show out of it holding his hands upside down and playing with the back of his fingers. Slim did "Laughing in Rhythm" and "Cement Mixer Puttee Puttee" and had lots of patter about imaginary drinks. He would do a "How High the Moon", where he would describe all the things on the moon, all improvised. I love the line he sang one night, "I bet moon never wondered how low, low, low you are."

+++++

Slim was in an older Bobby Darin movie playing, of all things, a musician! Bobby Darin plays a jazz alto player named "Ghost" Wakefield in the movie. The movie, directed by John Cassavetes, was pretty good. I love a scene in the film where the blonde, singing, love interest, sits in with the real jazz cats. The setting is a big party, and there is a very swinging band of all black jazz musicians playing. She works her way to the bandstand and wants to sing. Slim is on the piano, and he looks up at her and says, "Relax, baby."

In the middle of the tour, I had had a very good review in one of the London newspapers. Slim got it in his head that, whatever happened, he wanted credit for my discovery. It was quite bizarre. He kept going on about not getting credit for discovering Bobby Darin!

I loved his stories, though. I should have had a recorder. Slim said when he first got to New York, he lived in the park and "hung his clothes in the trees." He said he played for Frankie Newton. When "Flat Foot Floogie" came out, he said he would just go from bar to bar in Harlem and put nickels in the jukebox and play his single. A one-person PR campaign. But he was a great entertaining musician. Herb Ellis told me once, "Slim could play some rhythm changes on guitar."

Before we left Seattle, Slim borrowed a tux from Sarge, the doorman at Parnell's. It was a pink tux, and although Sarge and Slim were both about 6 feet 4, Slim's hands and arms were so huge the tux was a little small for him. It was quite a sight.

+++++

On our way back to Manchester, from some outlying area, I could see signs for Stonehenge. I started in about the mystery surrounding Stonehenge. Ernie Garside was driving and wanted to get home as soon as possible, so he stared at me and said, "We're not going to Stonehenge." But I kept talking and finally got Slim's attention, and when we came to the exit for Stonehenge, Slim said, "Ernie, take me to Stonehenge." It was so cool to be walking around Stonehenge with Slim Gaillard; it felt like something out of the *Hitch Hikers Guide to the Galaxy*.

+++++

We traveled all over England, Scotland and Wales, and at the end of the tour, we recorded in London for Alastair Robertson's label, Hep Records.[87] His record label was based out of Scotland and was a little like the New York label, Stash Records in the USA. A lot of the stuff on the label was from radio broadcasts during WWII.

We had Jay McShann[88] on piano, Buddy Tate[89] on tenor, a couple of English guys, and me. Slim had made up a song about the tour called; "It's Ok in the UK". It was a collage or collection of impressions from all the places with some Welsh words thrown in. He also did a remake of "Slim's Jam", a tune from his record with Charlie Parker and Dizzy Gillespie. At the recording, we are playing along, and there's a knock-knock, knock and Slim says, "Hey, it's little Jay Thomas at the door, c'mon in and blow some," then I proceed to play some alto. As a qualifier here, when I first got to England, I had checked the alto, and somehow in customs, my mouthpiece was lost! So, right away, I needed to get another. I walked down to Piccadilly Square and went to a music store and picked one out. Way too expensive! So, I got a cheap Yamaha mouthpiece; it did not sound too bad, but it could have been better!

BOOK TWO

1981 – 1997

"And whatever monkey that was
On my back
He jumped off just like that
Right into the deep blue sea
And I looked back over my shoulder
Thinking 'bout the sign
hanging up on the wall that said
Everything's gonna be alright
Everything's gonna be alright
Nobody's gotta worry 'bout nothing.
Don't go hitting that panic button
It ain't near as bad as you think
Everything's gonna be alright
Alright alright."
Song by Little Walter Jacobs
Big Mama Thornton   Kenny Chesney

CHAPTER THIRTY-ONE

Turning the Titanic Around

When I got back to Seattle, Jules gave me my pink slip and asked me to leave. So, I went off to my folk's motel, although I was still in and out of the Olympia house with Jules, and our son, Miles.

That Christmas, I was on my way to a family Christmas party on Vashon Island with Jules and Miles. We had already been to a party in the city, and true to form, drinking was involved. Some things are hard to fathom after the fact, but Jules and I had an argument, and I wanted her to be in the back seat with Miles. I knew it was safer back there, and this night we were in a cold spell, and there was a lot of ice on the road. I was motoring along with an alcohol buzz and high on methadone and was probably reaching for the weed pipe when disaster struck. I ran a stop sign, and a car was coming up a big hill diagonally, and we collided. I woke up in a field on the frozen ground, surrounded by sheep. I heard Miles crying, and I started to move, and people were already there and told me to lie still. Miles and Jules were OK, only a little banged up. Our station wagon was somewhere between a pretzel and an accordion, and even my saxophone that was in its case was totaled. It is a miracle that it was not worse for us. That is an understatement; the fact that Jules and Miles were OK was, in fact, miraculous. My collar bone was broken; the guy in the other car has a scar on his face to this day.

+++++

Slowly turning the titanic around

After a few days, I found myself at a lawyer's house discussing my DWI. While I was there, my old friend and ex-girlfriend of legendary Seattle painter Jakk Corsaw[90] showed up. (Seattle history buffs will recognize Jakk as the artist that designed the Globe atop of the P.I. Building.) Her name is of little concern here, and I will not break her anonymity. Suffice to say, she is and was as beautiful a woman as you would ever see as well as a great person. She came up to me and was bubbling over with warmth and love; she hugged me and said it was soooo great to see me, etc. I was embarrassed, and probably was, "stankin' like old Abe Lankin."

She started talking about how great SHE was feeling and talked about going to meetings, and I tried to follow her. Then she told me her story, or as they say in everyone's favorite twelve-step program, she started to "share her experience, strength and hope" with me. She was "twelve-stepping" me, and I did not realize it; that is the best kind.

She said she had been a nurse with a special license and could administer and handle narcotics. Her mother died of cancer in excruciating pain, and while she was taking care of her mother, she just gave herself a shot also. That started a quick spiral to the bottom. A little while later, she was busted and put in treatment. There, she hooked up with NA (narcotics anonymous).

I asked where she went to treatment, and she told me. But it was expensive, and I was pretty sure it would not work for me. To spend a lot of money on something that probably would not work did not seem like a good idea, and I had no money I could call my own. She gave me the telephone number of a program called ADATSA that was for people like me. I called that number and went through the process to see if I qualified for the program to get admitted. ADATSA paid for my treatment.

The treatment center was called Thunderbird, and it was way out in Rainier Valley. After I checked in, it took me about two weeks before I started to track. I related to it pretty well because I had read about Buddhism and various spiritual disciplines in my acid days, and this was a call to that forgotten part of myself. They had some very simple rules. Go to meetings, don't use in between, don't take the first one, and try to live a day at a time. Live in the present, and don't future trip. Just put one foot in front of the other, and most importantly, share YOUR experience, strength, and hope with others. "You can only keep it by giving it away." These things are so obvious, and we all know it's the best way, no matter what your story is, but with addiction, at my level, it forces you to do this. With my addiction, there were only three outcomes, jails, institutions, or death.

When I got out of the treatment center, Jules and I got back together, and we ended up in Bremerton managing the Chieftain Motel my folks owned.

CHAPTER THIRTY-TWO

Jack Brownlow, Dave Friesen, John Stowell, 1st Relapse

I got busy trying to reinvent myself, and I was regularly going to meetings. I started to play with Jack Brownlow[91] and Jim Anderson (son of my first trumpet teacher). I think Marty Tuttle was on drums, the drummer for the first edition of the Playboys way back.

We called the band *Panacea,* but we live in such an illiterate society, most people could not pronounce it, and only half know what it means. I was introduced to many "standards" by Jack Brownlow. It was a departure from my more straight-ahead playing. Jack often called tempos hard for me because they were in a zone where eighth notes were a little slow, and double-time was a little fast or felt contrived, so, in that regard, it was a real learning experience. Jack helped me pick out an upright piano that I moved into the Chieftain. I was trying to learn functional jazz harmony more thoroughly, and part of that process was to become more keyboard savvy.

+++++

I would watch Miles in the day; I guess I was a househusband. Jules managed the front desk and did the hiring and firing for the motel.

I started working more gigs. I worked at McCarver's in Tacoma, and I got a gig at a club in Gig Harbor that a friend of Dean Hodges owned. So, I started getting gigs more regularly. Things were going pretty well for a while, so my meetings began to seem like a good thing but not a necessity. Soon they became fewer and fewer.

Around this time, I had my wisdom teeth pulled. After the surgery, the Dentist was writing a prescription, and I can't recall if I steered him, but knowing my addiction, I probably did. He wrote a script for Percodan. Knowing my habit, I even have my doubts about the necessity of wisdom teeth surgery!

I'm sure he asked the question they all ask, "are you allergic to any drugs?" But I just stayed silent and did not say I was a hope to die, bonafide dope fiend. Instead, I figured I would take the Percs "the way they were meant to be taken." How did that work? The answer, Not well! I started in on a run that lasted for a while. At first, it was easy to scam the doctors in Bremerton; I had health insurance, so I could just keep going to them if I had to. I would put on my gigging tux and go thru all kinds of Academy Award level acting to score. A lot of creativity went into my stories.

+++++

During this time, I did a tour with David Friesen[92], John Stowell,[93] and the great drummer, Eddie Moore. We played in Los Angeles and Arizona, and I got to be close friends with John Stowell. I knew David Friesen from the days of the Queequeg and later the Llahngaelhyn. We played Yoshi's in San Francisco, which was a step up from when I lived down there before. (I later recorded with both David and John on separate CDs)

+++++

I still was not quite past that pesky problem with dope. I was not using street dope so much, but it is still the same thing. There is one problem after you have had some taste of recovery and been to many meetings; it fucks up the "using" pretty good. Around this time, I remember going to my folks' place on Vashon with Miles (without Jules). I had scored some Tussionex and took it when I got there. My plan was predicated on the idea that nobody would notice my high! Well, the scratching started up, and the lowering of my voice, followed by the pupils of my eyes getting like little pins. I think after 19 years, they definitely had the symptoms down. My mom, who had always been quite a good enabler, got up in my face and was pissed. She told me not to come around if I was going to do that. A little while after the tour, I ended up in another treatment facility called Ollala, on the Peninsula; it was better in many ways than Thunderbird. But hey, I already knew the ropes. My folks paid for this.

The psychiatric nurse at Ollala said something to me, after I started to track, what was necessary for me to hear. I was going on about all these personal problems and how I would solve them now that I was clean. The nurse fixed me with her gaze and said, "Wait a minute! I think you are a little confused; you are not here because of all these personal problems, you are here because you are an ADDICT!" with some emphasis on the word, addict.

So, when I got out, I was more motivated to keep it going this time. I started hustling gigs. Having Diane Schuur[94] as part of the band helped to score gigs. I also did some gigs with John Stowell, John Bishop, and Bruce Phares.

+++++

Before I go much further, I have to explain that no matter how much Jules and I loved Miles, we were saddled with too much negative history. I could never begin to make up for all the things I had done. As often happens when one person changes drastically, the whole thing gets out of balance, like a mobile. Anyway, even though we loved each other, neither of us had the communication skills necessary to fix it. So, with that, I will move to the next phase.

CHAPTER THIRTY-THREE

Becca Duran

A round this time, Mark Solomon, the guy shot at the Dizzy show when he worked at Parnell's, started a booking agency. I naturally went to Mark for work. He said he could get me some gigs but said I needed to have a vocalist, and he gave me some names. I already knew and eliminated some, but mainly he had one he wanted me to try. Her name was Becca Duran[95]. I heard a tape she was on with Bill Ramsay. Other than that, I did not know much about her. My first impressions were good when she drove up in a little sports car, and she was cheerful and attractive. And to top it off, she had a pretty hip book of standards and some special jazz things that she sang.

The rehearsal went very well, and Craig Hoyer, who was on keyboards, was also impressed. With Becca on board, I hit the pavement looking for work, and we got a couple of steady gigs right away.

One was a gig at the Eastlake Cafe, an old building with a deck looking out over Lake Union and featured many furnishings from the Art Deco period. We had a cool listening crowd of diners that seemed to like what we were doing. Our connection to the gig was Dean Hodges. As well as being the first-call jazz drummer in Seattle for decades, Dean was the most relaxed straightforward boss you could ever have. We played another club by the Tacoma Dome, had a few other little gigs, and even played the Jazz Alley in the University District.

Becca was single and attractive, and we had an instant kind of dance going. It turns out she had seen me once, years earlier, running a jam session at Parnell's, and took an instant dislike to me. Back then, she thought that I was arrogant and had also heard I was a junkie.

Anyway, I was in the first stages of recovery when I fell for Becca.

I might have just muddled along, but I had a sponsor who took me seriously and took the situation seriously. He said, "You have to do something. Making no decision might seem like an option, but would not be fair to anyone, including yourself." At this time, Jules and I had sadly parted ways as husband and wife. After all that we had been through, it was a gut-wrenching decision. Miles, my son, was three years old, and I'm sure it affected him. One poignant moment was etched on my memory when Miles asked me, "Why did you leave my mom?" That was a tough one.

Becca and I were then officially an item. We realized we needed a professional demo tape and promo even to begin to get serious about working. We went to a kind of sketchy studio, with Chuck Metcalf, Craig Hoyer, and Dave Johnson and recorded. While it was fun times, the demo tape was worthless for getting gigs. As professional commercial musicians, we were clueless.

We went back to the drawing board and got Nick Moore, an excellent piano player I used to work with in Pioneer Square, to produce a demo tape for us. Nick knew his way around studios, and with the help of Mark Solomon, our agent, we planned a demo tape. The recording was fifteen songs, in various styles, in 15 minutes. That's because agents and clients usually just skip around in a demo tape and do not spend time listening to the whole thing. Now they would get a good idea of our versatility.

I got my friend Milo Peterson to play guitar and even sing some rock n roll. Craig helped a little with the country part of the tape. Marvin, ever the practical person, said, "Why don't you include some foreign language selections for Becca to sing?" At first, we thought it would mess with the continuity of our heavily produced demo, but thankfully we included a few things Becca sang in Spanish, French, and Portuguese. The tape turned out great, and right away, we started getting gigs.

Unfortunately, we could not reproduce the audition tape's sounds because, after the recording, Craig left us a note on our doorstep saying he had joined the army! WTF.

We sent out many tapes, even to agents all over the world.

CHAPTER THIRTY-FOUR

JAPAN

We got our first real break from Japan. The demo tape landed on the desk of Mako Imaizumi, an agent in Shibuya, who happened to be friends with pianist Jorgen Kruse. Becca and I both knew Jorgen when he had gigged around Tacoma for years and was a good friend of Bill Ramsay. I had previously met Jorgen when he was running a big band at Evergreen college. Due to a divorce and other factors, Jorgen took a gig in Japan, met a Japanese lady, and decided to stay in Japan.

The agent asked Jorgen about us, and he said he knew us, and we were cool, etc. This is when the urging of my father to include foreign language material paid off. Becca could sing the hell out of the Edie Gorme *Trio Los Panchos* record, and we had included some of that material in the demo tape. Mako, the agent, loved it! Mako used to travel to Cuba to book musicians in Japan, and she had a real affinity for songs sung in Spanish.

Mako's agency, Washington Kikaku, booked a hotel in Nagoya that had a restaurant that was transitioning from a Hawaiian theme to French. Mako had provided their entertainment for several years and asked us if we could travel to Japan to play at the Nagoya Castle Hotel.[96] We took Curtis Brengle, a young Cornish graduate with great chops, and Milo Peterson, who could play drums and guitar.

Before going, I was having a rough time mentally and had what I thought of at the time as a "little relapse."

In August of 1985, we ended up at the 5 Star Nagoya Castle Hotel in Nagoya, Japan. What an adventure that was. The Nagoya Hotel sat right across from the Nagoya Castle. The Castle was from the Tokagawa period. It had manicured grounds surrounded by moats and featured a giant golden fish on top of the Castle.

The gig was easy, we did some standards, and Becca even sang a Japanese pop song phonetically. She is very talented with languages and could pull it off. We played the gig and did the tourist stuff also. The gig had three short sets with breaks between where we went to our rooms and cooled it. We were done at 9:00 every night, easy street.

+++++

When we got back to Seattle, I did a little tour with John Stowell, Bruce Phares, and Jeff Cumpston on drums. That time was the low point in my slight "relapse." I got drunk at our "going away party" in Nagoya at the end of the Japan gig. It was kind of comical if it was not so serious. It's like I had two equally powerful minds trying to wrest control over my body, like a silent movie of Dr. Jekyll and Mr. Hyde. I had the good "recovery Jay" in a bitter knock-down-drag-out fight with "bad Hyde."

Finally, I hit bottom and found myself totally beat and quite pissed off that I had allowed this to happen again. I knew if I went to another treatment center, they would essentially just reintroduce me to AA or NA. So, I went to an NA meeting up on Capitol Hill. I went in early and sat down, and somehow, I got boxed in. I was super pissed and hated all the people there before the meeting even started. They seemed to know each other, and it was a huggee, touchy-feely scene with a lot of laughter thrown in. That infuriated me even more! Luckily, I was boxed in because I might have split, thereby causing a completely different path for myself. When the meeting started, "*Sick Nick*" talked first; he later became my sponsor. He had me and the rest of the room in stitches. I know it has been said before, but laughter really is the best miracle drug! Nick had a completely deadpan and hilariously funny delivery and hit on important things while being out-rageously funny at the same time. *Wino Earl* was next, another NA recovery legend of the time.

At the end of the meeting, I realized I had gotten out of myself. Put in another way, for a brief time, I had been re-lieved of the "burden of myself." After the meeting, I felt way better. Somebody told me about a meeting at Pike Place Mar-ket the next afternoon. I was there the next day. At that meet-ing, I saw *Sick Nick* again. This kept happening, and eventual-ly, I was drafted into service and started doing hospital and institution meetings, including jail meetings. I also took over the Methadone treatment center meeting. That was especially good for me because I had such a history with Methadone. I got to see up close the level of denial capable by addicts. I had whole families of addicts coming into the Methadone meeting talking about how great it was to be clean while scratching their noses and nodding off. At the Jail meeting, I had people in orange jumpsuits talking about how great things were go-ing!

I went to meetings every day and did not use in between...
or since,

that was 11/01/85. My second birthday.

CHAPTER THIRTY-FIVE

The end of '85 was my new start, and Recording with Cedar Walton and Billy Higgins

One of the first things in the new Jay world was when my dad said, "How would you like to record with the Cedar Walton[97] Trio?" Are you kidding!!! Of course, that was like the coolest thing in the world. And that was right after pulling out of the spin. It was December, and Cedar came to the house, and we played, and I also sat in with him at Jazz Alley. His drummer, Billy Higgins,[98] was also very friendly to me. He was friends with Sal Nistico, and Sal had told him about me. Billy was a guy who had gone down as far as you could go with addiction. Billy shared some of his story with me. He was a fun guy to be around, could do the Michael Jackson Moonwalk, and loved to laugh. Billy had the chops and wherewithal to instantly recognize my situation and address me with humor and compassion. He told me things would be cool.

I learned some of Cedar's arrangements, and I brought a few myself. We went out to Triad Studios in Bellevue and spent the afternoon recording. I was super stressed when the actual recording happened. I was breaking out in Herpes and going thru all kinds of mental gyrations; (people in my corner giving me the smelling salts and wiping me down and massaging my shoulders and putting wax on that eye, so I didn't just bleed out!); that's what it FELT like to me. I was in a fight all right, but it had nothing to do with external reality.

On playback of a Bronislav Caper ballad called "Gloria", even I was impressed with the vibe and the sound of the tenor, and all of a sudden, the take stopped. I was standing there with Billy, hearing on the playback, "Something happened." Billy looked at me wistfully, shook his head, and said, "Nothing happened," meaning it was fine. Even though that was not the cut, we did get a good take of it. The next day I went in with a different game plan. After the first day, I said to myself, "Self, what would we like to do with Cedar?" The answer came back, "Just do tunes, and blow with a little less arrangement."

Boom! The following day was way cool, we recorded some standards, and I had a project.

Cedar, Billy, and David were a self-organizing unit. They reminded me of primordial hunters. They worked together as a unit, quickly inserting little vamps and knowing when to stay in one with a bass pedal and switch to four with the most contrast and effect. For example, I brought in a little arrangement of Secret Love with a part of the melody up a half step. Cedar was all over that. In the first chorus of my solo, they stayed in that pedal figure, and at the start of the second chorus, they inserted a break giving me two bars by myself, then they came in low to the ground swingin' so hard in four it made me feel like I was on a magic carpet. I like that teamwork in jazz; I think it also translates well for the audience.

Later Ramsay arranged a bone section as a sweetener for some of the cuts, and I had Luis Peralta lay down some percussion, also after the fact. That really lifted it to another level. (Peralta had been playing with Dizzy not too far back)

We sent it to a few record companies but did not know how to shop it.

CHAPTER THIRTY-SIX

Japan Again

Later in '86, we got another call from Japan, this time to be in Tokyo. Mako said our duty was to provide Jazz and Bossa Nova. Jazz! Whee, now we are cooking! Playing jazz for six months! So, in March of '86, we went to Tokyo; Becca, me, Milo on guitar, and Craig, who had managed to extricate himself from the clutches of the Army with an honorable discharge no less! We were a little short on details, but we just knew Jazz and Bossa Nova was right up our alley.

Luckily for us at the Eastlake Cafe, Craig had already done a couple of sequences on our brand new QXI sequencer, and we had brought our equipment along, of course. The *First Lady* club was in Roppongi, right across from the Tokyo Tower. Even though it was a brand-new club, it turns out we were the second band there from the USA. The first band was called the *Palm Springs Yacht Club Band*, and they came to Japan doing comedy and Dixieland. Even the name *Palm Springs Yacht Club* should have been a tip-off to the Japanese. Of course, the desert does not have a yacht club, and the Japanese could not understand the jokes, and they played Dixieland music. Their tenure was short-lived.

At the *First Lady*, we played alternating sets with a Filipino band, one hour on, one hour off, all thru the evening, and it was for dancers. We were in a hostess club. Whoops. Not exactly what we thought we would be doing. At first, we tried to do the old scuzzy Rock and Roll for the dancers. Songs like "Pretty Woman", and "Louie Louie", etc. But the Filipino band already had that covered. They were called Stars of the '60s. First Lady was a high-class hostess club, and they wanted current dance music from us. Craig got busy sequencing, and we were soon doing Whitney Houston, Janet Jackson, Huey Lewis, Chaka Khan, Madonna, The Eurythmics, Sade, etc. And we also learned many standards. Craig and I got into arranging for three-part vocal harmony with Becca, Craig, and me singing. We had really cool arrangements of "Straighten Up and Fly Right" and "The Java Jive" that Craig arranged. Craig was a savant when it came to his knowledge of a lot of tunes. He could also sing, and his arranging of vocals was at a high level.

+++++

Then I discovered Japanese coffee! In all my years as a junkie, coffee was not even on my radar. Japanese brewed coffee was super strong and quite an ass-kicker. We called it the cocaine of coffee. That, and the fact that there was discord in the band, had me going into some panic attacks. I would suddenly get the "fear" back in the room after the gig and think I was maybe going to have a heart attack or something. We had two tiny twin beds, and Becca would come over and put her arms around me. We did not get to sleep usually until the ravens started making their sounds in the early dawn. Man, the crows or ravens were loud; they sounded human at times.

+++++

We became pretty good on that gig. We learned enough material for several complete hour sets. We never stopped playing during our hour. That was a thing the club manager told us; basically, to play one hour-long medley. He said the Japanese would get bored if we paused between songs, and we could not have that! There was even no stopping as the bands changed. The lights would darken, Craig would go into Misty on solo piano, and the other band would slip onto the stage as we slipped off. I'll tell you that took some doing for me, considering I had a Trumpet, Flute, and Saxophone to move. The music never stopped.

It turned out that knowing current pop songs and never stopping also worked like a charm back in the states! The gig in Japan turned out to be a litmus test to handle a commercial variety gig.

We stayed at an old hotel called the Gajoen Kanko, located in Tokyo's Meguro district, for six months. This hotel was where the occupying brass stayed after WWII. It had murals painted everywhere on the ceilings and walls that were very old and probably considered antiques or treasures. It was part of acreage with a garden park that was a tourist attraction called the Gajoen Park Gardens. Becca and I fell in love with Japan, and we made a few friends also. We should have been more into the language, but, alas, we were a self-contained unit, and we had our hands full with the gig. Milo started picking up the language right away. Alas, Craig never hung out with us ever; we weren't sure what he was doing.

+++++

Our agent Mako had an assistant named Hiro, an ex-bass player who knew some jazz people. One night he took me to a club to sit in with jazz tenor sax legend Sleepy Matsumoto.[99] Rollo, my surrogate uncle, had been in Korea and had all kinds of stories about his time in Korea. One of them was going to Japan on R& R and checking out the jazz scene in Japan, and he talked about a guy nicknamed "Sleepy." Rollo was fond of telling tall tales as well as facts. It was often hard to tell them apart. In this case, he was telling the truth; it was cool to hear and meet Sleepy, and that it was not a "Fig Newton" of Rollo's imagination.

The agent said we were going to Badalando, "You know it?" I assured him that I did not know Badalando. It turns out it was the Anglicized pronunciation of Birdland. The club was an expensive high-end establishment, as far as I could tell. On each table was a bottle of Johnny Walker Red.

I went into the back, and Sleepy was sitting with his wife. They had a little chihuahua dog. If my memory serves me correctly, Sleepy had just turned 60. When I watched his show, it was astounding how good he was. He had a great sound, huge and projecting, a classic hard bop sound. Sleepy played on an old Berg Larsen tenor mouthpiece like Yusef Lateef used to play and currently played by Pete Christlieb and Plaz Johnson. He could play lightning-fast, and his ballads were beautiful. Even when playing a crowd-pleaser like "Tennessee Waltz" or "La vie en Rose", he always sounded great. Sleepy had to field a lot of requests, but he was unperturbed. He kind of sighed and said, "Takusan questo," on the mic. That translates to "many requests," referring to the number of requests. Danny Boy, whatever, he did it. His band was younger with a couple of black musicians, as I recall, and they played well.

My agent showed the Cedar Walton project to Sleepy, so he called me up to play. We played "Invitation", my sound was fine, but Sleepy was a jazz master! He was gracious and friendly to me.

On another off night, to hear jazz, I went to the smallest nightclub I have ever been to, to this day. It was called Sonor and was close to the Meguro train station. The band was good, and they were doing some Monk tunes like *4 in One and Trinkle Tinkle* and other tricky stuff. I talked to the sax player, who was playing alto and soprano. I asked him where he got the soprano, and he said it was a new prototype that Yanagisawa was making.

I got the Yanagisawa factory's address and went there taking my promo and mentioning Don Lanphere, who was my friend and a Yanagisawa rep. I tried to finagle being a rep and getting a free sax, but they were having none of it, but they did, however, give me a smokin' deal on a soprano. Yanagisawa is a cool company, and later they came to the hotel and brought me mouthpieces to try.

While I was there, I tried shopping the Cedar Walton project for Japanese companies. Some were very interested but did not bite for the whole deal. They got right up to the water, but they did not drink.

+++++

I was going to meetings regularly. The first one was a Japanese NA meeting out at the Yoyogi stop and was close to a university. Becca and I arrived at the meeting place, and I was early. It's funny because I could spot the other addicts right away, even with the cultural differences. That meeting was fascinating because words were not even that important; the important thing was to go there. To make an effort was the therapeutic part. When we observe ourselves practicing good mental health or caring for ourselves, it is powerful medicine in itself. The meeting was all in Japanese, except when they yelled, "Keep coming back" in heavily accented English. Often when someone would talk, there would be an eruption of laughter. I would laugh too! It was like a silent movie with no subtitles. Later, a guy came up to me and did some translating. One old guy got up and spoke, and the translator whispered in my ear, "Fierce gangster." Hmmmm, he just looked like a little old man to me. But I suppose Carlo Gambino would also have appeared like a little old man.

I asked the guy what the drug of choice was these cats were recovering from; really, that is not important. A drug is a drug, is a drug, including alcohol. But he informed me mainly speed. Hmmmmm, I asked about narcotics, and the guy said, "Oh, that's no big deal over here; a lot is just over the counter." I thought this cannot be right. That was a seed that was bugging me. I wanted in the worst way to find out if that was true. The 64-thousand-dollar question is, why was this bothering me? Fortunately, I was able to recognize the clear signs of danger ahead and steered away.

After that, I got my ass to some English-speaking meetings. I went to AA meetings right by the club where we worked. I think I could go on a break; it was that close. We had an hour off between the Filipino's set and our set. I never tried to determine if what the guy said was true about over-the-counter narcotics or a miscommunication.

+++++

My mom and dad and my niece, Anna, and my nephew, Bryon, came that summer and brought my son, Miles. That was a real joy I will never forget. Miles was just four, but he was smart as a whip and was digging Japan. He still liked to be carried sometimes.

We got a babysitter for Miles when we were at work. Her name was Mandy; she was half Welsh and half Japanese. She was cute as could be and very responsible. When we would come home, Miles was always in a playful mood, jumping from bed to bed, and we would sometimes go out walking even at 4:00 AM. We would go to the convenience store and get a late snack. The city is safe and virtually never sleeps. Earlier in the evenings, Miles must have had the sweetened coffee out of the vending machine. Vending machines are all over Japan. He was a live wire most nights.

Once, we were walking to a restaurant, and it was kind of far. Miles put out his arms like he wanted to be carried. I said, "No, you have to walk; we are almost there." He furrowed his eyebrows and puckered his lips in anger and kept making the signal for me to pick him up. I said, "No way, Miles, you're going to have to walk; the restaurant is close." He went on strike and stopped, and then he threatened me. He said, "I'm going to wake up all of Tokyo." I said, "Give it your best shot." He proceeded to let out a scream and even stripped the gears for a second, but when that was over, we calmly walked the rest of the way to the restaurant. Miles got pretty good with chopsticks, and he loved Ramen and Udon and Soba. He would have his arm all the way extended sometimes to drop the noodles into his mouth!

Becca and I were in Harajuku one day with Miles when we looked down the street to the shopping area, and there were thousands and thousands of people with black hair and Asian features. Miles remarked, "there sure are a lot of Japanese people here." We went to a big fair, and Miles got a giant pet beetle, and we also found Sami bugs that were huge, so this was cool for a kid.

When Miles left to return to the States, his babysitter, Mandy, did not come to say goodbye even though we tried to call her that day. Miles was distraught. As he was crying, he said, "Sometimes a guy would like to say goodbye." He was in love with her. When Becca and I were at the station, we looked across the other side and saw my dad and mom and niece and nephew and Miles right before they got on the train. I could feel a sadness in my gut, and Miles was also feeling it. We did not talk about that parting for several years, but it was intense because he let out a wail when I mentioned it years later.

CHAPTER THIRTY-SEVEN

Fall of '86, back to the US and Discovery Records

When we got back to the US, we started working for Mark Solomon's booking agency, playing company parties and society weddings, etc. With the material we had amassed from the six months overseas, we wowed them at weddings and functions. I did not mind the weddings; people always knew why they were there, and the management never worried about the till ringing, and they paid well. We also had a few other agents booking us. We traveled to Eugene and played at the River Valley Inn, located right on the Willamette River directly across from the City Center. While we were doing these gigs, I began writing material again. The last time I had been writing was in the 60s. Getting clean was the factor that allowed me the time and energy to start reclaiming my life.

We were working as a trio with Craig, Becca, and myself. It was the easiest to book moneywise. Craig had a personality clash with Milo. Becca and I got along with Milo better than Craig, but my first goal after getting clean was working steadily.

We used to go to Yakima and play at a place attached to the Convention Center called Johnnie's. That was not so great. They wanted a band with long rocker's hair! They could not understand why we would ever play some of the music we played and even were ABLE to play. The bar help and management wished that we would play music for the people they wished were there! This is a classic problem often described as the "chicken or the egg?" They wanted a sports bar for young, vibrant, drinking party animals. However, their clientele was older, sedate business people and older couples stuck in Yakima for the night.

We played there many times and found other ways to amuse ourselves, like looking for antiques or going out and finding the best Mexican lunches served out in the countryside to the workers in the fields.

+++++

The Cedar Walton project was sitting with no firm bites from record companies. Cedar had moved to LA during this period, even though he kept his rent-controlled apartment in New York. On one of Cedar's road trips on the coast, Billy, David, and Cedar were in their van while driving to a gig. Someone put on the project we had recorded. They hadn't heard it for a while, especially with all the sweeteners, professional mix, etc. They were happily surprised about how good it sounded.

Cedar contacted Albert Marx. Cedar had just done a project for Albert. Albert Marx then contacted me. He wanted the project on his label Discovery Records.[100] Albert was also knocked out by Becca's singing. Becca did a couple of numbers on the album. "A Little Tear" was a song where Becca had written an interlude that we played with voice and flute in harmony.

Albert was an old guy at the time, but his roots went way back. He recorded Benny Goodman way back in the day at Carnegie Hall. He started a label called Musicraft that, at one time, had Duke Ellington, Sarah Vaughn, and many big names in jazz. We were happy to have him on our side.

We titled the Cedar project *Easy Does It*. Hmmmmmm, you can see what I was thinking. That is one of the tried-and-true AA or NA sayings. In other words, don't get clamped. When it came out, it was getting play even at the local station umpteen times a day. That never happens.

The Latin cut of Cedar's arrangement of "Blue Train" was getting heavy play. Later I found out the Beastie Boys had grabbed (sampled) part of another tune on the album, a Cedar composition called Jacobs Ladder. I heard the cut on YouTube, and it had me on the album cover. However, they had sampled it and improved it in their minds at least. It was a little faster, had little of Billy Higgins, but a lot of Latin percussion. I had played all the parts, and it was obviously Cedar, but they replaced my solo with a more contemporary-sounding saxophonist. There was not much to do about it; I did not write the song. I suppose I could have investigated further, but by the time I started thinking those thoughts, it was no longer on YouTube.

Leonard Feather gave it a great review. He was very complimentary, and that felt like it could be the harbinger of an actual career in jazz! Things were looking up. I was getting some name recognition, which is especially important. Still, it was not immediately affecting my money bottom line or ability to get festivals or work out of the area. But it certainly felt OK and helped me get some jazz gigs, nonetheless.

Albert was old school, and he did not even make sure it was at all the stations. And when a Japanese company was finally interested in licensing the project in Japan, Albert growled over the phone and said, "Forget it, we already have distribution in Japan." Not quite the same thing.

Albert wanted another project right away with Becca singing. Because of the composing I was doing and Becca's ability to write lyrics, we collaborated, which was good. In hindsight, it would have been better just to do some classic standards rather than originals, especially for a first CD recording.

Jazz DJs are relatively conservative in many quarters, and our CD project was anything but conservative. We had a combination of synth and acoustic piano and all sorts of sounds not on your usual vocal album. Becca wrote Spanish lyrics about the "Disappeared" in South America for the song "Leaving" by Ritchie Beirach. We had the sampled sound of the engine running and a door slamming to signify the sounds of the Ford Falcons idling in the alleyway when police hauled off the young students into the night. We had a beautiful number called "L'fricaine" that had jungle sounds and a lion roaring, and Becca wrote French lyrics. I could just see the antelopes running and jumping on the plains of Africa. It was very ambitious for the scope of the material and the creativity that went into it. We were also trying to minimize the recording studio expenses. We recorded at a small studio run by Bob Meador. Bob could get a lot out of his little setup, but Bob's piano was barely doable, and while his outboard gear was OK, it was not in the same league as Studio X or Triad. We might have been better off getting a heavy-weight rhythm section, a great piano guy for Becca, and only doing standards in a major Seattle studio.

Becca's album *Hide and Seek* came out, and some people just loved it. We even received a letter from the Majestic Hotel owner in St Louis who heard it on Jim Wilke's national show, Jazz After Hours. We ended up going to St Louis and playing at the Majestic and using our old friend and guitarist, Danny Embry. But, by and large, it was not what we hoped. It did not get any play in Seattle, except the Jim Wilke show.

One other factor I should mention, Albert Marx died right before it came out.

Because we did not get much local play on it, I got into an argument with a station manager, never a good idea. I was passionate about the project. It took a bit of doing to mend that fence and turn the situation around.

Stay tuned.

CHAPTER THIRTY-EIGHT

Herb Ellis

As a result of the *Easy Does It* CD, I became involved with Herb Ellis.[101] Herb heard the CD and liked it. In the mid-80s, Herb came quite a few times to perform in Seattle. His road manager, Terry Holmes, was a good friend of mine. Consequently, I played a few gigs with Herb in Seattle with Buddy Catlett on bass. Herb was a witty guy, but sometimes he could be so dark it was comical unless you were on the other side of it.

I went down to Jazz Alley in the University District to watch a gig Dimitrio, Jazz Alley's owner, had booked for Herb. Herb did not like the drummer they had for him, so he growled at Dimitrio, "I can't play with this guy... get "tinki-boom," referring to the drummer he had before. Dimitrio had also booked Bill Smith on clarinet to be part of the group. Bill Smith used to play with Dave Brubeck and others and was on the University of Washington faculty. This did not sit well with Herb. On the gig, Herb refused to play when Bill played. Kind of awkward, to say the least. Bill Smith had an echo-plex he was using to loop phrases, etc. Pretty advanced techno stuff for the time. When Herb announced Bill the night

I was there, Herb got on the Mic and said, "And now ladies and gentlemen, we bring you Bill Smith- Smith-Smith Smith," gradually fading out. Then, when Bill played, Herb would just sit there with a baleful blue-eyed stare that made him look a little like Geronimo in one of those reservation pictures.

Later, I did a few gigs and festivals with Herb. The band included: Jake Hanna on drums, a swinging monster, and a very funny guy. Mel Ryne was on organ. Mel used to play with Wes Montgomery and was a great musician and an underground legend. Johnny Frigo was on violin. Johnny was very old but had a youthful spirit and was a virtuoso and also quite a comedian. Frigo talked about singing in a megaphone when he was younger. He said the song was a Rudy Vallee hit that had a humming part. When it got to the humming part, he would put the megaphone over his nose. Herb and Johnny went way back and co-wrote "Detour Ahead" together. "Detour Ahead" was a vehicle for Billy Holiday. Bill Evans also recorded it, as I did on my *Blues for McVouty* CD. The song bugged Herb a lot because everyone went gaga over Bill Evans's changes in his recording of this tune. Herb was kvetching about "Those are not the correct changes." Anyway, I was there when Johnny looked at Herb's changes and said, "Those aren't right!"

I was on one recording with that band. The session took place in Houston, Texas. The Justice Records company owner called me and said, "Who have you played with?" That caught me off guard, and I got a little defensive and just said, "Machito." This guy was a Johnny- come- lately rich kid, and he did not know Machito from a rolling donut. Next, the guy said he was looking for "gritty," and did I play baritone?

Oh well, you take them as they come.

They flew me to Texas, and most of the recording was already done, with little slots for solos, no ensemble stuff. And no choice of what I was going to play. I remember one cut was for me to overdub a solo on "Sugar Hill Stomp" at one of Herbs "rodeo tempos," up around 300+ MM. I only knew the song vaguely, and it was not a pretty thing! There were a couple of things that were OK. At the end of the session, the record guy wanted a blues. He probably would have been happy with a "Johnny Winter type, guitar god, pentatonic blues, jerk fest." But, instead, Herb just decides to wing it. Herb starts in, and we have no idea what he's going to play; the engineer stops it a little way in and says, "no, that's the hokey pokey."

Terry Holmes told me that Herb had asked Stan Getz to be on the recording, and Stan said sure, but his fee would be $100,000. Cedar Walton's wry understated comment when I told him this was, "Stan, (pause for effect) did not want to do that record."

At the end of the recording, I did two gigs with Herb in Houston. The first night was so unlike the recording. We had a blind drummer from Texas who was incredibly good and an excellent bass player. It was going great, and I thought maybe now I can approach the record company owner about a record of my own. It turns out he was not at the gig. The record guy already had a couple of people in mind. One was a jazz bassoon player! And the other was a trumpet player named Rebecca Coupe Franks.

We did play a gig in Hollywood after the CD release. As I remember, that went pretty well.

We did a festival in Colorado with the musicians from the recording, plus Franks. I arrived in Colorado after having been up all night. It was mid-morning, and the sun was just beating down. I felt like a vampire ready to go up in flames. Then to top it off, there was a street gig of a band that included 18-year-old Ryan Kisor on trumpet, just blasting out over the whole town. He was just horrifying; he was so good at 18. He was channeling Woody Shaw and Clifford Brown and was playing all over the trumpet; high or low was no sweat for Ryan.

It turned out to be a very anticlimactic gig for me. Because the record company wanted to promote Rebecca Franks, I was forbidden to play the trumpet! After the gig party, I quickly raided the shrimp, had some food, and then decided to head back to the hotel to sleep rather than do the required networking. My attitude was bad; it was, "network on this Mother F*+**>R." An old black tap dancer and I were the only ones riding the limo back to the hotel. We looked at each other like two old dogs that had just run the Iditarod. I was as tired as he was!

I also played a festival in the Ozarks with Herb and stayed in Little Rock, Arkansas, at Terry's place and Herb's house. My friend Terry had just gotten married and needed time alone, so I got farmed out to Herb's house. It was an interesting stay.

Herb had a history of alcoholism but was clean by the time I knew him. On the other hand, Herb's wife started juicing before cooking the dinner, so we had a wacky dinner. One thing led to another with several kitchen disasters. We ate very late at night. Herb and I just watched TV in the next room. I remember watching Mannix and Murder She Wrote back to back. Herb turned to me in the middle of the second one and said, "Pretty good, uh?"

He did have his lighter side, was a practical joker and a great storyteller, and sometimes got you on the ropes. I remember one time after an AA meeting, Herb and Terry were giving a newcomer a ride home when they pulled into the parking lot of a bar and said they always celebrated after a meeting. The poor girl freaked out before they said they were only joking. Herb could be difficult, though. Terry said Herb had to go off on someone every day.

I remember Herb telling me who the next president was going to be. Herb said Bill Clinton was going to be president, and I had never heard of him. Herb said he was from Little Rock and would be president. I filed it away, giving no thought whatsoever to that prophecy.

CHAPTER THIRTY-NINE

Bill Ramsay, Chuck Israels

Also, around this time, I started a band with Bill Ramsay called Los Altos. The same idea as Tenor Dynasty, only with four altos, Denny Goodhew, Rams, Jim Coile, and myself. Travis Shook or John Hansen piano, Doug Miller bass, and John Bishop (Origin records founder) on drums in the rhythm section. Ramsay started cranking out some charts. Bill was always a good arranger. Ramsay wrote all the big band charts for Ernestine Anderson on the album; "You Made Your Move Too Soon". That album got Ernestine a lot of radio play and was a big hit for her.

I also got busy and started writing. At first, my arrangements were a lot of harmonizing the melody, but I eventually got better and got Russ Garcia's book on arranging as a kind of handbook. I bought a little Fostex multi-track analog recorder. I would put all the horn parts and piano down and then sit back and listen to them. My initial criteria were, is something jumping out at me? If there was, I did not consider that a good thing. I learned that each time you added a 1st or 3rd part, the previous part would lose some fidelity. To get around this, I would lay the inner parts first and the bottom and top last! Digital technology and midi have made this kind

159

of approach obsolete now, in the same way that we don't physically lift the needle on an LP record anymore when we transcribe.

We worked a few gigs, but not nearly enough for the effort involved in putting that together.

+++++

And at this same time, bass player Chuck Israels[102] came to Bellingham to teach at Western Washington University. Chuck played with Bill Evans after Scott Lafaro died. That was a cool time in Bill's career. Even though Bill looked skeletal and was using heavily, I loved the music from this period.

Chuck was also on a record with Coltrane and Kenny Dorham that was always a favorite of mine. Even with a very disjointed Cecil Taylor providing piano accompaniment, it was a terrific record! I know, I'm aware I'm on dangerous ground here, but I can hear what's going on during the recording of that date. The inclusion of Cecil Taylor probably was an A&R man's invention to try and sell records. Chuck Israels certainly was not on board for Cecil, and Dorham had many piano players he would have preferred to Cecil Taylor. But, sometimes, it is the grain of sand that produces the pearl, and I loved the way Kenny and Trane dig in to assert and find their way over the broken groundwork laid down by Cecil.

Israels had a book for a small, big band and had been the writer/arranger and leader of the National Jazz Orchestra in New York City, featuring Tom Harrell and Sal Nistico and many top players. Chuck was the precursor of Wynton in the way he seriously showcased Ellington and Strayhorn.

I hit it off well with Chuck, and in addition to his little/big band, I was also doing a trio with Chuck and Dave Peterson, and later guitarist Danny Embry. Occasionally Chuck would bring me to Western Washington University to play with his band at the school as a clinician and guest soloist. Chuck had specific requirements to become a jazz person; one was to be familiar with jazz styles and phrasing and vocabulary evident in classic jazz recordings. My standards are not so rigid based on my R&B background, but I understood where he was coming from, and I guess I kind of passed muster because I played with him for several years off and on.

Chuck is a real New York intellectual and has always played with the best of the jazz players in America. Chuck has no love for the ever-changing fads of popular culture. In Chuck's world, R & B and pop were not something he paid much attention to; the Beatles were just a minor distraction or novelty band. I admire Chuck's single-minded ability to cleave to his vision.

As I said previously, Chuck had charts for a big band, and he reached out to the greater Seattle jazz community to put a band together to play his music. I can't remember the original personnel, but I know he had Bill Ramsay on lead alto, Dave Peterson guitar, and Dave Peck on piano. At the rehearsals, Chuck was very particular about how he wanted his arrangements played. Chuck was also a real taskmaster when it came to tempo fluctuations. He would not stand for rushing or dragging. That band might have had one or two gigs. I had fun and got along fine with Chuck, but the band was not destined to continue in Seattle. Chuck wanted a certain kind of vocabulary and time feel, and fundamental ethos that was definitely a New York thing, so he had no patience for those who did not have the same dedication and experiences he had. And vice versa, the band had no patience with his no patience!

After that, I continued playing with Chuck in his no-drummer trio, bass, horn, and guitar. Chuck plays with great time and conviction, and I learned a lot from being around him in this period.

CHAPTER FORTY

Willie Thomas

Through the years that Chuck Israels was at Western teaching, I was busy playing with several bands. In today's world, that's the way people stay active in music. In the old days, the goal was a steady gig with one band, but today most people are very diversified with teaching, playing, and recording.

I got a call from Chuck one day to do a recording in Seattle as part of a sextet. The recording was going to be for *Jazz Player Magazine*, and he wanted me on saxophone. Dave Glenn was the trombone player. Dave is a New York trombone player who used to play with the Mel Lewis Orchestra and moved to Walla Walla to head up the jazz department. Dave has a great big, fat bone sound, ala J.J., and can read flyspecks, and is a monster arranger as well. Dave Bailey was on drums. Chuck had always been extolling the virtues of drummer Dave Bailey. I was familiar with Dave Bailey from recordings with Art Farmer and others. Maybe Hod O'Brien was on piano.

Chuck was also excited about a trumpet player who had moved to Orcas Island named Willie Thomas.[103] I will never forget my first meeting with Willie. I was getting set up for the recording, playing a few things on tenor just to get my sound squared away with reeds and a little general warming up when I heard this ridiculously good trumpet playing. I looked over at an older white guy who looked like he had spent too much time in the sun in the past; he had on a funky floppy kind of a fishing hat. He noticed I was staring at him, so without much preamble, Willie stopped and said with a pronounced southern accent, "Hey, Willie Thomas here, bet you wanna know what I was doing?"

Never to pass up an opportunity, I said, "Yes," and Willie went into a somewhat hard-to-follow explanation of stacking half-diminished chords and how they wove into each other. That was my introduction to Willie T.

We became friends. There is a non-verbal way that we learn a lot about people in seconds from almost indiscernible cues. Pretty soon, Willie and I were sharing personal history, and it turned out we had a lot in common. Willie played in a band with Frank Strozier and Walter Perkins, Bob Cranshaw, and Harold Maburn, and they were popular and had some hits. The band was very comparable to Cannonball Adderly's band and Horace Silver's band. Willie also played with Slide Hampton when the other trumpet player was Freddy Hubbard. Willie played with Woody Herman and was on the Al Belletto band when Carl Fontana was the other horn player. Willie, as a player, was serious business. At one time, he was married to the young singer, Jerri Winters, who had been making quite a name in New York for herself. There is a nice picture of her on Willie's Wikipedia.

Alas, Willie got into coke. He eventually became a dealer and at one time had a separate apartment for his stash! Willie told me when he was riding high, he would go up to Harlem and sell to guys on the Basie band.

A historical perspective is in order here. In the old days, Diz and many others not associated with drug abuse still enjoyed a toot now and then. Coke was not demonized like it is today. Almost all the Latin guys I played with occasionally had a toot. With that in mind, Willie was not a real pariah for dealing coke. However, like alcohol and all other drugs, about 10% of people get addicted. Soon, Willie recounted the inevitable fall. He said, "One day I graduated to the all coke diet. I would put coke on my grapefruit in the morning. I was in Central Park one day trying to heal somebody with a feather and some string" pause, "some things happened, *then I was mailed home.*"

I use that same line for what happened to me in New York.

When Willie got back on his feet, he started teaching jazz in schools and got whole areas of the country organized. He was like a traveling salesman/shaman, "The Music Man" for jazz in schools. While not in the limelight any longer, Willie still honed his chops and had the horn in his face daily his whole life.

In 1996 I got another call from Chuck about playing on a new book of Willie's that would be part of the Hal Leonard publishing house and be titled *Jazz Everyone*. It featured a rhythm section playing simple jazz phrases designed to be played by ear. It was a "call and response" kind of teaching that I thought was genius. So, I spent a day laying the phrases down with Willie.

Willie's second wife was his helper in the business of selling his jazz curriculum. She was also an heiress to the UPS fortune! Also, on that project with Willie was a young trumpet player from Germany named Oliver Groenewald. He was studying arranging with Chuck, and he was helping with this project. More about Ollie later.

Anyway, when I say Willie Thomas, Jazz Shaman, there might be something to it. Once at the Port Townsend Jazz Camp, baritone sax player Gary Smulyan helped Willie demonstrate his "pentatonic pairs" and how it could be used for jazz players on any level to immediately get the "vocabulary and actual bebop sound" of jazz into their playing. When I saw Willie before his presentation, he grabbed me like his long-lost brother, and Willie put his tongue in my ear! Ha. I was shocked, of course, but worse was the fact he had a pro-digious amount of garlic on his breath, and afterward, for a whole hour at least, my head vibrated.

He was absolutely the funkiest 85-year-old you could ever meet. Terrell Stafford told me a similar funny Willie story. I guess Willie came up to Terrell at some trumpet workshop or event and said to Terell, "You make any babies yet?" Terell said, "We're tryin'." Willie puts his finger in his mouth and then presses it to Terell's forehead. Terrel said he did not know what to do! An 84-year-old can get away with murder.

Terrell, a little later, became a proud father. I'm not saying there was any connection... but...

CHAPTER FORTY-ONE

Cedar Walton, Billy Higgins, and Blues for McVouty

My next main CD project was *Blues for McVouty*, with Cedar and Billy. This time I had Chuck Israels on bass and a very savvy guitar player named Dave Peterson. Dave Peterson is a NW legend and a fantastic musician. Dave was at Western Washington way back when big band trumpeter Bill Cole was the Jazz Department head. Dave has a golden touch with everything he touches musically. He wrote one big band arrangement that is still one of my favorites! Dave plays relaxed and has a natural lyrical sound, ala Jim Hall, but can also play funky as anyone. Cedar was in town again at the Jazz Alley, and he agreed that he and Billy would go into the studio again to record. We recorded for two days. We decided to call it *Blues for McVouty* in dedication to Slim Gaillard and because of the funkiness of the title song I wrote for the session.

Becca and Billy did an up-tempo version of "Everything I Love" that I liked a lot on this CD. Cedar ran through it once before the recording, and at the end, took his hands off the keys and exclaimed, "Whoa, that's a lot of changes." Anyone familiar with Cedar's tunes, such as "Bolivia", knows that

Cedar was very comfortable with plenty of changes. "Blues for McVouty" is from a Lester Young lick that Rollo showed me when I started to play tenor. Another friend of mine, Dean Leggit, harmonized my tenor solo, and I overdubbed a whole sax section. We laid down several tunes with just one or two takes.

Stash Records owner Bernie Brightman picked up this CD for his label. Bernie made a very cool cover for the CD.

Becca and I went to New York, where we met with Bernie. We stayed with my old friend, Dr. Roscoe, on 51st Street.

We hired Cliff Gorov, a jazz record promoter, to work on the CD. That means he called Radio Stations and Reviewers and suggest they check it out, hopefully, play it or write a review. There were some radio-friendly cuts, especially the title cut, "Blues for McVouty".

But this is where you get into the sausage-making aspect of how the music industry runs. In an ideal world, you would think that a project would rise, or fall based on its merits, or if people liked it or not! Not so. Radio stations and reviewers usually get over 100 new CDs every week. After a while, if they don't recognize the artist, they rely more on their friendly promo service. We are not paying the radio d.j. as in the past but are paying a third-party intermediary. Also, to get a review in a jazz magazine like *Jazz Times*, the sure-fire way is to buy advertising space.

This CD certainly helped me, but not in a direct financial way and only peripherally as an artist. The limits of using stars (well-known musicians) on your album are it is not an accurate representation of the band you can field at a gig or festival. Plus, Seattle is not a place to further your jazz career. No matter, it was still fun to record, and I learned a lot from just being around Billy Higgins and Cedar Walton on these two projects.

+++++

I still had a nagging problem in my backyard, and it was the fact I had left my last conversation on a sour note with the station head of our local jazz station. So, I decided on a campaign to get back in with the station. I observed one of the most politically astute musicians on the scene, and I duplicated his moves. The station, being a non-profit, was having a fundraiser. I called and volunteered to go to the station and answer phones on their fund drive. I also brought cookies and coffee to the station. At first, I thought it might be too transparent, but no, it worked like a charm. They were excited to have me there, and my theory is that even though what I was trying to do was transparent, it was like kissing the pope's ring. What I was doing was recognizing their powerful position and paying homage to it! Thus, I started getting radio play in my backyard, as well. In Seattle, that is not always easy. Seattle has many good players, but very little local music plays on the main daytime radio.

CHAPTER FORTY-TWO

Gearhead and Randy Jones

I have to mention that after I got clean, I developed another habit that has some of the aspects of addiction but has also been fun and profitable for me.

That is the "searching for gear" habit. (gear = musical instruments)

It started around 1985 in earnest, but I had also got into it a little with Mark Doubleday way back, once scoring a flute for $100 bucks, worth much more. Well, I then started to get hip to vintage saxophones. Freddy Greenwell always talked about his old Conn 10M sax. I began to notice that many cats played 10M's. Sal Nistico played a 10M on the classic clips playing with Woody Herman, and the movies of Dexter in Copenhagen were when he played a 10M. Other sought-after saxophones are the Selmer MKVI and Super Balanced Action tenors. With all these saxophones, different vintages have different sound qualities and based on that, the price fluctuates wildly. Then there are the mouthpieces. Saxophone mouthpieces got bright and loud for a while, but if you are at all a jazz music freak, like me, you have a sound you're after in your head. The saxophone sound in my head is definitely more into the Stanley Turrentine, Dexter, Trane, Fathead Newman spectrum.

So, soon I was out hitting pawnshops looking for stuff, and I started to check the newspapers. I saw an ad for a vintage Conn tenor in the paper. I called and made an appointment to meet him at the Scarlet Tree, a restaurant and bar famous for funk music. The guy shows up, and the horn looks good, has attractive engraving, and seems like it's in pretty good shape. I got it for a couple of hundred bucks.

When I got it home and looked at it in the light closely, it looked gold, even though tarnished. I played it, and the sound just came tearing out of the horn. Right away, I needed info on this horn, so I called a place back East called USA Horn. An old guy got on the phone and offered me $1000 for it, told me to pack it up and send it to him. Then, I got thinking, Hmmmmm. Wow, that was too easy; maybe a little more research would be in order.

Next, I called a guy I had already dealt with concerning mouthpieces and asked him about it. He was a gruff talking person and put many people off. For a while, he was the king of vintage mouthpieces. He came on and offered me $1100 right out of the gate. He said pack it up and send it. Done deal. At this point, I decide to put on the brakes for a second. For the time being, I'm just cooling it with this horn. Later that evening, I get a call out of the blue, and it's Randy Jones from the Midwest. Randy just said, "Hi, I'm Randy Jones[104], and I hear you have a gold-plated transitional Conn... (pause) ... I want it!"

Now we're talkin'.

He asked me what I wanted for it. I decided to cut to the chase and said, "How much is it worth to you? I have offers of $1000 and $1100 already."

He said he could pay $1600 and said he would rebuild it and probably sell it for a lot more. That was ok with me. He also said a funny thing, and he said, "Don't play it." Well, I packed the horn well, put it in a box, and sent it to Randy. He got the horn, called me, and said it was not gold plating; it was gold lacquer. It was gold over silver plating, and the lacquer was flaking off in places. So, I said, "Ok, what is it worth then?" He still paid me $1100.

Well, at that point, we established a connection that included some trust. Randy asked me if I was into this sort of thing, meaning, of course, the hunt! I said yes, so he gave me a list of stuff he was looking for and said what he would pay. The list included old Bueschers of a particular vintage, Conns, and Selmers at the top of the heap. His list included all the desired serial numbers.

In addition to hitting all the music stores in the area and checking out their trade-in stock, I also had quite a pawn shop route. Jules and I shared custody with Miles, our son, and almost every week, I would drive from Seattle to Olympia. There was a pawn shop corridor by Fort Lewis, and I hit a string of them in Tacoma as well. There were a couple of pawn shops in Olympia, and sometimes I would stop in Kent or Auburn. You might think, how did I have the time for this? Most of my days were free, and my nights were teaching and gigs, and I was very quick in the pawnshops. In the store, I would go right to the area with musical instruments. Sometimes the owner would say, "What are you looking for?" and I would answer, "Saxophones, trumpets, flutes, clarinets." Time, all total, just minutes in each store. I also religiously checked the newspaper ads. What started as a hobby blossomed into quite a sideline business. Now, this has changed because of the internet and eBay. Today pawn shops sell on eBay, and they have a better idea of their items' value.

It became a pastime and passion, with a little of the adrenaline rush that can be addicting. It was also a great feeling to get over on pawnshop owners instead of being at their mercy like I was in my earlier life. Sometimes I would see these pathetic addicts and other unfortunates, and boy, did I have an attitude! It was, get out of my way Muther%&^**^ After I had sent Randy a dozen horns or more, I also sent him a CD I had recently done called *Blues for McVouty* with Cedar and Billy and Chuck Israels. Randy put that on his playlist in the shop, and we became friends.

+++++

At one point, he told me his friend from the University of Northern Iowa, Bob Washut, was getting married and coming to Seattle for his honeymoon. I think I recommended a hotel and said I would take him around when he got here. Bob Washut stayed in the hotel at the Pike Street Market with his new bride. I contacted him and asked him if he would like to go out and hear some jazz. Coincidentally, I was playing at the Pike Place Public Market Festival with the Latin band, Sonando. That was in the afternoon, so it was a leisurely stroll for Bob and his new wife to walk thru the scenic market and catch our band. At the time, there was a cool little spot to hear music and hang in the evening. It was a bar called Salutes in the Vance Hotel in downtown Seattle. Salutes had great food and a warm, friendly atmosphere. That night I took him there, and it was a very cool time, with a great mix of people, black and white, young and old, all there for the food and the music. Floyd Standifer, my old teacher, was there, and many more people from the jazz community. I sat in and had a ball. Bob also had a great time. He asked me if I was interested in coming to Northern Iowa University, where he taught and where Randy's shop was. I, of course, said yes. I have found this has been the circuitous path to a lot of great connections. Later, when I first got involved with Kohama and the Japanese, it resulted from this infernal gearhead hunt!

Iowa was really fun. I stayed at Doc Tenny's house. Doc Tenny was famous for resurfacing mouthpieces and eventually had his own line of mouthpieces.

I brought some of my special charts and some from the SSCC band. The Northern Iowa band was killing, and they played my arrangements better than my professional band in

Seattle. I did clinics and had an extra gig that Tenney got me. The concert went great, and I had a nice write-up in the local newspaper. I bought a Super Balanced tenor for a steal from Randy. I also picked up a tenor that Randy had rebuilt for me. A Conn 10M of the correct vintage. It was super fun.

+++++

Often in Jazz music, the actual sound is the message as much as the notes played. Coltrane was a mouthpiece nut, and there have been many players that worked on their mouthpieces themselves. Johnny Griffin and Frank Wess, and more. Because of my interest in these vintage mouthpieces, I sometimes buy one that I sell later to buy another (kind of a cycle there). Now I sell them by putting up a demo of the mouthpiece, or horn for that matter, on YouTube and putting the video on an eBay auction. Because of the fees and hassles, I often skip eBay and go directly to social media with the videos. Strange, but compared with my "music performance" videos I have on YouTube, my "gear videos" get a lot more attention. I still help sell horns for musicians or wives whose husbands have deceased. And, probably half of the saxophone players in Seattle are playing horns I found for them.

Part of the reason vintage gear is valuable is that back in the day, they made instruments before what some call the decline of crafts in America. This was before "student gear" became a way that companies made more $$. Old Meyer saxophone mouthpieces were about $15 then and now go for $1000. Conn, King, and Selmer companies only made professional horns. Currently, student instruments are often produced by people with no connection to the music or the craft. We know that when it comes to flute head joints, for instance, hand-cut is best, same with mouthpieces. Often today, there is no "handwork." The exception to this might be the manufacturing of top-of-the-line instruments in Japan, where one craftsman is responsible for start to finish.

Even the material has changed; for instance, the vulcanization process of hard rubber mouthpieces is shorter these days to make manufacturing cheaper. The hard rubber is soft and mushy and hard for people to even cut an accurate facing.

Sorry about the gear side trip. My wife Becca will not sit still any longer for an A versus B listening test. Sometimes when sax players start in on a gear conversation, eyes roll, and other musicians move away quickly! Ha.

CHAPTER FORTY-THREE

Luis Peralta, Becca, and Evolution

One evening, I received a call from Luis Peralta. Louis had provided "sweetener" percussion tracks for the *Easy Does It* project. Luis said he was having a get-together at his house and invited Becca and me along. I knew the bass player Miguel Garrido, a musician from Argentina because we played together in a band called Sonando. Also on hand was a young Rick Reed on acoustic nylon string guitar.

Luis' place was a small servant's house behind a mansion. The place was tiny, so it was very crowded with the five of us and our instruments. We played, and it was instant magic. For one thing, it was incredibly soft, and Brazilian music comes alive when it is super intimate and quiet. The music was like a lover's whisper in the ear. Everything was subtle and soft but with irresistible South American grooves at the same time. Miguel and Luis could lock into many South American rhythms. The feel of Partido Alto and Bayoun with these two South Americans underneath was incredible. Rick Reed was way into Flamenco and various comping styles from South America, so it was lots of fun. Before we knew, hours had passed. We set up another time, and rehearsals became a regular thing.

I started bringing in tunes, and we would slowly begin exploring how we would play them. In this regard, the composing was more of a group project than an industry-style situation. In the "industry" situation, the person bringing in the song would have it in a legible form, have all the hits notated, and have a final arrangement to run down with time being closely monitored. No wasting of time in that world. The way we did, it was halting and by ear, trying many beats and tempos, changing the form, and modifying the changes. Everything was up for grabs, and one tune could take hours of rehearsal and then still not be finished. It was exciting and creative and did not rely on musical notation symbols. It was rhythmically sophisticated as well.

Soon we became a group. We called ourselves *Evolution*.
I applied for many gigs through a book that listed all the festivals in the area, but we never had enough work to make a living. However, we played reasonably often. This was the newer model of being a musician; there was never one band that could provide enough money to make a living. It had to be a combination of bands, and usually, some other stuff thrown in, like teaching.

I was now without my junky habits, so I went overboard compulsively with recording Evolution. Bob Meador's little studio was getting all my spare cash. Evolution went into the studio repeatedly. Soon we had a ballooning project. This was before pro tools, so it was difficult to fix things in those days. I remember we were recording a song, and the time went into a slow-motion glide, and the measure stretched unbelievably. I loved the take except for that spot. When I pointed it out to Luis, he said, "Oh, that's just a caress." Hmmmmm, well, I put my little brain to work and decided the solution was to add Luis doing a big cymbal roll during that spot. It worked well, and it was making a fix by adding something rather than cutting. That band went thru several stages. I think Luis was feeling some tension from my ambition and desire to do things with this band. Louis was very spiritual and could be described as an "Ecstatic." It had worked for him, and he did not see any reason to change. I had some of my old addictive behavior at work and was agenda oriented. Also, I was looking for a guitar player that had more of the jazz harmony vocabulary. Rick was great, but I looked for a little more of the jazz vocabulary that players like Dave Peterson had.

CHAPTER FORTY-FOUR

More Top 40 Gigs and the Four Seasons Hotel, Maui

During this time, we were still doing the "variety casuals " for Mark Solomon. On one gig at the Four Seasons Hotel in Seattle, Olympia pianist Barney McClure and bandleader, trumpet player Fred Radke, who were working in the atrium, came in on their break and caught a little of our set. We were doing standards and Top 40, and then we went into one of our tricky, three-part vocal arrangements. Fred Radke was booking Four Season Hotels all over the US, and there was a new one opening on Maui. Fred hired us to play in the lounge with our band, *Travelin' Light*. Becca sang the hell out of the song, "Travelin' Light", and we had been going by that name on all commercial gigs since Japan. That spring of 1990, we were at the Four Seasons in Maui. We played there for 11 weeks.

+++++

My good friend, Gene Argel from the Seattle Queequeg and Llahngaelhyn days, was living on Maui, and his trio was playing out on the deck of the dining room of the Four Seasons.

Through Gene, I met some players on Maui and played a few times at "Blackie's" in Lahaina. Blackie was a real character and made his money in Newport Beach, California. Blackie's was a heavy drinking establishment, and Blackie loved jazz. Gene and the guys were doing all kinds of cool stuff. Milton Nascimento, Horace Silver, standards, and whatever they wanted to play. Blackie would go up in his signature bright orange shirt, and the band would launch into the vamp on Killer Joe. Blackie would tell people if they were Canadian, "hit the door," if they wanted a medallion of beef, "hit the door." He would go on to list all the offenses that would get you kicked out and banned. One of the times I played there, he must have dug it because he came to my commercial gig at the Four Seasons. I met him out in the hotel's expensive rock garden, and he looked around and said, "Good place for a fire" ha, not one to mince words with what he thought.

I hooked up with some of the jazz players on Maui through Gene. Players like saxophonist John Zangrando and pianist guitarist Shiro Mori. As a result, I did a couple of really easy hotel gigs where you just played The Saints or something like that and walked tourists to the beach. Total gravy train. Five minutes of playing and ka-ching! It did not hurt that at this time, my CD, Easy Does It, was getting pretty heavy airplay all over the US, including Hawaii. A happenstance meeting on the beach with Bob Fulton, the young heir of Robert Fulton, of the steamboat engine, and I had the use of his alto flute for several months, even using it on a song on one of my CDs.

The Four Seasons was an important gig for rekindling our relationship with our Japanese agent, Mako Imaizumi of Washington Kikaku LTD. The Maui Four Seasons' opening was a big enough deal that she was there as a guest. When she saw us performing at the Four Seasons, we were back on her radar for future work in Japan.

+++++

On the opening night at the Hotel, they had vocalist Mel Torme backed by a big band put together by Fred Radke. Fred has the Harry James library and name and leads the Harry James ghost band. An acerbic jazz guitar player who will go un-named once referred to Fred as "the white Harry James!"

Mel Torme was fantastic, and many of my friends were on the band, including arranger Milt Kleeb and saxophonist Bill Ramsay. Bill was playing tenor and sounded just marvelous soloing and occasionally filling behind Mel. Bill has a huge, massive tenor sound, broad like Dexter, melodic, and funky. Bill, like Freddy Greenwell, improvised with little illuminated pieces of melody rather than just running changes. I went to the rehearsal, and that was an eye-opener. Mel knew every speck of his charts, and he even had it down to what kind of sound he wanted out of his saxes. Mel hated the bright funky-pop-sax sounds so prevalent in LA and exacerbated by flame-throwing sax gear. Mel made all the sax guys play subtone!

As a side story, for this gig, Bill Ramsay and Milt Kleeb were rooming together. Unsure about food arrangements, they went to the store to get peanut butter and bread as soon as they arrived. I guess Fred had neglected to tell them about being comped at the restaurant. When Bill was at the desk the day they were leaving, the old childhood friend of Fred Radke that was responsible for getting Fred the job of booking all the Four Seasons came up to Bill and said, "Whadddayu think of this place?" with a smile and twinkle in his eye, Bill, with a dour look answered, "It would have been nice to have had food." The CEO was flabbergasted and said, "You should have just gone into the restaurant; we would have comped it." Unknown to the band, an employee's dining hall had delicious food free for the band. Bill was so pissed he wrote a letter to Fred in protest. Most of the band signed it.

Fred's bassist, Peter Vinikow, was feeling his oats because he read all the charts down and fit with Mel's rhythm section perfectly. Peter got the attention of Mel's rhythm section for his outstanding abilities. So, even though he worked with

Fred exclusively and had a good living from Fred's gigs, he also signed the letter. Whoops. He went from a good living to zero overnight.

+++++

For a second, Becca and I even thought of making a move to Maui, but once, on our off day, Becca and I wanted to see a movie, and the only thing we could find was a Teenage Mutant Turtles' movie. Plus, the endless sunsets were getting her down. Every day I would go out to my deck before work and take a picture of a majestic sunset. I said to Becca, "Hey, check out the sunset." The first 50 were great; then we were done with them!

The swimming and surf were a real plus. One day I got the fins and snorkel and swam to the nude beach. As I stealthily made my way through the water and got closer to the shoreline, I noticed they were all guys! Oh boy!

After 11 weeks, we were ready for home and a return to our ongoing musical projects.

Chapter 31 - 33

Jakk Corsaw

Dave Friesen

Jack Brownlow

Corsaw's P. I. Newspaper Logo

John Stowell

Herb Ellis

Chuck Israels

Dave Peterson

Jan Stentz

Red Kelley

Freddy Greenwell

Barney McClure

Chapter 38 - 45

Nagoya Castle Hotel

Gajoen Park Gardens

Nagoya Castle

Wedding Palace

Sleepy Matsamoto

Four Seasons, Maui

Traveling Light Band

Four Seasons Resort, Maui

Bill Ramsay

Travis Shook

Herb Ellis

Jon Wikan

Willie Thomas and Jay

CHAPTER FORTY-FIVE

Japan, Round Three with Bob Nixon and Danny Embry

We received another call from Mako. She offered us a job outside of Tokyo in a "Wedding Palace" followed by a stint at the familiar Nagoya Castle Hotel.

We brought Danny Embry, a great guitarist, to play bass at the Wedding Palace. Danny played with Brasil 66, which made Mako very happy because she was a big fan of Latin music. Danny and I also had a history playing with Chuck Israels in a trio setting. Bob Nixon was on keyboards and was also in charge of managing our sequencer and all the instruments hooked up to it. Today, it would be a cinch, but then it was formidable with all the gear, connections, and error possibilities.

I first met Bob when my first jazz teacher, Floyd Standifer, took me to a rehearsal at Bob's house in 1965. Bob knew many tunes, understood how changes moved and had many different sets of changes for standards. Bob was a serious musician. He played at Parnell's and was well-liked by old-timers such as Eddie Lockjaw Davis and Sweets Edison. These were musicians who just called tunes and expected others to know them, or at least most of them. Bob was a real character who sometimes reminded me of John Cleese's character in Faulty Towers. I still miss Bob.

We had my old friend from England and the Slim Gaillard tour, John Boucher, on drums. John is a helluva smart guy and was getting into Brazilian drumming. Brian Kennedy, a young bass player from Seattle, was to play the second half of the Nagoya gig. We arrived at Narita airport, and Mako had a van pick us and our equipment up and transport us to our digs in Kashiwa, the Wedding Palace location.

Bob was on a new vegetarian diet with his wife, Pam. The agent took us out to eat after dropping off the equipment at the compound where we were to stay. Immediately we ran into a snag. Bob was trying to decipher the menu. That was pretty hard to do when we could not read Japanese and barely understood Mako's English. We ordered a soup that was supposed to be only vegetables. After a few bites, Bob pulled a piece of meat out of the soup, and it was quivering on his chopstick before he dropped it onto the table, declaring in a loud voice in front of our startled agent, Mako, "I don't eat dead animals." Oh boy, we were off and running.

We got back to our digs, and it was unbearably hot. We only had these swamp coolers that we had to keep filling with water, and still, the cooling only went about three feet up from the floor, so we had to stay down low.

+++++

The Wedding Palace was an interesting place, mainly designed for picture taking. It was like Branson, Missouri, where all the country stars do their shtick. Most of the buildings were just facades. Doorways went to the back of the billboard. The fake buildings were very realistic, and they had pathways that they covered with rose petals and all kinds of cool shots like that. A lovely garden and a little pool, an imitation of a country setting, all suitable for traditional and more modern weddings.

They showed us the hall where we would play, located on a stage facing the guests. This hall was the only real building for the wedding participants to enter. We had special songs that we had to perform by Elvis and others, and Becca was still singing some songs in Japanese and Top Forty and Great American Standards.

Oh, I almost forgot one funny story from the evening of our arrival right after dinner with Mako. Back at the pad, Bob desperately needed to make a phone call. We were all tired, and I'm afraid I was not that helpful. We had telephones of various colors in the house. Bob could not make head or tails out of reaching an English-speaking line, let alone a long-distance line. So, Boucher and Bob set out on foot to find something that would work. Unfortunately, I set Bob off on the wrong course because I said I thought he needed a white phone. They went into town and were having no luck with communicating with anyone. Bob finally got frustrated, ran up to some Japanese people, pointed at his white tee-shirt, and yelled, "white telephone!" Bob was a sweet, harmless person, but tall, and if he was upset, he could seem menacing! I'm sure that eventually, they figured out the international phone booths. These days with cell phones, it is rare even to see a phone booth.

Danny's mother visited, and they had a ball sightseeing. Danny was also quite an avid golfer, and I think he hooked up with some people that took him golfing. We settled into the routine of playing the gig and sightseeing during the day.

Japan is a great country, but sometimes a little strange to Westerners. I noticed that they tended to put many people on a task that only one person would do in America. For instance, gas stations in Japan. You drive in, and they meet your car with about four guys yelling, like a celebration. They attack the job full-on, cleaning, checking fluids, pumping gas.

And then when you leave, they will often step out into the road and stop traffic for you.

In this spirit, we had about seven guys in grey suits in charge of the band's sound system. One night one of the guys touched a setting on Bob's gear. Bob was immediately in the guy's face, and with a contorted face and veins popping out of the side of his neck and choking with anger, Bob told the guy, "NEVER touch my equipment again, EVER!!!" Sometimes Bob was not an easy person!

Part of our job was eating at the hall after the gig, ostensibly to be with the guests. The hall had different sections, even a prime rib section and a seafood section with sushi and lobster. There were at least eight stations in this big hall. In Japan, all fruit is costly, and every night Bob would scarf as much food as possible as we all did. But he went one step further and would pile his plate as high as possible with fruit to take to our digs that were right across the parking lot. So, Bob has his plate piled high and is ready to sail off into the night. Well, the guy he yelled at earlier sits down at his table before he can leave, and is sobbing and says, "Bobu you my teacher," more sobbing "You song just like Carmen Cabellero"... more sobbing. Bob, to his credit, knew we were teetering on the verge of an international incident. And Bob just sat there smiling and trying to calm the situation. Becca and I observed this and were howling with laughter after we got outside of the building. The Japanese sound guy had "lost face," and that is a no-no in that culture. So, in fact, it was a delicate situation.

+++++

Next, we went to the Nagoya Castle Hotel. The hotel was directly across the street from one of the huge stone Castles built in Japan's Feudal era. It is massive and surrounded by moats and had two giant goldfish sculptures on top of it. When one gets close to a Castle like this, it is evident that any invader would have to be very strong and determined. The

Nagoya Castle Hotel is an easy gig with three sets with long breaks and finished at 9:00 PM. after which they give us a very nice dinner. The dining room even had Stephan Grappelli playing in the background. Very civilized indeed
When Pam Nixon came with their baby, things were happy camping.

+++++

Boucher, who I said earlier was way into Brazilian rhythms, hooked up some grooves with our bass player Brian Kennedy that were way more authentic than the traditional bossa nova beat that is generic in commercial jazz played at weddings, etc. Boucher is a funny guy and, on this trip, he got some cool pants with pleats that bagged way out at the sides and five-toed shoes and a headband with a red sun on it and was wearing it in the hotel. Immediately they told him that the shoes and pants and the little coat were for "workers" and were not considered "polite attire" in the Castle Hotel. Also, Mako, our agent, informed us the headband had WWII overtones.

John and I got into Younker, the invigorating energy drink used by Japanese businessmen. Younker has a Tincture of Viper in it and a whole lot of stuff, none of which will get a person high, but is used for energy and stamina. Anyway, after a set in the lounge where Boucher and Kennedy launch into a real cool South American groove, on the break, I get a loud knock on the door, and Bob is furious with Boucher. He said Boucher "is on the shit!" referring to the viper juice concoction. I calmed him down, and the band went about finishing the month-long engagement at the hotel.

Bob was very supportive of Pam's pottery making, and they went on to Korea, where there was an area famous for pottery that Pam wanted to experience. Mako helped them set this up. Mako, who was very relaxed, surprised us with her take on Koreans. She said they look normal but have "black hearts." The anti-Korean sentiment is part of Japanese culture though not a universal sentiment. Japanese culture is still mysterious and full of nuance and contradictions.

CHAPTER FORTY-SIX

Sonando, Barney McClure and South Seattle Community College Jazz Band

When I returned to Seattle, I was busy trying to book Evolution. Also, I started getting more gigs with Sonando, a band more on the Afro Cuban side of the Latin music spectrum. We used to rehearse regularly and soon put out a CD of songs we had down. The material was a combination of originals and reworked standards. I had played with some excellent Latin bands, including Machito, but I did not know some of the basics, such as clave. Sonando's leader, Fred Hoadly, was really into Cuban folkloric music, almost entirely based on clave. My problem was when the clave was not being explicitly played, I tended to flip clave, which in a Cuban folkloric setting will get you excommunicated! None of these bands paved the way financially, but all together helped a lot.

+++++

That summer, I got a call from Barney McClure. Barney is the piano player who played a lot at Parnell's. (And also, for some time, was mayor of Port Townsend.) Barney was not only a good piano player but also a natural politician. He had a very natural, facile way with the piano and knew a ton of tunes. Once when Barney was playing behind Zoot Sims, he was soloing and playing a lot of notes, and Zoot looked up at the bandstand and said in his very dry way, "I'm sure glad he's doing that." One other comment from Zoot, "I wonder if he is getting paid by the note?" Don't take these as put-downs; Barney could really play and was quite a communicator. Audiences, as well as musicians, loved his playing. Barney also used to back Ernestine Anderson a lot.

Back to my story, Barney had talked himself into a Community College job running a big band. Barney had no desire to continue and offered to hand it off to me if I could finesse it with the college. It so happened that Becca and I were living in the south end of Seattle, and the college was South Seattle Community College. I started teaching the SSCC band course in 1993. The band was incomplete when I got there. We had just a few charts and incomplete sections and no lead trumpet player or credible drummer. As my father always said, "A big band is only as good as the drummer and lead trumpet player. "

The school had an excellent culinary department but no real music department. The band was mainly for students who wanted easy credit. In other words, nobody went to this college to study music! So, I got my dad, Dick Thorlakson, and Don Glenn and all kinds of big band people and put together the band. I had John Boucher on drums, and soon we were kicking the asses of other community college bands. It essentially became a community rehearsal band; we did have the occasional SSCC student, but not many. I always played in it. And I would get the good, rising star high school students and offered them head-start college credits for those motivated high school students.

This band was a lot of fun. We played for some school events, and we were good PR for the school. We played on the Sea-Fair Parade float at the end of July, and that was a real kick. One summer, our float broke down, and we had a parade by ourselves, through town pulled by a big truck. We also got little festivals in the summer and played some Sundays at the New Orleans Creole Restaurant on First Avenue. For the school, we played for the big graduation at the Seattle Convention Center every year. Teaching at SSCC got my foot in the door for education, and even though I did not have any "traditional" qualifications, I was able to do the job based on my years of big band experience.

My father, Marvin, was integral to running the big band. He could find charts like no other. He was a chart sleuth; if there was a chart out there, he could find them. Marvin was soon in contact with different people around the country, basically horse-trading for additional charts. Syd Potter was also a big help by giving us boxes of extra charts he had. I know there were many copyright considerations here, but most of the country's rehearsal bands do this. We did have access to original charts by band members and also bought many special arrangements. We did buy a ton of charts over the years, so I don't feel that we did not support the cause, but yes, we also did trading. Another consideration is that some arrangements were no longer available, and then we would pay Syd to do transcriptions.

Travelin' Light and Evolution were still playing casuals for companies and big socialite weddings, but I was definitely moving in a more "jazz artist" direction.

CHAPTER FORTY-SEVEN

Jon Wikan, Buddy Catlett, Travis Shook

During this time, I got hooked up with some young cats that were to affect me profoundly. I got a call from a young pianist Reuel Lubag, and he wanted to get together and play. He said he had a bass player and drummer. Perfect! I invited them to the house, and he came in with a short, muscley guy with a big smile and an Alaskan drawl named Jon Wikan. When we started playing, I remember it felt really good. The swing thing was spot on even though I thought it sagged a little in the time, but it sure was fun for me. They had a thing, and it was based on the Ray Brown trio and Monty Alexander, and Oscar Peterson. After all the floater jazz and various styles I had been doing, it was refreshing to get back to quarter notes and swing time. This was kind of old home week for me and a return to those roots of Stanley Turrentine and Gene Ammons, etc.

They were students at Central Washington University over East of the mountains in Ellensburg. We played often, and Ruel even made a little CD with this band. Ruel was also a Cedar Walton fanatic, so my recording with Cedar was a big deal to them. I'm about twenty years older than Ruel and Jon, but based on my amount of "clean time," we were not so far apart in psychological makeup in a lot of ways.

I remember one gig where they invited me to Ellensburg to play with them at a tavern. My friend from way back, Betty Cheney, the artist, was visiting from New York. It just so happened that her mother lived on a ranch over in Ellensburg, so I gave her a ride to her mother's place before the gig. When we got to Betty's mom's place, everything is beautiful; warm weather, blue skies, aromatic, perfumed air, just a joy to be alive.

Shortly after our arrival, a truck drives up, and it's her brother and his partner who are beekeepers. I notice there are sure a lot of bees around the truck. The guys are just brushing them aside like it's nothing. I shook hands with Betty's brother, and we are walking towards the house when I feel this heavy vibration going on around the top of my head. One of the guys reaches over to grab the bee but not before it stings me on the very top of my head. I'm almost incapacitated by the pain coming down like a giant shower cap made of stinging jellyfish. While I'm speechless with agony, the guys are calmly discussing whether I got stung or not. They get stung multiple times every day, no big deal.

I went to the gig and had an incredible night. I started thinking about that bee sting at the top of my head. I guess my body flooded my system with endorphins and might have also "woken up" the crown chakra that yoga people talk about! Don't worry; I probably won't carry around live bees to sting myself on the top of the head.

Jon is a guy who is not shy and can work harder than most and is smarter than hell. A very formidable combination. I laugh at the camouflage that Jon has. Jon had a big goofy grin and behaved like he just showed up from Alaska. Ha! People fall for that and are disarmed. Jon is an extremely thoughtful guy about politics and understands everything from a combustible engine to the stock market and computers. He taught himself how to do a website in a day. Jon gave me my first computer. He literally dragged Becca and me into this century. (In 2020, he is building a recording studio at his house.)

+++++

Jon once took me commercial halibut fishing in Alaska. We both had worked a gig the night before, but early the next morning, we flew into Alaska and stayed at his Grandparent' place. Once on the boat, I saw that we had line and hooks all tangled up, and my job, while Jon piloted to the fishing grounds, was to untangle it and bait the hooks. Yikes, I barely have the patience for a knot in my shoelaces. On the way to the fishing grounds, we camped on a little island where, Jon informed me, the most brown bears on earth lived. Grizzlies! Jon taught me about a whole new level of endurance and work ethic on that trip. I got very seasick on the boat, and Jon just laughed. I saw a fat, little iceberg, and Jon let me jump onto it. Unfortunately, the photo he took just looks like I'm standing in the snow! While I was on the iceberg, Jon said, "Jay, you better get off that; these icebergs can flip over." I moved very quickly and carefully off that berg.

When Jon went to New York, he had a list of people he wanted to play with and have as friends. That is an entirely different way of thinking than I have. And guess what, Jon met these people and now has a thriving musical life in New York and tours often.

+++++

During this period, I tried to get more conversant with standards, and I used to sit in with bassist Buddy Catlett at the Sea-Tac Airport, 13 Coins restaurant. Buddy, of course, knew a ton of tunes. He usually had Jack Percival on piano, who played for years with Harry James at the Frontier room in Las Vegas. Buddy Rich played with that band as well as Jake Hanna. When I could, I would hire Buddy Catlett for quartet gigs because as well as being a monster player, he also was a mentor to me in musical and non-musical ways.

One night I went to the 13 Coins, and there was some unbelievable piano playing by a real young cat. It was a player from the East Coast named Travis Shook.[105] Travis had been to a Patterson, New Jersey school and was just on fire. He was super facile and hip.

Travis taught me something about practicing. Travis would stop off at my house when he would drive into Seattle. Travis lived in Olympia, a little over an hour from Seattle. As I listened to him practice, it was like listening to Tai Chi. Travis would practice Bach super slow. That was why he could play so fast. Just lightning speed, but he practiced super slow.

I also used to go to Lofurno's to sit in with Buddy.

Lofurno's was a great Italian restaurant in Seattle run by an old boxer who loved jazz. It was a colorful, smoke-filled place with delicious food and strong drinks (I hear). Currently, there was no drinking for the Jay-man.

One time, Bill Ramsay and I got a gig at a brewery in Yakima, and I hired Jon Wikan on drums, Travis Shook on piano, and Peter Vinikow on bass. We drove across the mountains, stopped off at Wikan's house, and then went to the Yakima gig later. Wikan was getting better and better. Travis and I looked through all of Jon's CDs, and it was almost all Mel Lewis! That's a great thing, but Travis said, "Hey, what about Tony Williams? What about Billy Higgins?" Jon was like a sponge, and before long, Jon was going into a lot of new directions while retaining that ability to feather the bass drum and really swing in that traditional foot stompin' feel. Ramsay was happy with Jon also. Bill had played with many great drummers. But once at a gig, he turned to the drummer and said, "Can you play with more DRUM drum." What Bill wanted was more skins and not so much splashing cymbals. Jon filled the bill because he had the skin part of the drums covered.

Jon also was starting to be a "tippin" drummer. Tippin' is sitting forward in the time. A difficult concept for many. Ray Brown once gave a clinic and demonstrated swing by creating a line on the floor and leaning as far forward without toppling over. Then Ray said, "this is where the swing is at!" Jon was tippin.

+++++

Also, at this time, Jessica Williams, my old friend from San Francisco, showed up, and we started playing some gigs, and we recorded three CDs together. So, there were lots of things cooking at that time. It is funny, but when writing this book, I have noticed how much harder it is to document what was happening after I got clean. Before, there were undoubtedly important things, but way less in number and usually one thing at a time. After getting clean, I entered the modern world, where to survive and make a living in music, you have to be awfully busy. Or really lucky and talented.

CHAPTER FORTY-EIGHT

Rapture and More About Travis Shook

In 1994 Becca and I moved from the Sea-Tac area back to the Wallingford District just north of Lake Union. Jon Wikan had recently graduated from college and took a room in our house. We played a lot, and Jon was getting established, and I was gigging and jamming regularly. I decided to do another project using the rhythm section of Travis Shook, Phil Sparks, and Jon Wikan. My previous CD, *360 Degrees,* had some of the same people on it but was more of a hodge-podge of personnel, recorded in many separate sessions and different size groups. That CD was picked up by my old friend, Alistair Robertson of Hep Records.

Now I was ready to settle down and do a quartet album with this rhythm section. We were playing together and trying things out, and it was a real group collaboration. The arrangements were put together informally in a session/rehearsal setting. The project had a lot of drive and was quite different than most other projects coming out of this area. The drums were up in the mix, and we had Travis adding a lot of sparkle to the proceedings. Phil Sparks was sitting on top of the beat, and everything felt great. We recorded the

Harold Land composition Rapture and the new project I decided to call *Rapture*.

It was an exciting time for me.

Jon had a friend who worked in the office at Verve, and he was playing the CD when a bigwig walked by and heard it and said, "Jeez, that's great! who's that?" When the reply was Jay Thomas, somebody immediately dismissed it, 'cuz it was irrelevant if it was not one of their in-house musicians. At 40 plus years of age and living in Seattle, I was starting to realize I was not in the demographic or profile sought by most of the big record companies. New York was becoming the only city for serious jazz players to launch a recording career. As far as the jazz magazines and critics are concerned, Seattle is pretty far off the beaten trail. However, a Canadian company, Jazz Focus Records, released the Rapture CD. We did get the CD out there, and it even got good local play and, as usual, good reviews around the country.

+++++

A little aside about Travis Shook: Travis was and is a beautiful player. He won a big jazz piano competition in Jacksonville, Florida. I had mentioned Travis and the way he practiced. When Travis went to the Florida competition, he brought all that to bear on the situation and completely dominated his competition. You see, Travis had a lot of *street* in him as well as talent and pedagogy. Travis had done a ton of playing and transcribing, basically putting it all together the old-fashioned way. He lived in a house of musicians on the East coast and playing with the best New York players elevated his progress. He is, and was, the real deal in so many ways. As a result of the big win at the competition, Travis received a Columbia recording contract to do several albums. Now we enter the parable part of this story. Travis makes a bold move and hires Tony Williams on drums with Ira Coleman on bass. From a sustainability standpoint, there were many players he could have used where he already had a "personal connection." Jazz is a tough business and has a geographical bias towards New York players and recordings. At this stage in his career, living in Olympia, Washington, was not doing him any favors.

At first, Columbia decided to promote him like the "Young Lions" blueprint they had from Wynton and others. The promotion emphasized Travis as a contest winner and all his schooling and awards. For better or worse, the public is way into "street" when it comes to jazz. In hindsight, had they emphasized his relationships with people like Buddy Catlett and his humble beginnings and innate ability to learn and thrive on his own, it might have been a better strategy.

Larry Coryell's promotion was just the opposite. When Larry went to New York, he was all over the place playing. He formed a band with young cats and started playing music that had a resonance with youth influenced by Beatles and R&B as well as Coltrane and Bill Evans.

There was a big picture of Larry in the Downbeat magazine. Larry was resting in between takes on a Chico Hamilton recording. Larry looked like he had been up for days, sporting the two-day beard so popular in Italian fashion magazines. Larry was in greasy Levis that looked like he slept in them, had bedroom hair, and was lying on a bench. Larry was promoted as having a connection to the blues. Larry exuded androgynous sexuality and lined up with the "from the street" code that the public and critics expected.

Even if Travis Shook is not a household jazz name, when all is said and done, Travis is one bad cat!

BOOK THREE

1997 – 2019

"Pretty hard to describe, but I had an expanding appreciation and feeling of being a very lucky guy to be welcomed into this," jazz family" and experience a lot that most outsiders do not get."

Quote from Jay

+ +

My New Family

Kohama, Atsushi, Daisuke, Goh, Shuhei, Yuki, Tsutomu, Yoshiro, Masanori, Yoshihiro, Nana, Maya,

And the entire CUG Jazz Orchestra

And The East West Alliance

And The Sax Friends Band

Plus

All of their friends who have made me welcome for almost 25 years

CHAPTER FORTY-NINE

1997 Nagoya Castle and Meeting Kohama

I should back up a few paces to 1997. In the summer of '97, Becca and I were contacted again by Mako to do another Nagoya Castle Hotel hit. This time we decided to have piano and bass players with Becca and me. We got Geoff Harper on bass and Josh Wolfe on piano. Geoff is legendary for his spirit and creative weirdness. Josh was a young guy but had a streak of genius ability. Josh was learning the language and knew more Japanese than me by the time we hit the tarmac in Japan. Josh took lessons from Jerry Gray and took Jerry's "tune learning" to heart, and his repertoire of standards was ever widening and in any key. He was also way into thematic improvising, making it possible for him to play at a very high level without playing a lot of fast lines and other flashy mannerisms. Josh had one fly in the ointment; he was drinking heavily. Geoff was more on the straight and narrow at that time. He could not bring his acoustic bass, so he got an electric bass at the last minute. Too bad because Geoff has a great big fat sound on upright. Perfect attack and great feel. We rehearsed a little before we left and had some arrangements ready for the gig.

+++++

I decided before I left that I wanted to score a good flute. The Japanese are known for their flutes. Muramatsu is a brand that James Galway plays, and Prima Sankyo is another excellent brand. I played my friend's Mateki, and I had it in my head that I would try and get a Mateki. I had the hotel contact the leading music stores that had pro flutes. I also found the Muramatsu showroom in Nagoya. I set out to find a store called Uemura, located a few subway stops away by train. In the store, I saw they had all kinds of flutes. Miyazawa, Mateki, Sankyo, Muramatsu, and I asked to try the flutes. At the time, even though I had an affinity for flute, in no way was I even close to being a pro player or even a good doubler. Trumpet and flute have a very similar embouchure. In the past, I would often play flute on R&B and pop gigs, sometimes humming into the flute as I played. So, I imagine the Japanese people in the store were not too impressed with my flute playing!

In the states, I was on an instrument finding kick at this time. I started going to pawn shops at first. I actually got a Prima Sankyo flute in a pawn shop in White Center (rat city) for 100 dollars. Needing money, I sold it for $1000. It turns out with the pointed key arms and other factors; it was worth $6000 new. Earlier I found an Armstrong Heritage model flute for $100 and was told by Chuck Stentz that they listed for $3000. However, with the Internet and eBay, these days, it is much harder to do. So, I was already looking for vintage saxes and mouthpieces. I was addicted to the gear finding and trading game now.

Back to my story…

I could not speak Nihongo (Japanese) well, so I had a little one-page promo sheet on myself that had some highlights of who I was, including the recording with Cedar Walton. This is good in Japan because Japanese people who learn English in school can often read and write English even if speaking it or hearing it is more problematic.

I saw some vintage saxophone gear in Uemura Gakki for ridiculous amounts of money. I was thinking I could do some horse-trading and get one of those real pro flutes without having to go so far into my pocket. So, the second time I went into Uemura's, I flashed a vintage Otto Link mouthpiece to the clerk behind the counter and asked, "Do you know what this is?"

+++++

Enter Kohama…

They quickly called the saxophone teacher down from upstairs. Yasuhiro Kohama[106] is his name. Kohama put the mouthpiece on his horn and blew it, and said, "good." Hearing Kohama play, it was apparent he was a jazz player.

Kohama was also a gear head! Kohama could speak a little English, so I used him to facilitate a deal where my son, Miles, who was coming soon, would carry over a MarkVI Tenor Saxophone, and then we would trade for a Prima Sankyo Artist Model flute.

Miles had been to Tokyo before, and I wanted him to come again now that he was 16. I told him he had to read Shogun as a primer. Miles was an avid reader, so that was no problem. I found a Mark VI tenor for $1500 for Miles to bring over. Today that same horn would be worth around $8000 or $9000. If a horn has original lacquer and is in the five-digit serial number range, the price can skyrocket. So, we had this deal cookin'. When Miles showed up with the horn, we did the deal down at Uemura's shop. Kohama came down again to inspect the horn, of course.

Then, I said to him that I would like to play together sometime. I will never forget that moment; Kohama took out a card and wrote, Star Eyes, Wednesday. I said I would be there. The Nagoya Castle hotel gig finished every night at 9:00, so the following Wednesday, Miles, Geoff, Josh, and I set out for Star Eyes.

It was a warm summer night and armed with a map, we soon found the Star Eyes club. As soon as we walked into the club, Kohama quickly came up to the door, and he said, "you play now."

That is certainly a change from how it usually goes in the U.S. when inviting players to sit in. It usually entails waiting while they play a set. Or at least a couple of songs, and then you are called to the bandstand. This time it was, bam, now! You're on.

I will never forget, the song was "Lover Man", one of the earliest songs I knew by heart from playing with Dick Thorlakson in high school and even earlier. Dick would play the piano and shout encouragement.

Star Eyes is an ideal sounding club; it is all wood and has excellent acoustics. For horns, this made it very easy to play. They had a grand piano, and the piano player this night was Koji Goto. Koji is a great piano player I have since seen performing with Marcus Printup and Big Daddy (alto player from Lincoln Center). The bass player sounded great and played with gut strings and a high-strung bass, and the drummer had a nice tight drum kit sound. Also, there were no mics or other impediments in the way. I launched in and had a ball and got "house" (applause) as well. My chops were feeling good from playing at the Castle every night. I recently worked on a thing that I call splitting the thirds, and that was just showing up in my playing. Next, they called, "It's You Or No One", boom, I also knew that one. And so on. On the break, or maybe it was the end of the night, Goh, the bass player, asked me if I had ever heard Coltrane live. I said yes, and this impressed him. I asked Goh who he took lessons from, and he replied, "Paul Chambers." Since Paul Chambers had been dead for a LONG time, I quickly realized that they were, like me, learning from the masters via recordings.

The Japanese are some of the heaviest, after-gig hangers I have ever met. Kohama asked us if we would like to get a bite to eat. Off we went to a Chinese restaurant. We had to split up into several cars to fit all of us. I rode with Kohama and noticed the baby seats in the car, so I knew that he was a dad also. I do not remember what we talked about at the restaurant, but we were soon all laughing and having a fantastic evening with chaos, translating, and great food. They gave us a ride back to the Hotel, where we sat in the lobby for a while, talking and carrying on. The conversation never lagged because Kohama was always asking questions. He has an insatiable curiosity about people.

For the rest of the gig at the Castle, we hung out every day. We went to cool record shops and other music stores. And then they took me to an area called Osu, which was a cheap shopping district. There they took me to Komeyho, an upscale pawnshop. They had many used instruments that were so cheap; I had to pinch myself to make sure I wasn't dreaming. I had already spent way too much on two flutes, and now I was staring at the mother-load of flutes for incredibly low prices!

In the days following, I gave some lessons to students at Kohama's store.

+++++

This gig was a lot of fun also because of Josh and Geoff. Those guys would go on long walks and take Miles along where they got into all kinds of "trouble." The convenience stores have many skin magazines and various explicit cartoons and things; they are very into sex, just like the rest of the world. In Japan, it is a funny combination of over-the-top explicit photos, but they also have censors to make sure the penis is airbrushed. Anyway, as a lark, Geoff found this gay magazine called Samson that showed older businessmen having sex, obviously with air-blown stuff to get by the censors. Well, Geoff got a total kick out of it, and since this made Geoff happy, we liked it too! Geoff also went around the nightlife district and took the cards from phone booths of girls promising a great time. He took these cards and made business cards out of them on the blank side.

Once, we were with Geoff when he showed the Samson magazine to a Japanese person and asked where we could find another. The guy looked at us with disgust and muttered, "Baka baka baka baka." We walked away asking ourselves what's with the baka baka baka. It turns out it means stupid! Josh and Geoff would go to Karaoke bars, and Geoff would bellow out songs he did not know. They often closed the Jazz Inn Lovely. The Jazz Inn Lovely is a great jazz club that has been going for 50 years now.

We had a lot of fun. The Castle Hotel had an athletic club, and we had privileges there. It was fun to see all these quiet businessmen's reactions to Josh, Miles, myself, and Geoff's loud laughter.

We were very naughty.

+++++

On one of the last nights, we went to a club called Swing, and I brought my horn. A guy named Atsushi Ikeda was playing there. Atsushi is a Tokyo alto player and had spent a lot of time in New York. Atsushi loved to play fast. When they launched into Cherokee, I asked Josh, "how fast are they going?" After checking his watch and tapping a few beats, Josh said, "350 MM and faster."

Swing is not a particularly big club, but it is deceptive when it comes to sound. It was not easy for me to get a pleasing sound on the trumpet and play over the band. I think I was a little freaked out by the tempo I had just witnessed. Anyway, after I played, I met Atsushi. I had Miles with me. Atsushi gave me a very lukewarm handshake and said, "You must be a good family man," some icy Tokyo shit! I thanked him while inwardly pissed at what I took as a big sleight.

Oh well, I didn't let it get me down. I have been to enough jam sessions to know that sometimes it does not go so great, and I also have had them go really great.

The last night in Nagoya, we all went out for a huge party. During the evening, Kohama asked if I would be interested in playing with his big band. I said, "of course."

At the end of the night, when we were all saying our good-byes, Miles, who was very emotional, broke into tears when we were saying goodbye. He said, "We might not ever see these people again." I said, "Don't worry; we probably will."

CHAPTER FIFTY

Song for Rita

B ack home, I was busy teaching at South Seattle Community College, playing gigs for parties, and generally keeping
busy playing. We made changes to the band, Evolution,
adding Vineet on guitar and Mark Ivester on drums. Vineet, I
first heard down at the 13 Coins at one of Buddy's gigs. I was
amazed at his vocabulary and the perfection of his time feel,
and the way he placed his eighth notes was magic to my ears.
I also saw him at Lofurno's at another Buddy session. Mark
Ivester played with Sonando and was familiar with Latin and
funk and many contemporary drumming styles. We were finally able to do more harmonically complex material, and
Vineet took a lot of the pressure off me of being the only soloist.

We added a piano also. We had Jovino Santos Neto, who
was new in town, come by a few times. Jovino was Hermeto
Pascoal's piano player and was schooled by Hermeto for
years in Brazil. For piano, we finally settled on Josh Wolfe, a
very creative guy who had versatility and fit nicely with
Vineet.

The last piece of the puzzle was Chris Stover on trombone.
Chris was part of the Central Washington class that included

Ruel and Jon Wikan. Chris played bone on Latin bands and, in addition to being an excellent bone player, was also a fine arranger and composer.

We played some festivals and gigs, and we also completed the recording started with Louis and Rick Reed. Like the earlier band, we worked on the music collectively at rehearsals.

"Song for Rita" started as a phrase Becca sang to me. I only needed that phrase, and the thing ballooned into the tune, "Song for Rita". The beats, Partido alto on the A sections, Baou on the bridge, was arrived at by trial and error and at Miguel and Louis's suggestion.

I still like the CD, *Song for Rita,* and every time I hear it, I get a warm feeling for that time in my life and happy with what we created.

CHAPTER FIFTY-ONE

Kohama and C.U.G.

In the early fall, very late one night, my phone rang. I thought, who in the hell is calling at this hour? I hope everything or everyone is all right! A voice on the phone said, "I am Kohama. Can you come to Japan?" I said, "certainly," and asked him if I could bring my dad, Marvin.

In March, we flew to Nagoya and met the band for the first time. The big band was called C.U.G., meaning *"Continued in the Underground Jazz Orchestra."*[107] Kohama, the bandleader, like many top jazz players in Japan, had spent time in New York, the jazz mecca of the world. When Kohama was in New York, he studied at the *University of the Streets* run by Barry Harris. Kohama also took private lessons from many famous people such as Jimmy Heath and others around the Barry Harris studio.

Kohama told me he was at the Village Vanguard on a Monday evening listening to the Mel Lewis band. For those reading this and not aware of the Vanguard Monday night tradition, Thad Jones and Mel Lewis started a big band that met and played on Mondays in the early '60s. When Thad left, it became the Mel Lewis Orchestra. After Mel died, it became the Monday Night Band or Vanguard Orchestra. The band features top musicians living in New York, and Monday night means that even the "Broadway show players" can partake.

Kohama had an epiphany, and the heavens parted for him when sitting in front of the Vanguard Orchestra. He heard the history, the soul, the skill, the continuity of the band. Plus, all the musicians playing together without exhibiting their egos, but each soloist celebrated their individuality and unique expression. He told me he could not stop crying. Kohama had an almost religious experience and vowed to create a similar band in Japan. He had found his life's calling.

Shortly after my dad and I arrived in Japan and checked into the hotel, we were off to a rehearsal. Besides the classic big band charts, there were many by the pianist *Shuhei Mizuno*. By the prodigious amount of arrangements for the band by *Shuhei*, CUG has a unique sound that separates it from bands that do not derive their sound from an in-house arranger. I also brought a few of my charts.

The musicianship in the band was high, but they had a few weak spots here and there. They were not in a hurry when they rehearsed, and as soon as something got tense, Kohama would immediately call a short break. The difference between rehearsals in the US and Japan is a cultural one. Japanese musicians would not say, "Hey, I think you are out of tune." In the US, it's just, "pull out; I think you're sharp." Or, "you're dragging or rushing in this section." The communication in the Japanese band was deep but indirect. Any criticisms would entail a conversation.

I saw this right away, so I was cautious when Kohama asked me for advice in front of the band. I was Kohama's tool to introduce various suggestions and criticisms without upsetting the balance in the band. The players had a lot of bebop phrasing, so I tried to introduce a little more of the greasier Basie and blues-based folk elements. I also was a tuning policeman and had the band play softer. Not a big deal.

+++++

One of the first stops on the band's schedule was a village on the water, famous for pottery and poetry. It turned out one of the band musicians was from that village, and he was featured on a special poster they had of that venue. My dad and I went to a pottery gallery before the gig, and I got a beautiful little bowl. We were sitting around in the artist's studio, and they put on *Rapture,* my CD with Wikan and Travis. I remember the piano player, Shuhei, had big eyes for Travis' playing. Shuhei asked me how old he was! *Shuhei* had been part of a "Young Lions" promotional push in Japan, ala Wynton, and the Boys.

After that first gig, we were eating delicious food in a big restaurant or banquet room, and the night was magical with a giant full moon. Marvin and I were both on our lips from jet lag when all of a sudden, we heard a scream, looked for the source, and spotted the roadie, *Take,* standing on a chair dressed in a jockstrap with a little animal in front. Everybody hesitated for one moment, forks and spoons and hashi (chopsticks) midair and, after a slight pause of a second, the buzz of conversion started in again, and nobody paid any attention. I knew then we were not in Kansas anymore. *Take* had two roles in the band: hard-working roadie and "Court Jester." Years later, when the CUG band came to Seattle, *Take* did a special dance for Seattle outside of Tula's, where we were performing.

On that tour and subsequent tours, my dad Marvin tapes everything. He had a Dat recorder at that time, and when we listened to the recordings after the gigs, I could see some nights were very special, and then sometimes it was also handy to hear areas that needed improvement. But Kohama was not in a hurry. CUG means, *Continued in the Underground* with the emphasis on "continued." As Kohama said, they did not want to be a "flash in the pan."

Now I am on my 43rd tour with the band, and it has survived and continued to grow and improve. Today it is a going
concern. Never content to just coast along, the band has continued to evolve. Some personnel changes as expected, but
many of the same people from my first tour are still with the
band. Usually, bands have their heyday earlier, and there is a
decline, not so with CUG.

One thing I should mention is one of the charts they played
was "Sunset and the Mocking Bird" by Ellington. On that
chart, the sax section channeled Duke's sax section sound so
good; it was uncanny and kind of spooky.

The band was very patient with me. I had absolutely no
Nihongo (Japanese) at my disposal and did not even have the
presence of mind to bring an English /Japanese dictionary.
With this first tour, we traveled in two big vans and went all
over Japan. The tour was a couple of weeks and change.

I think I might have brought a horn to sell. I usually did.
And I probably bought a flute or sax at Komehyo, the used
instrument shop that Kohama showed me earlier the previous
summer.

+++++

Near the end of the tour, when we were out on the road, we
played at a little town on the coast. There we picked up a
trumpet player who was my age or maybe a little older. He
had been famous in Tokyo way back and played with a top
Tokyo-based big band. He sounded great and had a thick,
dark sound and could play in all registers and played with an
authentic swing style.

That night after that gig, the band very quickly packed up.
Everybody pitches in, and it goes fast that way. Then the food
started to be put on tables, including a giant fish. It turns out
that this trumpet player was now a chef. *Tomomi*, the trombone player, almost had tears in his eyes when he told me that
the trumpet player had been to the fish market at 6:00 AM to

get the particular fish he was now preparing for us. It was a big Tuna and very fresh sashimi grade, and he carefully sliced it for us. Since then, I have seen documentaries on searching for the best fish early in the morning at their huge fish markets. Being a novice in Japanese culture, I did not realize the depth of their dedication to excellence when it came to fish and other food preparation. In Nagoya, the band used to go to a big chicken restaurant after gigs, and we ate every part of the chicken. I ate chicken sashimi as well, that is raw chicken. You would not do that in the USA!

I was slightly embarrassed at this restaurant because they were playing a CD I did with Jessica Williams. It was hard for me to ignore that and stay in sync with my surroundings. We settled into eating, and then the trumpet player said, "stop the music," so they turned the CD player off. And then he started to serenade us with his trumpet. He played "Taking a Chance on Love" at a medium tempo with all kinds of color and expression, and it was magic. *Goh*, the bass player, quickly put his hashi down and jumped on the bass; *Tomomi*, the bone player, jumped on drums; *Toru*, also *a* bone player, jumped on piano and *Shuhei*, the piano player, had picked up a flugelhorn. That was a magical jam session. Not only did it sound good, but we were just playing for the love of the music and each other. That is rare and strong when combined with skill. It reminded me of the Hobbit scene where they had the magic party with the elves in Rivendale.

Pretty hard to describe, but I had an expanding appreciation and feeling of being very fortunate to be welcomed into this *"jazz family"* and experience a lot that most outsiders do not get.

+++++

On the way back to Nagoya, we stopped off at a family-owned farm of one of the band musicians. It was a beautiful Japanese-style house, warm and wooden and sturdy. His mother asked me if I knew anything about tea. I said I liked tea. But she was a tea master, and that was a whole different story. She asked would I want to do a tea ceremony. I said, sure. But I was immediately starting to get nervous. I sat facing her, and she began to lay the utensils out and slowly heated some water. Then she lovingly cleaned all the utensils and seemed to go deep into herself. After the water heated, she put in some tea. In this case, it was powdered green tea or matcha that went into a lovely little, hand-made ceramic bowl. Then she took out a small bamboo whisk, delicately worked the water and tea, and then went into a quick motion to mix air into the liquid, putting a little foam on top. She presented me the bowl with both hands as an offering. This was also done in slow motion as part of this ritual. I was transported to a different level of consciousness.

It was a completely transcendental, ego-less experience and very powerful.

My dad and I went back to Seattle with many new friends and a bunch of memories and impressions of a place that is at once modern and ancient.

Jay Thomas

224

CDs, Partial list

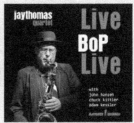

225

CHAPTER FIFTY-TWO

Twelfth and Jackson Blues

Back in Seattle, I was using Jon Wikan on drums and John Hansen on piano, and we had an upcoming gig at the Cotton Club in Vancouver, Canada. I knew about Russ Botten as an excellent bass player, and he completed our quartet.

Our engineer was Jim Wilke[108] from Seattle. In 1965 Jim did a live radio broadcast of Coltrane at The Penthouse on the same night Jan Kurtis recorded the album *Coltrane, Live in Seattle*. There is a bootleg of the radio broadcast that overlaps some of the Impulse album. When Jim asked Coltrane for his OK to broadcast live, Trane didn't say no, but he did ask Jim's astrological sign. Jim said, "Taurus," and Trane immediately said, "OK." I read somewhere that those born under the sign of Taurus have pleasant voices and appreciate the arts - maybe that's why Coltrane said OK! Previously issued from Jim's Penthouse broadcasts: Cannonball Adderley, Jack Wilson Quartet with Roy Ayers, Wynton Kelly Trio & Wes Montgomery, The Three Sounds, Gary McFarland, Ernestine Anderson, and Joe Williams.

I don't remember the first time I was on Jim's show, but maybe from The Jazz Gallery, which The Seattle Jazz Society operated in the 70s at Eastlake and Fuhrman. That space was the Llahngaelhyn before SJS took it over. I've been on his show many times since then! Jim has been recording and streaming jazz in the Seattle area and Internationally with his Jazz After Hours show for over 50 years, and he is still going strong.

+++++

Vancouver, Canada, is breathtakingly beautiful and a very international and cosmopolitan city. The choice of restaurants, especially Chinese, is off the charts. And I loved the disparity in the dollar when it was about perusing pawnshop purchases. A little harder for musicians when it comes to being paid.

Anyway, we set up at the club and played through some of the music new to Russ. Jim Wilke was in another room to isolate what was going onto tape from what he heard live. The resulting CD from the two gigs had a great, funky feel. John Hansen wrote a tune called "Midnight Stomp" that was very cool. I brought a blues called "Twelfth and Jackson Blues", and it had some aspects of a cross between Trane and Stanley Turrentine.

We recorded over two nights. Being on the road and recording served to provide more focus. We did not have all the mundane cares of being at home and the everyday routines that we fall into, so it focused our whole time up there on fun and the recording.

+++++

While in Vancouver, I also had an interesting and scary non-musical experience. Becca and I loved to go way out on Hastings Street to a place called The Pearl for a brunch of dim sum. We would invariably eat way too much and then walk back into the city on Hastings Street, where all the pawnshops

229

were. It was about a three-mile walk with virtually a dozen or more pawnshops. This time, I went into a pawnshop and recognized a French-style professional flute case, always a good sign. I looked at the flute, and it said Takumi. I thought for sure it was probably special. It was $100 Canadian, so I bought it.

I might have even tried to haggle them down with some B.S. Anyway, I just could not wait to research the value of the flute. As we walked up Hastings towards the city, I saw the Lon McWade music store, and I knew they had many high-end flutes. Becca and I went in and asked about Takumi. The clerk said they were good, but they were selling more Haynes and Powell those days, and they did not have any Takumi anymore. He still could not give me an exact price on one, but his mentioning it in the same breath as the other big-name pro flutes just whetted curiosity. I went upstairs to where the repairman was supposed to know a little more.

Upstairs the guy said, just wait here a minute. He came back with a big grin and said, "Good news, the flute is worth about $6000. The bad news, it was stolen from this store!" At that point, a very tall, Canadian Mountie clapped me on the shoulder and proceeded to question me. I told him I had just bought the flute and showed him the receipt and everything. As it turns out, there was never a police report filed on it. That is why the pawnshop was not aware of it being hot. Pawnshops have to list all the items with the police department before they put them up for sale. It had a girl's name written inside the flute case, which also got me thinking something was fishy. I would have tried to get to the bottom of it in normal circumstances and would have had serious questions, but at this time, I had no visa, so I was too nervous to contest the flute issue. In those days, you had to have a work visa even to do a small jazz gig. That would also entail a bureaucratic mess. Today you do not need a work visa if you are a musician traveling up there to play. The Mountie said to me, "Mr. Thomas, when you travel to Canada, and a deal seems too good, then it is." My thought then and now is, "what a mor-on." Pawnshops are the same everywhere, and I had done nothing but purchase an instrument from a legitimate busi-ness. It was on them to register with the police all items for sale, to see if they were stolen.

Back to the recording.

The CD, *12th and Jackson Blues*, came out on Jazz Focus, a label based in Calgary, run by a wacky psychiatrist I met on a Jessica Williams recording earlier in Portland. It got a little bit of play, and we sent it out to reviewers, etc. It did not do so much on the radio stations but had good reviews as with my previous CDs. Later on, Nat Hentoff saw it sitting around and decided to play it and completely freaked out on the feel of it. He called and interviewed me, and I ended up with a great article in the *Wall Street Journal*. We had a lot of fun recording that CD. Some of the youthful optimism and talent from John Hansen and Jon Wikan can be heard in this CD. Wikan had his sights set on New York.

CHAPTER FIFTY-THREE

Billy Wallace

I first met Billy Wallace[109] at a jam session in Seattle. Billy was an older African American who, at the jam session, was playing atrocious alto saxophone. His sound and chops were not great, and he was super arrogant and standoffish as well. Not a particularly auspicious beginning for a friendship.

I started to hear about Billy from others who were impressed with his piano playing. Soon Billy was playing gigs around town on piano and pissing off all kinds of people. Bob Nixon was playing a gig, and Billy walked up and told Bob his changes were wrong on a particular song!

But Billy persevered and was soon playing a long-term gig at the El Gaucho restaurant with Floyd Standifer, my original teacher, and mentor. Billy was also playing a lot with Clarence Acox and others at the New Orleans Restaurant on First Avenue. Some of his background histories were also a topic of discussion. Billy had played with Clifford Brown and Max Roach, and many others. Billy was reportedly a Karate expert, and it was rumored he also packed a piece. Billy was some serious, "old school" action! My first gig with Billy was at

Stars, an upscale restaurant/sports bar located in the heart of downtown Seattle. There I got a better understanding of him. Billy looked at me slightly bored and said, "What do you want to play?" So, I called a standard. With no preamble or count off, he launched into an intro, and it was easy to enter and play the song. One after the other, the evening progressed like that. I would call the tune, and key and Billy would start. I quickly learned he knew any song I called. What was so cool is, he thought of each song as an arrangement with an intro and an ending composed on the spot. Sometimes he would do little stylistic backgrounds, which were easy to handle and made the music more open harmonically.

The guy who booked Stars was John Simpson, a car dealer who liked Billy Wallace and Floyd Standifer. Billy must have thought I was OK because John hired me to play with Billy repeatedly.

On one gig Hubert Laws was there. Hubert sat in for a whole set. That was a real treat. On the break, Billy came to the table where Hubert was seated with his companion, a Japanese woman. Billy launched into Nihongo with her, and I started to think that Billy had many talents. However, he was still a handful at times and not very friendly. Once, I said to him, just trying to be friends, "Gee Billy, you sure know a lot of tunes." Instead of the usual response, which would be thanks etc., instead, he said, "two thousand tunes, and a thousand with lyrics." Whoa, that is undoubtedly impressive, but also illustrates Billy's condition. Today it is popular to speculate about who, or who isn't, on the "spectrum," referring to autistic or Asperger tendencies that include lack of awareness of social cues and occasionally some real smart savant-like abilities. Another time on a gig, I asked him about karate, and he got up and had me stand up as well, and he said, "now come at me." I complied and started closing the gap between us. Immediately he had me checkmated physically. He told me when I got inside a certain distance from him, he "owned me." After that demonstration, I became a believer.

Once, Benny Green was in town, and he made it known that he had big eyes to meet Billy. The truth was, I, like most others in Seattle, did not know the full scope of Billy's abilities. On one trip to Japan, I was in a record shop, and there was a Billy Wallace CD.

The last time I saw Billy was in Montana. John Simpson had moved to Montana and was working at a car dealership there, and also booking jazz as a sideline hobby. In addition to people he knew and liked, John was booking people like Scott Hamilton. I went to Montana several times to play with the groups he assembled. The pay was always right, and I dug the musicians he paired me with. The last time was with Billy Wallace and Chuck Kistler. Chuck is a bass player who I often play with in Seattle. Billy had moved from Seattle to Las Vegas and then to Denver, where he was currently residing. The Montana mini- tour turned out to be a fun time and was an eye-opener regarding Billy's ability. Chuck was a big fan of Billy, which helped also. The time feel of the trio was swingin' and easy and never drug even without a drummer.

I think Billy might have been at the beginning of what finally got him, Alzheimer's. The reason I say this is, Billy just kept playing with no eye on the clock. The sets would not have stopped had John Simpson not stepped in. Same with the end of the gig, Billy's foot was stuck on the gas pedal, and we just kept motoring along past the end of the gig until John called it.

On this tour, I once called "I Loves You Porgy", which is a song I love. I rarely call it because most piano players do not know it. Billy started into a medley of all the Porgy and Bess tunes. He not only played the melody and chords, but he also played all the inside moving parts and counter melodies that Gershwin had written, and Gil Evans had orchestrated. It was a little miniature orchestra that Billy conjured up with his ten fingers and a piano. I had to restrain myself from breaking out in tears. It was an awesome demonstration. During this tune, Chuck and I just stared slack-jawed at him.

On the gig, Billy, all of a sudden, was very uncharacteristically friendly to me. I mean actually friendly. He told me he really liked my playing, and he appreciated that I still practiced. He thought that was the key. Without putting anyone down, Billy said that was the problem with Floyd and many older musicians; they just stop practicing. With Billy on that gig, we played stuff like "Serenade in Blue", and "I'll Take Romance", and many others that he talked me through.

Shortly thereafter, Billy was diagnosed with Alzheimer's, and there was an article written on him about how he could still play well, remembered a ton of tunes but did not know what was going on, day to day. He passed shortly after. Since then, I have read articles where Herbie Hancock mentioned him as a force and a musician he would get together with when Herbie was a young player in Chicago. And Harold Mabern talked about being taken under another piano player's wing and being shown many things. Harold was talking about Billy.

A funny anecdote from my last trip was Billy going off about Trane. Billy, like some older black musicians, was not a big fan of Trane.

He said, "Von Freeman was way better!"

CHAPTER FIFTY-FOUR

Wikan, Wataru, Keezer

On one of my earliest trips in Japan, one night I was playing at Star Eyes, and a young, very tall and very pale, and an exceptionally well-dressed guy came up to me and said in heavily accented English how much he liked my playing. Enter Wataru Hamasaki! He shook my hand, and my initial impression was like meeting a very suave, young Count Dracula. His skin was so white it was almost luminescent, like porcelain. And he was dressed all in black in an ultra-modern suit. He asked about my mouthpiece also. I had a tenor mouthpiece I had purchased from Bob Carpenter, a famous refacer of vintage mouthpieces who happens to live right outside of Seattle in Bothell. On the next tour, when I saw Wataru, he had a vintage hard rubber Brillhardt like I had the first time we met. (But I had moved on several mouthpieces by that time!)

+++++

I had a stock line I would use on musicians in Japan, and it was if you come to Seattle, you can stay at my house. This young guy I had just met turned out to be a very natural sounding tenor player, originally from Nagasaki and was studying medicine in Nagoya. Wataru had about 20 students and was playing gigs as well as becoming a doctor. His playing was smooth. He had transcribed a lot of stuff like Shoeshine Boy by Lester Young and was also familiar with some of the Warne Marsh, Lee Konitz material. Wataru comes from a family of doctors, and I think they even have a hospital. So, he did not hurt for resources even though he was doing fine on his own. I noticed in the Japanese society there is a real hierarchical pecking order kind of baked in. And just the way we are here in the US and other parts of the world, there are many signals and cues that are almost beneath conscious awareness. These help us identify where everyone belongs in this hierarchy. Wataru took me to lunch, and we also went shopping. I noticed the deference people showed Wataru wherever we went. He is an "alpha dog," for sure, and he sends those signals out. So is Kohama, for that matter. I asked Wataru about his suits and the clothes he was fond of. Tsutomu, the lead trumpet player, also wore them. So Wataru took me to a clothing store in the Osu district of Nagoya.

Osu has many covered streets that are only for pedestrians. Both sides of the street have nothing but one business after another. There are many clothes stores, tea shops, produce markets, hat shops, hardware stores, pharmacies, virtually everything. And Osu was an inexpensive area where one could get a bargain. Osu always has a somewhat festive vibe with happy shoppers on foot and many outdoor food stalls and lots of mouthwatering smells. After hitting a few places with Wataru, I was styling. I have never really been into clothes, but Wataru helped me remedy that, and now I am, "lookin' good." After seeing Wataru at a few jam sessions and gigs and a few lunches, we became friends.

As I said earlier, I had invited him to come to Seattle. So, he informed me he was planning on coming! I informed Becca that we would have a guest. Wataru showed up in Seattle, and we put him in our extra room upstairs. Wataru and I practiced together, and I took him to all my gigs and jam sessions. He played in my big band, and I even brought him to the UW Jazz Camp. Everyone liked him a lot. Clarence Acox, from Garfield, hired him to play at Tula's jazz club when his regular tenor player could not make the gig. Clarence had heard him when I brought him to the Wednesday night gig at the New Orleans restaurant. Even the management of Tula's was happy with him. He was well-spoken and a good player and very handsome and well dressed. (He was also a chick magnet).

Wataru had been soaking up everything and showed me some transcriptions. I thought they looked too hard to play and didn't make much sense to me, but there was something vaguely familiar about it. They were some of my solos from the gigs we had been playing! That's not something I encourage, but it surprised me, and I suppose flattered me a little even though I am operating with few illusions. Wataru got to be friends with Wikan, and Wikan was always trying to improve Wataru's English in funny ways. Wataru came back to my house after hanging with Wikan trying to pronounce "take the skin boat to tuna town" and other stuff equally as funny and risqué. We had a lot of fun. The name that had him frustrated was Marilyn Monroe. That one came out a little lopsided. As funny as we like to think of foreigners struggling with English pronunciation, it still is way better than most of us can do with their language. At one point, Wataru got a Super Balanced Action tenor from a friend of mine, so we were thick as thieves at that time.

+++++

I think Wataru came to Seattle at least three times, maybe four. One summer, Wataru came to Centrum jazz camp. Besides, being a student, he also played second tenor on the festival big band that Frank Wess directed. That same summer, Motchie, the great Japanese bari player, was also at the camp. Gary Smulyan had started to teach at Centrum, and Motchie had big eyes for Smulyan.

+++++

Now Wataru is famous in Japan, tours regularly and teaches. For recreation, he scuba dives and now has taken up golf in a big way. Wataru is married to a very good bebop piano player.

Musically, Wataru represents Ishimori saxophone gear and plays Ishimori mouthpieces and Ishimori horns. Ishimori's saxophone shop is probably the most famous on earth. I don't see him much anymore, but occasionally I see him at Okazaki Jazz Street. He has his life now and has found his niche and has moved on. Also, Wataru graduated from medical school and is now an Ear, Nose, and Throat doctor. After he got his degree, he was freed to pursue saxophone with all of his energy. That medical degree was for his parents, I suspect!

Wataru can really party and hang. One night I was with Kazuyoshi Kuroda, the drummer, after a gig that he had played with Wataru at Jazz Inn Lovely earlier. Wataru called Kuroda san and was looking for his cell phone. Turns out Wataru was speaking on his cell phone!

When Wataru was a student, Becca, Marvin, and I were invited to Wataru's house for a Bar-B-Que and to play some flute duets. I think this was late in the summer. Anyway, we played the duets, and then a couple of attractive girls came by who were friends of Wataru's. Wataru abruptly stopped the duets, and then he went out into his postage-sized backyard and started clearing the grass by hand. He just moved like a whirlwind, grabbing chunks of grass and just pulling and cutting. Next, he set little chairs out. Then Wataru started a fire with big chunks of charcoal pieces of wood. We had a scrumptious feast with many unfamiliar dishes. He whipped it up in no time. It was magic, all under the stars. At the end of the dinner, we went out to the alley and lit off sparklers. The sparklers were a childlike innocent end to the evening. It was a delightful experience that I will never forget.

+++++

Wikan, shortly after moving to New York, started playing with Geoff Keezer. Geoff is a guy I had been hearing about from players like Travis Shook. Geoff played with Art Blakey early on when he was maybe only 17 or 18 years old. He also worked with Art Farmer and was the pianist in the Ray Brown trio for a while. Geoff is a formidable talent and was a prodigy who just kept going. One of the very best ever.

Keezer also speaks Nihongo and used to live in Tokyo. These factors came together, and Wataru and I pooled our money to record with Wikan and Keezer and a bass player named Matt Closey. The name of the album is called *Accidentally Yours*. An appropriate name because in as much as we plan, so much of life is happenstance or accidental. We recorded a song of mine and a couple of Wataru's and some Keezer songs and arrangements. It turned out good from the standpoint of having a great feel. This rhythm section handled that nicely.

CHAPTER FIFTY-FIVE

Milt, Rams, and the mid-nineties

The band I had a helluva lot of fun with was the Ramsay Kleeb 10-piece band fronted by Bill Ramsay and co-led with Milt Kleeb. Milt was a person who, early on, was large in my life. If you remember, in Chapter One, the first band I was in was the Playboys. All of the charts we played were written by Milt. One of Milt's band configurations was Alto, 2 tenors, bari and trumpet plus rhythm section, and vocalist. When I started out in high school, my dad got the entire 8-piece band library from Milt and then recruited kids from his friends who were private music teachers. At one time, we wanted Milt's daughters to dance in front of the band, kind of like go-go dancers. That did not go anywhere. Milt's daughters were beautiful; Candis and Karen and were twins. Dave Johnson, the drummer, and I went over to Milt's house once when Milt and Judy were gone. I think Dave and Candis probably kissed and made out a little. I just stared at Karen and did not do anything! What I did notice was Milt had a very hip record collection featuring a lot of Coltrane. Pretty advanced for a big band guy circa WWII

241

+++++

The Ramsay/Kleeb Orchestra was a mid-90's band that continued on into the 2000s. Milt was an arranger, sax player active in big bands and arranging going back to WWII and before. Milt taught himself to arrange with natural talent and because, as he said, "the arrangements I could buy were not very good." Milt understood that arrangements were best if every inner part was fun to play and made melodic sense. Many arrangers write with little regard for the inner voices and how it feels to play them.

In WWII, Milt arranged and composed music for the troops. Milt worked for a general who wanted a new show every week. So, hewas very busy arranging and playing for troop entertainment. The big band era was in full swing, and Milt was writing in that style. Milt married the general's daughter, who was an excellent singer. Her name was Judy and Milt arranged many songs for her. Later, Milt wrote arrangements for the Boyd Raeburn band.

+++++

Bill Ramsay was also a good writer of the self-taught school. Besides playing with Basie, Bill also played in the Grover Mitchell band and contributed some charts. That band was full of great writers as well. Bill also did all the big band charts for Ernestine Anderson for the album that had her hit song, "You Made Your Move Too Soon." Bill arranged the trombone sweeteners for my album *Easy Does It* that started me on my way.

+++++

As an aside, when I was just a kid, my dad played with Milt in a smaller big band, and he took me to one of his gigs. I remember going to sleep in his overcoat and being awakened at the end of the gig. Another time when I was just starting to play jazz my dad took me to hear Milt's band. We went thru the kitchen because it was a private event. We watched a few songs. My dad, after a tenor solo by Rams, said to me, "that's that New York sound!" My Dad sometimes played in Milt's small band. Milt continued through the years to write for big bands and occasionally played shows because he was an above-average reader.

+++++

In the '90s, Bill Ramsay teamed up with Milt, and Milt started writing for a ten-piece band. Milt was on Bari and Rams lead alto.

Pete Christlieb began coming up from LA to play with the band. The other tenor was Jim Coile, who had been busy in LA for years before returning to Seattle. Before that, Mike Edwards played tenor. Much later, Travis Ranney took the second tenor position. Travis was sometimes called "little Pete "by Rams. After the first time, Pete and Travis played together Pete kept saying afterward, kind of talking to himself. "I couldn't shake him." That hardly ever happens because Pete has a huge sound and is one funky and fast M. F.

First, we had Gary Shutes on trombone, a guy who had experience in New York. Gary was replaced by Dan Marcus, who relocated to the NW after playing lead bone on the Ray Charles band. Dan later married Bill Ramsay's daughter. Bob Panerio was the first lead trumpet, but shortly after, Brad Allison became the lead trumpet when he returned from Las Vegas. Brad had been very active in Vegas and was recognized for his strength and endurance and his musicianship. Brad was playing the Tom Jones show where the book was so difficult, they had two lead players. One night something happened to the other lead player, and Brad did the whole job himself, and they thought, " Hey we don't need two lead players." I loved playing with Brad. We both had Calicchio

243

trumpets that not only are on the bright side, but Calicchio's have a lot of color and core. Brad is one of the most solid cats I have ever played with. Chuck Deardorf played bass. At first, it was Barney McClure on piano and then John Hansen.

+++++

For the bulk of the time that I had a blast with this band, it was Jon Wikan on drums Chuck on Bass with Hansen on piano. The big gun on the band was Pete Christlieb. Pete is an excellent tenor player, and I like to say he has no "natural enemies "in the saxophone world. Pete played for 17 years on the Tonight Show band. He is on many recordings, notably Steely Dan's The Deacon.

The brass, for only three, puts out a lot of sound. I loved playing with Brad. We had similar equipment, so the blend was right, and the phrasing was never a problem. All the saxes doubled nicely on flutes and clarinets so Milt could really get into his arranging. With Rams and Christlieb, it had a loose and funky feel and was quite loud as well! Milt arranged "I Won't Dance" and a fast Rhythm tune called "Big Daddy" that featured Pete. Pete has a great sense of humor and some really cool stories. Pete's dad was a famous bassoon player in Hollywood studios. Pete got to be on the set of Cleopatra and said that they had an acre of bassoons. Pete's dad had a party one time, and Pete's job was to park the cars. Pete said he took Stravinsky's car for a "joy ride."

+++++

In this Rams-Kleeb band, along with the music's high quality, there was a lot of laughter and camaraderie. Rams and Pete were both very funny, and Milt was always deadpan, like a silent movie character. If something tickled Milt, his eyes would twinkle. At the end of the band's run, Milt got very hard of hearing. And it was amusing to see Rams try to get

Milt's attention. One time Milt had a squeaky baritone reed. Rams was yelling, "Milt...Milt....Milt ....Your squeaking! We used to play a lot at Red Kelly's in Tacoma, and we played at Tula's in Seattle and some festivals and occasionally at Port Townsend. We also played at Brother Don's in Bremerton. These were not especially big venues, but the people ate it up, and I had some real fun times with this crew.

We did a recording in 1997 called *Kelly's Heroes*. The CD had solos by everyone in the band and featured some of Milt's writing. Rams is a great lead alto player. One of the funkiest and most swingin' I have ever heard. Bill recorded a CD on lead alto in Japan with the Frank Wess big band when they had all the old Basie guys still alive on the band.

After *Kelly's Heroes*, the band still worked occasionally. When Wikan moved to New York, we had Gary Hobbs on drums. Gary used to play with Stan Kenton and has been a mainstay in the fertile Portland, Oregon scene for a long time. Gary is a great drummer, but the hookup that Wikan and Hansen had was special from all the playing they did together in this period.

The band had all the power and guns of a big band but a small group's sensibility with shifts in meter and reharmonization underneath the soloists. It was a band with a lot of solos.

Later, for a short time, Milt and I had the band together. Milt wrote some new charts, and we recorded a CD. After Milt passed, he left me his library of charts.

CHAPTER FIFTY-SIX

DURKEE

During the 90s, I was busy recording. I played on other people's projects as well as my own. And I also did some work recording for Muzak. Seattle had the dubious distinction of being the Muzak capital of the world, and I got in on the tail-end of it. All kinds of elevator music, as it is often called, was recorded in Seattle. For me, recording is always fun. It's like the old punch line about sex; even bad sex is great! The Muzak sessions were sometimes four to six hours long, and occasionally all day. I often paired up with Dan Marcus to lay horn parts down. I would play trumpet, alto, and tenor, and occasionally flute. Dan would put down bone parts. We had our choice of being paid by the hour or paid by the song. We always went with pay by the song! We took the gamble that we would be fast, and fast we were! The engineer quickly fell into it with us; it quickly became a very guttural shorthand; after a little flub, it was just, "getcha in," and boom, he would roll, and we would be in again where we had the mistake, until the next error. Unbelievably quick out in the trenches of the music world. I'm amazed when I get into jazz

246

recordings where a big discussion ensues after a little mistake; can or can't we get in, and the engineer puzzled where to get us back in. Kind of ironic how much better those "industry" guys are than the "art calls." I was flying into Anchorage one time, and the music in the airport started to get my attention, and then I realized, hey, that's me!

+++++

Through Luis Peralta, I became friends with Norman Durkee. Durkee would often show up just to hang and lend support for the band during the Evolution days when we had Luis and Rick Reed. And, on some cuts, Durkee even played for free. Almost unheard of in the Durkee universe. Durkee was a guy who was at the top of the heap of $$ making musicians in Seattle because of his recording and producing commercials.

A little about Norman Durkee. Norman grew up in Tacoma and went to Berklee School of Music in the '60s and was a fine pianist. He was a huge guy; I mean massive as in tall and big—almost a giant. Luis was a little skinny guy, and the two of them were odd-looking together. They had a routine. Luis would ask Durkee a question. Why is the sky blue? And Durkee would take off on flights of metaphysical fancy.

One time after one of Durkee's breakups, Luis decided to take Durkee to Cannon Beach on the Oregon coast. Luis had a girlfriend down there and assured Durkee that there were all kinds of girls in Canon Beach just waiting to meet him. So, in Durkee's big Lincoln Continental, they set off to Oregon. Durkee was hungry on the way, and Luis pulls out some bee pollen and other esoteric health food snack items, and that does not fly with Durkee, who wanted real food, of course.

When they get to Cannon Beach, Luis is to go off with his girlfriend, but they need to get a room for Durkee. Luis says he knows of a place. Durkee looks it over and says, "No way! This is a dive." So he goes to the most expensive hotel and gets a room right on the beach. Luis and Durkee no sooner get into their room to admire the view than outside of the window, two young women are wrestling on the sand. They were getting frisky with each other and pulling down the tops of the other's bathing suit and exposing their naked breasts. When Luis told me about this later in a solemn tone of voice, he said, "Jay, that was quantum physics, we made that happen." He continued with a little sadness in his voice, "we could have created an angel."

Back to my point about recording. Durkee was one of the ad music industry kingpins, and he had some very big clients like Campbell Soup Company, U.S. Bank, and many others. I loved working for him because he did not ever have me do takes over and over again. Even if I thought I could do it better, he would just say, "I think we got it." I would most often go to his digs in the Marlborough Apartments, a very cool old vintage building. I would go into his apartment, and he would put me in the hall with a great mic and headphones.

Sometimes he had me do fun stuff also. One time he had a project going that was very unusual. He told me, "Don't play in any key or any tempo." That was not easy to do. It turns out Durkee had some other people doing the same thing. Later, he put them together like a collage. And it worked really well!

Durkee got his start in Seattle when they auditioned people for the musical *Hair*. It turns out Durkee was perfect for it. And he later stepped into managing the biggest studio ever built in Seattle, Kay Smith Studio.

+++++

About the middle of 1998, Durkee approached me for a gig with a band he was putting together. It would be a gig backing clowns, acrobats, and singers and providing atmospheric music for dining—a bizarre kind of circus in a tent. The theme was "love and chaos," and a lot of the music was inspired by spaghetti western music and Nina Rota. Nina Rota composed music for Fellini films. I recommended musicians for the band, we rehearsed, and soon we were doing a show five nights a week. The show was called *Teatro ZinZanni, Love, Chaos, and Dinner.*

After a few personnel changes, it settled in with Jon Wikan on drums and Dan Marcus on trombone. That made it one of the most fun gigs I have ever had. Dan and I went to every thrift store in Seattle and got pots and pans that represented every pitch and built an instrument that he would play on the show. Wikan was a constant rip, rig, and panic guy, playing the drums with a vibrator and all sorts of stuff. Jon had a great ear and could hum just the wrong note to destroy a chord. We were like little gremlins or the Katzenjammer Kids in the old cartoons. Norm Langill, the head boss, sometimes would get alarmed at our antics and wanted us to reel us in, but Durkee protected us and wanted it to remain fresh and chaotic, and spontaneous.

Not only did it pay well, but we got a splendid multi-course dinner at the end of the night. I played that show for a year and a half before it temporally closed.

When it re-opened again, it was a completely different animal. What used to be free-wheeling fun by six and seven musicians was now played by four musicians and tamped way down. They removed the chaos and made it just a musical "industry endeavor."

Coincidentally, Durkee's ad business, with the after-effects of midi studios and home studios cropping up everywhere, just evaporated overnight, and now when Norm Langill said jump, Durkee had to comply.

CHAPTER FIFTY-SEVEN

Jim Knapp Orchestra

Jim Knapp[110] is a trumpeter and arranger originally from the Midwest who came to Seattle in the early '70s to create a jazz department at the Cornish School of Music. I had been to Cornish much earlier when I was in high school to play with a combo run by Floyd Standifer, and it was a place that was kind of loose. I saw Mark Doubleday there one afternoon in the '60s; he was searching out a practice room! Anyway, Jim Knapp soon made Cornish a competitive jazz department. Gary Peacock, Julian Priester, Art Lande, and many great players taught there. Carter Jefferson was the sax instructor for a while, and then Hadley Caliman. In those heady early days of the Cornish jazz program having a master's or doctorate was secondary to real-time practical jazz experience. Cornish had a connection to the avant-garde as well as traditional jazz. John Cage did some of his famous work at Cornish. The counterculture connection holds to this day, with many young students from all around the country coming to Cornish to study based on Cornish's open-minded approach to academics.

Jim Knapp is a very good trumpet player; actually, I would say more than good. But most know him from his composing and arranging. Jim had already been busy writing when he was in the Midwest. An anecdotal account is that Jim McNeely heard Jim's music being performed and said, "that's what I want to do." I'm not sure of the truth in that, and it was a long time ago, but I can believe it. There are still recordings of the music Jim wrote when he was in Indiana and Chicago. When Jim took over the Cornish jazz department, he formed the Composers and Improvisers Orchestra band. They had many great players, including Denny Goodhew, Dave Peterson, Chuck Deardorf, and Jim played trumpet.

They brought clinicians out to Cornish, such as alto player Anthony Braxton, composer Carla Bley, and pianist Cedar Walton.

I played with the Carla Bley big band at Cornish a little later.

+++++

My story concerns the band Jim put together in the '90s. Jim started writing for three trumpets, two bones, French horn, four saxes, piano, bass, and drums and then put together a band compromised of some young players that were able and willing to rehearse and perform Jim's music.

The band was: John Hansen piano, Phil Sparks bass, John Bishop (of Origin Records) drums, Brad Allison, Jack Hallsey, and me on trumpets, Karen Halsey French Horn, Hans Teuber alto and soprano, John Goforth tenor and flute, Mike West tenor, Greg Metcalf baritone, Jeff Hay and Dave Bentley trombones.

The music was unique and had real orchestral aspects of lush, complex harmonies with lots of mixed meters and conducting. We had a chart on "Donna Lee" that had a lot of Bird thrown in through the band and a trumpet soli that was doable only with dedication and practice. Jim also leaned towards

251

some of the Lennie Tristano type line playing. Like starting the same line in several places and similar devices. We used to do one piece that was a Palindrome. It was a line that was the same forward as it was backward. We recorded with that first band, but there was still an unsettled feeling in the band regarding commitment levels and who blended well with one another musically and personally. That recording also had some problems in the studio with the musicians hearing each other.

After that recording, John Bishop decided to leave because he was getting so busy with Origin Records, his record company. At that point, I stepped in and strongly recommended Jon Wikan. Goforth was replaced by Rob Davis, and Hans Teuber was eventually replaced by Mark Taylor. Phil Sparks has been in and out of the band, and for a while, we had Chuck Bergeron, a recent New York transplant on bass. We had Chris Stover on bass bone. Eventually, Verne Sielert replaced Jack Halsey on trumpet. Those were the Golden Years of the band.

We played some festivals, Bumbershoot, Earshot, and played Patti Summers club, The Drum School, and Tula's Jazz club. It certainly was a labor of love and not a commercial enterprise. It made me very proud to be part of this band.

We did our second recording at Bear Creek Studio. Chuck, our bass player, got his friend, John Fedchock, to be on hand to monitor what was going down and be mission control to keep us on track. John Fedchock was an excellent choice for this role because John has tons of experience with big bands in New York. He is a wonderful arranger in his own right and only slightly less anal about the details than Jim.

We recorded over several days, and the studio was a great environment, located in Woodinville, Washington, in very rural surroundings. We could look out the windows and see cows and horses. The main room has nice high ceilings, is made of wood and is pleasing to the eye and has a natural warn but present sound. I don't usually listen to what I've recorded, but this one still makes me happy when I hear it.

I loved the Bear Creek album because I had lots of solo space and the pleasure of hearing voicing and musical phrases that were completely new! Believe me, when I say that does not happen often. For me, I loved playing Knapp's arrangements. Often the third trumpet would have the melody, sometimes with French horn or trombone or tenor. 1st and 2nd trumpet usually did parts together. Sometimes I would be on flugelhorn and in harmony or unison with voice. Jim split up the parts in interesting ways.

+++++

I played some of it for Scott Robinson, the baritone player with the Maria Schneider Orchestra. He completely flipped, and it really got his attention. Scott had come to town leading the backup band for Bobby Short. Scott is a complete monster bari player but was playing tenor on this gig. There is nothing that Scott does not play. He plays excellent clarinet, and there was a documentary on PBS about him where they talk about his contrabass sax, one of the few in the world. In the documentary, a rabbit is running around in the sax. I took Scott to Northwest Winds, run by a reclusive genius instrument repairman named Brad Wherry. I was fiddling with something, and I heard a beautiful cornet sound and brilliant jazz lines. I turned around and was shocked to see Scott playing one of the cornets off the wall. Probably not playable by me. The Civil War-era ancient funky mouthpiece did not stop Scott. Scott wanted to go to the Wind Flutes at Magnason Park. I live here and had never heard of them. We walked down to where they were on an icy, windy January day, and sure enough, these giant flutes stuck into the ground were making deep, resonant flute sounds from the gusts of wind off the water. The duck and geese probably dug it! Next, Scott wanted to look for old sci-fi paperback books, mainly for the vintage artwork that used to be on the 1950s and '60s book covers!

+++++

Going back to the recording at Bear Creek, another little side-show event concerns Chuck Bergeron, the bass player. Chuck was bringing a lot of players into Tula's Jazz Club.[111] Tula's is a club started by Mack Waldren, who ran bands in the Navy. Tula's is the one place in Seattle that featured jazz seven nights a week, and local players could have a stage. (*Sadly, closed in 2019*)

Mack is very friendly, but he is also a person that, as they say in nature, "has no natural enemies," Mack is a tough SOB. Anyway, one night, Chuck Bergeron and Mack were drinking after the bar was closed. Some macho stuff surfaced at one point, and Chuck was into some sort of strength game with bending your opponent's wrists. Chuck could probably "take" most of us. But he got into it with Mack. Chuck must have looked too serious for Mack. Without breaking much of a sweat, Mack broke Chuck's wrist.

We did the Knapp recording with Bergeron in a cast. I remember Buddy Catlett telling me once that the bands he worked with told him right away they liked the boom boom boom best, not the Bibbety bobbity boom that bass players can sometimes gravitate towards. Bergeron was forced to do the boom boom boom on this recording, and I laughed because I thought it was great! I'm sure he would disagree and probably have choice words for me! I had a lot of fun playing with Chuck. He is on my early CD, *Live at Tula's*, and I even ended up playing on a tune on one of his CDs.

+++++

Sorry for the side trip, now back to my narrative concerning the Jim Knapp Orchestra. The thing is, we were in the wrong city for making a big splash on the jazz scene. But it was a strong group with highly developed arranging of the first order. There is only one Jim Knapp. Jim has a theory book with his take on harmony, and many people smarter than I have embraced it.

Now, Jim is arranging for a string collective orchestra called Scrape. I went to one of their concerts, and it is unique and quite a revelation to hear. I know Seattle is known for Nirvana and Soundgarden and Pearl Jam, but the real artistic giant, Jim Knapp, has been a well-guarded secret.

Oh well, Van Gogh only sold one painting in his lifetime!

Jim's wit is formidable and shows up in his song titles; one of his titles is "Combos in Indiana". So dry it reminds me of the Zoot Sims quote, "You can really have a lot of fun with these musical instruments."

Also, at the time of the Knapp band, I was playing the Teatro ZinZanni show and was to do a second Japan tour.

CHAPTER FIFTY-EIGHT

Bud Shank, Centrum & Roy Hargrove

The Northwest is a wonderful area for people who love nature. It has a lot of the sophisticated qualities of big cities without dirt and traffic jams. At least it was way back in the late 90s and early 2000s when many people relocated to this area. One musician who moved up here was Bud Shank.[112] Bud was a jazz alto sax player from LA who was on many records in the late fifties and was also co-leader of the LA Four, a Quartet with Ray Brown. Bud had done very well for himself in Hollywood studio work and real estate investments. Bud moved to Port Townsend, a little town over on the Olympic peninsula. Bud took over the Centrum Jazz Camp[113] located at Fort Worden in Port Townsend. The camp was started earlier with help from Barney McClure, mayor of Port Townsend. Barney was the pianist who often worked at Parnell's and was sometimes part of Ernestine Anderson's rhythm section.

With Bud as director, the Jazz Camp/Festival grew by leaps and bounds. I used to play there with the Festival Big Band, and often at one of the clubs on the weekend. The clubs were not "jazz clubs" except at the end of the week-long camp when the town turned into one big jazz club featuring jazz at every restaurant and tavern. One year they brought Mel Lewis out with Dick Oats, lead alto, Kenny Werner, piano, and Dennis Irwin on bass. I played the second tenor chair on that band. It felt great to play with Mel propelling the band. And sitting next to Oats was fun.

Right after the *Rapture* CD came out, in addition to having the big band gig, I also had a club gig in town during the festival. The band I had was Vineet on guitar and John Hansen on piano, Phil Sparks on bass, and Jon Wikan on drums. We were still playing a lot of the arrangements and tunes from the *Rapture* album.

It was a strong group, and soon guys from Ray Brown's band and Roy Hargrove's band started to show up to sit in, Greg Hutchins and others. We were having a ball doing standards and some Dorham tunes, all kinds of stuff. Dan Marcus and Travis Ranney were sitting in as well.

+++++

I should say that I possessed a reasonably healthy ego at this time in my life and did not follow who was who in the jazz world. Since it changes so quickly, a lot of these guys were unfamiliar to me. I mispronounced some names, but everyone was happily chugging along, and, as I said, the music was powerful and swingin'. So, I was caught by surprise when, on one song, all of a sudden, people in the audience start to clap and cheer, and Roy Hargrove[114] marches out from the back of the stage, playing tonics and fifths on his horn as high as he could play.

I looked over and thought WTF??
All the other cats had asked to sit in, and of course, I said sure! No problem. Well, this was a different story. Dan Marcus then kind of set me up; he whispered in my ear, "I guess you won't be playing trumpet anymore tonight." I immediately said, "fuck that!" I'm almost like a chameleon where I

257

adapt to whatever surroundings I'm in. Roy was an interloper, and the adrenaline took over. Before Roy's antics, there had been such a nice feeling and balance, and all of a sudden, "my gig" had turned into the Roy Hargrove show. It then turned into one of the old westerns where the sheriff, a former bad boy, hung up his six-shooter. But of course, when the town starts to get shot up with intoxicated cowboys and usually, one, in particular, he has to take the six-shooter down once again to restore law and order. For me, it was a big deal, but for Roy, probably just one night out of thousands, quickly forgotten.

Anyway, I went after him. I talked real softly to him in a slightly high sweet voice. "Yeah, you sound beautiful man, I love your sound (pause); we used to sound that way in the '60s." I went into that "junkie mode" epic, insincere compliments while smiling, speaking softly, etc.

I called "But Not for Me" with Trane changes, and we went at it for a while on an assortment of tunes. Bobby Shew was there listening and drinking and gave me thumbs up. Doug Ramsey even mentioned it in a feature he was doing about Roy in *The Texas Monthly Magazine*. My dad was there with his recorder. The recording sounds ok, but music is not always better with adrenaline pumping away, contrary to popular belief. I heard a researcher talking about this effect in the athletic sports arena. What he said was that "over-arousal" is usually the undoing of the highest level of performance. Roy had been misbehaving that night, and it did not work well for him in many ways. It was exciting because that stuff does not always happen to me. Usually, we behave much better, but Roy on coke was just brazen.

I played with Roy again down at Tula's one afternoon, and it was completely different. We actually got on really well together. *(Roy just passed in 2018)*

CHAPTER FIFTY-NINE

University of Washington

In 2000, during my tour of Japan, I was just reeling over the election. First, I heard Gore won... then the next time I check, George Bush has won. Wow, I'm thinking to myself, what's going on with our country?

Then I get a call from Marc Seales at the University of Washington. Marc is a very good piano player and a friend since the Parnell days. Marc told me, my old trumpet teacher, Roy Cummings, who worked at the UW, died suddenly. Roy was a kingpin in the department and ran the jazz band.

At the University of Washington, the Studio Jazz Band (big band) met down in the basement. Up and down the stairs was quite a trek and sometimes difficult and tiring. Roy had a heart attack on the steps, and the papers he was carrying were still fluttering when he was already halfway to Valhalla!

Marc asked if I would agree to be the interim instructor while they searched for someone. These days all university jobs require a nationwide search. I said yes but let him know that I was from the "No-School" and asked if that would be a problem. He said they would overlook that and give me a special rating based on my experience.

259

The UW band was actually quite good. When I started, I noticed quite a draft at the rehearsals; it seemed like they were not thriving. After a couple of weeks, I said to someone, "get the door." No, it's not a Buddy Rich prelude! I had to talk to them and set them straight about what we were about. I said that Roy had been my teacher too and that I had been his friend, and in no way, shape or form was I happy about getting a job because of Roy's death. I said I was not concerned too much about what they thought of ME. I wanted them to know I really liked and cared for THEM and wanted with all my being for them to focus on the music and working together having fun while learning.

+++++

Teaching at the U of W was really an eye-opening experience about working in a bureaucracy. Roy had done so much that was off the radar. Roy did not always fill the school in on what he did for the program and how he kept it going with recruitment from the high school area. Roy knew of all the good young players and also had quite a thriving trumpet studio.

Unfortunately, I was only getting a fraction of the pay I would have had if I were officially hired for the job. No benefits like health insurance etc. No recognition of what the job actually entailed. I remember one of the administrators said, "we need to expand the job." If they had only known what Roy used to do in the background, they would have known it was already a lot more than met the eye.

+++++

I let the band recommend some of our charts, even though sometimes, to my chagrin, they chose stuff that I did not like. But I felt part of my job was to let them know the fluid nature of art and jazz; in other words, anything that we did not like we could change or delete. They chose Stan Kenton's Malaguena, for example. There was not much I liked about it, but we changed some figures, deleted some sections, and did a lot of things to it, and it turned out fine.

A big band is really an excellent way to get many kids learning to play jazz together. Obviously, there will be many different levels as far as the actual "jazz playing" is concerned.

+++++

Stuart MacDonald was in the band, and he sounded professional even as a very young guy. I had a solid lead trumpet player, Cesar Amaral, who had the range and endurance for just about anything I could throw at him. I got access to a room with stacks and cupboards full of charts and culled through for Thad Jones's stuff. Those are fun but challenging to play. My main objective with the band was getting the rhythm section to "feel" right. I was on the drummer a lot to find that magic spot where the tipping happens. This is challenging in a big band because a lot of times, just the volume and the size of the sound if you're not careful, becomes unwieldy and starts to pull back.

+++++

I did not interface very well with my fellow faculty members. Part of my background, the dope shooting past and the lack of formal schooling, made me feel like an outsider. To this day, I have no real idea how my year and a half at the school was perceived by others at the school and the community.

+++++

There were some bright lights. I had one young student in the UW program who was only 15 or 16 ... his name was Aaron Parks.

Aaron was a young whiz kid, an actual genius. Aaron was way ahead of the game and found himself at the university at a really young age. Aaron could just focus and devour entire styles of music systematically. Aaron went through phases where he would just learn all the Trane stuff, and then he would go into Art Blakey. etc. He had a prodigious ability to organize information and deal creatively with what he had just learned. Chops were not a problem either.

I got to see first-hand the jealousy that some of the kids had towards Aaron. I talked him into being in the big band, and he was amazing. But I had one of the future band director hardliners say to me, "he just does not play in the style." True, he did not sound much like Count Basie. On top of being a genius, he was nice and wanted to do his best for the whole band, so Aaron was not a problem. I also heard that because his parents got behind him, especially his mother, comments like, "Oh, his mother does everything." As if his mother was playing the piano.

They were such brainiacs, the whole family, and I became friends with them. They had an apartment right by a cineplex. I practically forced them to come to a Jackie Chan movie with me! My lesson was that many things are fun that does not have a ton of intellect involved.

Aaron's parents realized they needed to get Aaron to the jazz mecca, New York if he was going to really hit his stride (like Joey Alexander's parents). So, they moved to New York. Aaron went to the jam sessions at night, and just like Benny Green in earlier times, it was only a matter of time for Aaron to be heard. As a result of this exposure, he was hired by Terrance Blanchard, with who he remained for years.

I got a kick out of how the mouths suddenly stopped their gossipy, jealousy-driven, backbiting tone. Suddenly, it was, "we always knew how great he was," and so on. After glowing articles in Downbeat and Jazz Times, the city he hailed from quickly took possession of him and vicariously benefited from his success.

+++++

While I was working at the University of Washington, I turned 50. All of a sudden, I had inklings that maybe I was not a "kid" anymore, and the old refrain of my mortality reared its head and in an added way. I had seen an old friend recently in this period, a guy named Bob Woll. Bob was a gifted musician I first met at the Reno Stage Band clinics, also known as the Stan Kenton camps. Bob played accordion, he was very good, but everyone said, "dude, you gotta move to the piano."

At an early age, Bob worked all the time with Lee Wuthenow, who now is a respected player in Portland. Bob and I were close for years growing up. Bob had seen the light and cleaned up before the rest of us. Bob no longer was chasing the dream and had gone into church music. Bob had given up the clubs and gigging in bands.

Back to my story, Bob said to me, "how are you feeling?" when we met after years. I thought what an odd thing to say. Then he explained to me that he had Hep C. DAA Da-Dat DAA (theme from Dragnet!) After the flat five chord had exploded in my mind, I asked him how he found out. He said he was tested, and it came up positive. It turns out they were not screening for Hep C when I got clean. I checked for AIDS immediately because the addict community was really impacted by that disease. I had a clean bill of health! Well, to make a long story short, I checked with Group Health, and they had not done a test for Hep C. I scheduled an appointment, went in, gave a blood sample, and waited for the results. Sure enough, it came back positive for Hep C.

I knew when Bob said he had it that I MUST have it, because as bad as Bob's past was, mine was worse. So, now I'm 50 with a ticking time bomb on top of my own mortality to contend with.

I had already been thinking about this on one of my trips to Japan. I'm lying in my hotel room there thinking how fast the

50 years have gone, especially the last 20 years, and wondered what I would be doing twenty years from then. Then I thought of my dad in the next room and wondered what he was thinking about at 70 years of age! I had not reached the stage of evolution yet where I could clearly see the only way out of this dilemma is to just live to the fullest and stay in the present!

More on the Hep C later.

+++++

Going into 2000 was undoubtedly a heady time for America. I could see it among my friends as well. I had two friends who were constantly day trading on stocks and doing quite well.

I remember 2000 New Year's Eve, the going rate for musicians was $1000 a man. Usually, New Year's Eve is double the money we are accustomed to earning. Becca and I and Vineet and Bob Nixon had a job at the Four Seasons in Seattle, and we got some very long green for this gig thanks to Becca, who negotiated the contract.

As soon as we got into January and Bush got in, watch out, everybody in the tech stocks got hosed. The following year it was hard even to get any NY Eve gig! As it is today.

+++++

I continued to teach and rehearse bands at the UW and SSCC, and I had a plethora of gigs, side-man recordings, and other projects. Kohama called me for another tour. He also needed a bass trombone player, so I brought Dave Marriot to Japan with me. Dave is an exceptionally talented trombone player who has an innate ability to play fast and generate bebop lines. He is also an accomplished arranger. Dave and I went to Japan, and we started playing gigs as a sextet and in the big band.

We did a recording. The recording had a producer who was into what he thought was a vintage recording style, so we were not close to the microphones. There was no overdubbing or fixing either, and in the age of midi and pro tools, that's kind of silly.

The recording showed problems that were persistent issues in the band that had not yet been solved. But we had a ball nonetheless, and it was cool to bring Dave to Japan.

Dave and his brother, Thomas, came through the Garfield program in Seattle. Garfield is the top inner-city school located in the heart of the Central District. This area used to be mostly black before recent gentrification. At this point in time, there was a busing program that brought kids from other districts into Garfield. It was also a school that had a fast-track program that brought in many gifted students. There was a core of about 260 high achieving and scholastically superior students that went to Garfield. Plus, it had a history of Quincy Jones and other famous musicians who went to Garfield. The director, Clarence Acox, was from New Orleans and was recruited because of his charisma and association with an award-winning marching band out of New Orleans. Clarence was also a drummer.

Dave and Thomas Marriott (trombone and trumpet) had the good fortune to be enabled by a very influential dad. (kind of like me.)

Dave Marriot Sr. was a very socially minded person who could solve problems and get people to work together. Dave was a facilitator and a mover and a shaker. Dave Sr. and his wife, Helen, organized the Band Parents of Garfield; this really kicked their program into high gear. They organized fundraisers and activities that were the blueprint for how other schools do it now.

Once, I played a gig with Sonando at the Bellevue Jazz Festival. After my gig, I walked to my car and heard Roy Cummings' All-City High School big band performing. A young trumpet player took a solo, and he quoted Harry "Sweets" Edison with a great sound and a long string of quarter notes!

I went up to the back of the stand, got his attention, and gave him the high five. That was Dave's brother, Thomas, on trumpet. Thomas and Dave were part of the outstanding young musicians I had early on in my big band at SSCC. Dave is an accomplished arranger and educator. Thomas went on to win the Carmine Caruso competition and is now a very successful musician, recording and performing extensively.

CHAPTER SIXTY

Garfield

One day, I received a call from Clarence Acox about Garfield Band III. Garfield is a well-oiled jazz machine or was back then. Garfield is still a contender but not as much when, in its heyday, it had a feeder program out of Washington Middle School. The band director at Washington Middle School was an ex-military African American band director named Bob Knatt. Bob basically ran a jazz boot camp for his middle school kids. Quite often, Bob's bands would be better than all the High School bands in competitions. I heard them once, and they had a couple of trumpet soloists that came out and played transcriptions they had done themselves and knew by heart. What a great foundation. They also swung like crazy. Bob was a very tough nut, and he once told me, "I talk to them in a language they can understand." In other words, failure was not an option. And, if they did not do the work, they were out-a-there! Some kids could not hang, and there were crying and various dramas, but for many who stuck it out and thrived, they will always hold Bob close to their hearts. Mr.Knatt cared for the kids and prepared many for the lives they chose.

Even though Bob was not from a jazz background, he had checked out the classic jazz bands and players and figured out right away how to teach it. So, when these kids went up the hill to Garfield, they were already quite good and already far along the jazz trail.

Clarence taught bands I and II, and those bands met during regular school hours. As an aside, many school band programs have to meet at the crack of dawn before school! Anyway, the Garfield program was flourishing, and they did not want to turn kids away, so they had a band III that met after school. I was contacted and asked if I was interested in running the after-school band. Well, "of course" was my answer. So, for two days a week, I met with band III after school at Garfield. The first year there were so many kids that I also had a band IV with just four altos and a rhythm section. When I worked with them, my priority was getting it to "feel good." That meant straightening out the time feel in the rhythm section and getting the kids to subdivide and play phrases with the right time feel and articulation. It seemed to work, and we usually scored at the top in competitions.

I had a long run at the school; it was a good ten years. It was fun to see the "bright lights kids," that had the same awakening to jazz as I did, travel through the bands, and later go on to careers in music. At the end of my tenure at Garfield, it got to be a little too much to handle when I had too many kids that could not play and had behavior issues. Before, I had kids in band III at a level where they could have played in Band I. They were my "allies" within the band. The culture and level dropped after Mr. Knatt retired from Washington Middle School, and the school zoning changed at the same time. Now Garfield had to split many of the "advanced track" kids with other schools. In the heyday, there were approximately 260 advanced kids at Garfield. It is no coincidence that many of these same kids made up the core of the award-winning jazz bands Garfield fielded over the years.

The last few years were different. I did not get any help from within the band, and at that point, my skills at "controlling" the kids became the issue. I don't have the skills for dealing with kids with behavior problems. So, even though I enjoyed aspects of the teaching, it was also quite a relief to have that time to myself. These days I'm spending a lot more time practicing and playing for my personal development.

I make a joke out of it. I got out of there safe. I didn't hit anyone or French kiss anyone either! (but, I might have said a bad word or two.)

Sometimes I do miss the bus rides back from a festival when they "won." The excitement and optimism of youth are intoxicating.

CHAPTER SIXTY-ONE

CUG in Seattle

After a few tours in Japan, I had the idea of bringing the CUG big band to Seattle. I first approached John Gilbreath at Earshot. In the fall, Earshot has a jazz festival that runs for three weeks, where many bands play in venues all over the city. John has an adventurous and forward-thinking policy that brings stars and lesser-known jazz groups from the US and other countries to Seattle during the festival. John was immediately on board with CUG.

This was the start of eight months of work and planning to pull this off. I enlisted the help of Becca, my wife, and we worked our way through a myriad of details. There was the issue of getting visas for everyone and getting permission from the International Musician's Union. There was also the problem of transportation and housing when they arrived. I think that Kohama had some help financially from the City of Nagoya.

One of the things that we needed was a letter from our mayor to show the government officials in Nagoya that this was a real deal and important. The immediate problem was how to get the mayor to write a letter. After some thought about it, the idea came to me of calling Dave Marriott Sr. As I said earlier, Dave Marriott was a real power broker in Seattle. Dave said, "Just write the letter, and I'll have the mayor sign it." Boom, that was done! So now it was the part of the modern music biz that is somewhat painful. That is, trying to find jobs and ones that pay. I contacted many of my friends who were schoolteachers and got a few gigs lined up at High Schools and Universities.

On September 11, right before the Japanese were to come over, Becca woke me up and said, "we're being attacked." We watched with the rest of America as the Twin Towers burned and then fell to the ground.

The band was scheduled to come in October, and, of course, September 11th is when the tragedy struck. Kohama called me and asked if it was safe to come. I hesitated only a minute and said, "yes, come," thinking in the back of my mind as the rest of us in America, "Fuck those motherfuckers, we will not be frail and frightened."

Many of the CUG band members felt the same way, but everyone respected those that bailed after 9/11. So, I had to get local guys to fill in some chairs.

Dan Marcus played trombone, Greg Shroeder played bass bone and Dave Marriott, who had already been to Japan, played bone. Travis Ranney played tenor, and part of the time, Galen Green played tenor. So, we did have a multicultural experience. It was fun at the first rehearsal to see the U.S. musicians perk up when they started to play Shuhei's arrangements. It was strong, modern writing.

+++++

People were impressed with the band's energy and spirit, and we had standing ovations on almost every gig. That usually never happens in Seattle. We did a chart of Ornette Coleman's *Happy House* that featured a lot of free improvisations, and people just went nuts over it.

271

The band stayed at the very funky University Motel. It was inexpensive, so they rented suites. They were happily cooking and having quite an adventure.

I got us one gig East of the mountains, and when coming back, one of the van's brakes went out. Tsutomu, the lead trumpet player, drove the van, with a braking problem, all the way back to Seattle, over Snoqualmie Pass at night in the fall!

We played on Vashon Island, and we also had a couple of early morning school gigs. There is always drama in a situation like this. Two of the bone players forgot their mouthpieces! Luckily Brad Wherry's shop, NW Winds, supplied several New York Bach mouthpieces. Also, one of the trumpet players showed up with no horn. I borrowed a horn from my Dad. Once again, we have a strange combination of "wrapped real tight" and "loose as a goose" when it comes to the Japanese musicians!

+++++

Kohama has quite a support network in Japan, and three women who played with his sax group, the *Sax Friends*, came and helped sell CDs and were part of the adventure. Also, a photographer named Jinsan chronicled the whole trip in pictures. The little Roadie, *Take* was also on hand. Before we played at Tula's, *Take* danced in front of Tula's, he said it was the dance he made up for Seattle. He is the person that earlier dropped his drawers at the big dinner party in Japan.

At another gig, the band was roaring through a super-fast Thad Jones' chart called *Fingers* when the band stopped on a dime and sang Happy Birthday to me. Pretty cool.

The spirit of the band and the group consciousness is what makes CUG such a force. Instead of an ordinary big band, with many separate little islands of consciousness, CUG is in it all together. When they play, it truly is all for one and one for all. That, and their familiarity on a personal level with jazz and jazz's history, also makes the band special. They know all the classic records intimately. I would say more so than many musicians in the US. Later, this became a real inspiration when I started filling in the blanks in my jazz knowledge.

Shuhei, the piano player/ arranger, is a fine player who can go in many directions. He can go into McCoy influenced things with pentatonic shifts through key centers like nobody's business. But he also has a great fondness for Bud Powell. One day I heard Shuhei play a blistering version of Shaw Nuff in octaves as a sort of warm-up. The thought came to me immediately, "self, why don't we know this?"

When I got back to Seattle, I got busy and started transcribing more bop, including Shaw Nuff.

CHAPTER SIXTY-TWO

More Recordings and Learning Directions

The transcribing got me deep into the bop idiom once again. I put a band together with Rob Davis, a fantastic tenor player with the idea of playing bebop heads. We played these heads with no reading; we taught ourselves the old-fashioned way, by ear and memory.

This group ended up with a live recording, *Boy, What a Night.*

Every situation has a lot of signposts for what to do to keep the music moving. I know Coltrane talked about going back at the same time as he was blazing a trail forward. He once said, "I'm all the way back to Sidney Bechet."

In this period, I also realized that I needed to clean up some other weaknesses like playing fast and being comfortable in *I've Got Rhythm* changes. In today's world, part of the *I've Got Rhythm* changes problem is young players, and the not-so-young players play too much in a style that is outlining too many of the changes. People paint themselves into a Sonny Stitt corner. And accompanists usually play too many changes. "*I've Got Rhythm*" changes can be way more fun and looser if we get into the folk element of jazz, "Second Balcony Jump," for instance!

I had come from a background where I played a lot more modern stuff, Boogaloo and Dolphin Dance, various Wayne Shorter tunes, etc. So, going back and trying to find myself in some of these more traditional jazz backdrops has been a challenge. Going back started by checking out some different approaches and designing my own program to increase my technique and rhythmic understanding. We did a quartet CD, *Live at Tula's, Volume II*, with Jon Wikan, John Hansen, Paul Gabrielson, and me. It was again recorded live by Jim Wilke and was a real learning experience. I think one of the things we tried to do was "Inner Urge" by Joe Henderson in 7/4. I have loved the tune "Inner Urge" and liked playing it and had learned it in 1968 from the recording.

I thought; this should be no problem. Wow! I came to the realization I could not even play "Come to Jesus" in 7/4. So, I started down the road to becoming fluent in other time signatures other than 4 and 3. I had to break it down and approach it as a total beginner. I know a lot of great cats ask me, why? Many feel that playing in 7/4 has nothing to do with what they want to do in jazz. I respect that, but I like the challenge. One thing that playing in another time signature does is to get me out of the rut of playing all the familiar "pets."

Going way back to the '60s, I had learned a tune by Eddie Harris in 7/4, "1974 Blues". But we played slower over a groove that made it possible for me to shuck and jive my way thru it better. Eddie had the 7/4 like a little clave with a bap bap on the 6 and 7, so you could think of it as a syncopated measure of 4 followed by a measure in three with "one bap bap." It is one of the tunes we recorded for *Live at Tula's*.

Are we having fun yet? Ok, enough of this and back to the story.

CHAPTER SIXTY-THREE

SRJO and the "Old Timers"

A round this time (I'm a little out of order in my story here), I became a founding member of SRJO, a band that started in 1995 and is still going strong. SRJO stands for Seattle Repertory Jazz Orchestra.[115] The band's mission is to play classic Ellington and Basie and other famous bands of that era for audiences in the Northwest. They also bring national Jazz Stars to Seattle to play with the band. The band was started by Garfield jazz band director Clarence Acox and University of Washington saxophone teacher Michael Brockman. Clarence and Michael used their organizing skills to build the band and, with their board of directors, developed the SRJO into a serious organization on every level. The band started in 1995 and had some venerable old-timers in the band; Don Lanphere, Bill Ramsay, Floyd Standifer, Buddy Catlett, and Hadley Caliman.

+++++

Don Lanphere[116] was a saxophonist who spent time in New York way back in the early fifties. He had the good fortune of

276

being a last-minute replacement for Allen Eager, who did not show up for a Fats Navarro recording date. Lanphere at that time was living the high life that a lot of young white beboppers had adopted, opiate addiction being one aspect and heavy drinking also a standby. Don also had the distinction of being with Chan before Charlie Parker stole her from him! I loved hearing his stories from that period. Don played with virtually all the big bands and was active on the New York scene.

Don hailed from Wenatchee, Washington, a very scenic little town in the mountains, where his father had the music store. Don returned to the NW and, after some struggle, got clean and found Jesus. Don was a relentless self-promoter capitalizing on his New York bebop history and his prodigal son story. He created a lot of opportunities for himself and his band that way. Don surfaced in Washington State again in the late '60s, early seventies. Don was writing contrafacts on standards and playing them along with Abersold play-a-longs! He also mentored a young trumpet player named John Pugh. Lanphere was also fond of playing super-fast.   Later Don became the go-to teacher for young sax players in the Seattle area. Mark Taylor and Travis Ranney both got their start with Don.

Don tried to "bring me to Jesus" one time when I was younger. My dad was a founding member of the Magnolia Rehearsal Big Band, and once, when I was sitting in at a rehearsal, Don was also on the band. Before I went to the rehearsal, someone gave me some powder that was supposed to be coke, and it had been cut with angel dust. Or, as they call it in Washington DC, "Hinkley." I should have known better; it stung my nose like hell, not something coke would do. Anyway, the angel dust made my eyes cross; it also interfered with my perception of balance, making it difficult to read music. It also made it difficult for me to seriously consider Lanphere's pitch to me. Lanphere was telling me about the "Jesus High" while I was trying to ride out the angel dust high that was sucking up all my CPU, and I had no time for Don's pitch.

There is a funny story about the Woody Herman band taking a detour on one of their tours. The piano player and straw boss, Nat Pierce, said they were going to stop off in Wenatchee to see an old friend! The band had been riding for a while, and I imagine they were eagerly awaiting the stop, maybe score some grass have a little party; whatever.

So, the bus pulls into Wenatchee, and Nat Pierce calls Lanphere. Lanphere shows up, and Nat asks if he has been gigging. Don, with a beatific smile on his face, says, "yes." Nat says, "who with?" and Don replies, "Jesus." Nat yells, "Hey guys, back on the bus!"
Red Kelly, bass player, and wit said it succinctly, "the trouble with being born again ... is you always come back as yourself."

Don did a lot of nice things for me. I later recorded with him. But he always had a way of getting to me also. When I recorded with him, there was a great chart by Knapp on "Love for Sale"; it was right in my wheelhouse for hard bop, funky, etc. After playing it at the rehearsal, he took that away! He had me playing two things with Jay Clayton; one was soloing on "I Remember Clifford" and another playing background obligato. Well, it probably made me a better person.

Due to health reasons, Don turned me onto a gig up in Anchorage, Alaska, that he used to do. It paid well and was part of the festival they have each spring called Jazz Week at the University of Alaska. Also, I finally got on the teaching faculty at Centrum Band camp run by Bud Shank. Lanphere, saddled with increasing health issues, mentioned my name.

As much as he used to drive me crazy, I loved the guy, and he was one of my big supporters. He did a lot of really nice things for people. One story I like is about when Charlie Rouse passed. Rouse had met a lady in Portland, Oregon, and she and Charlie were happy together until he got cancer and passed while in Seattle. Don and Bud Young from Buds Jazz

Records were giving Charlie support at the end. After Charlie died, he was to be buried in Portland, but the cost of having him transported was astronomical. Don and Bud decided they would just drive Charlie to Portland. They put Charlie in the back seat, put his favorite hat on him, and drove him down to Portland. I love those guys for doing that. Like many people with a background in intravenous drug use, Don had a silent killer running in the background, Hep C. Don's liver was shot, and unfortunately, he was not a good candidate for a transplant. Credit should go to Michael and Clarence; they kept Don on the SRJO almost to the very end.

+++++

SRJO also featured Bill Ramsay[117] on baritone. I have mentioned Bill before in this narrative. Bill was the guy who brought the old school wit and humor to performances and anchored the band with one of the best bari sounds I have ever heard. You can listen to Bill's bari sound on some Basie recordings on YouTube. Bill was also a mainstay of the Grover Mitchell band based in New York. Bill had quite a commute from Fife, Washington to New York City.

+++++

The other old-timer was my old teacher, Floyd Standifer.[118] Floyd, off of Quincy's band, brought more depth and credibility as a real jazz improviser to the band. SRJO is not only a big band that sounds good, but what makes SRJO special is the excellent local jazz players that Seattle is proud to have and support. It is a band of personalities, and in the case of the old-timers, local legends. In our area, the High School bands that rehearse every day and have some talented players can be incredibly good, but we have the improvising "old guys!"

+++++

Buddy Catlett[119], I also have mentioned previously. I loved Buddy. We both were getting into recovery at about the same time, and we played many gigs together. Greg Williamson of Pony Boy Records, Buddy, and myself did a trio recording titled, *Here Comes Buddy*. Buddy was a repository of good cheer and common sense. Many younger players, including myself, availed themselves of Buddy's wisdom. I did an Art of Jazz concert with Buddy in 1997, and Buddy sounded sooo good. That Wilke recording was lost for many years but will be a new CD titled, *Upside* (2020)

+++++

The other old-timer was Hadley Caliman.[120]Hadley was a sax player originally from LA, and he had been through it all. I had an album of his way back in the vinyl days, and Hadley sounded great. He had one song on the album called *Kicking on the Inside*. He wrote it for his pregnant wife, but it had a double meaning because he wrote it when he was in San Quentin. Hadley really paid the price but came out the other side a strong, beautiful cat. Hadley had so many stories. He told me of being in the LA County jail when they brought in Miles and Art Blakey. I guess this was back before Miles had his throat injury, and, in those days, he did not have the macho commanding presence, and they played a prank on him involving a big mean-looking dude!

When I lived in the Bay area, Hadley was at the top of the heap along with Manny Boyd. Hadley would often work in bands with trumpeter Dr. Eddie Henderson. Hadley became a NW fixture when he was hired at Cornish School of Music to teach saxophone. Hadley was a great teacher, and many players became good from studying with him.

Hadley also played with SRJO until the end; he played with cancer, and I loved the fact that he was still on the band performing up to the very end. There is a funny story of an SRJO concert with Hadley playing the role of Paul Gonsalves on "Diminuendo in Blue". Gonsalves had re-energized the Ellington band with a famous recording where he took chorus after chorus, each one funkier until the crowd was going completely wild. Well, SRJO was going to play that chart at the next concert, but, at the rehearsals, Hadley kept coming in early. Finally, Mike told him, "Hadley, don't come in until I signal you, no matter what." Well, at the concert, Mike forgets to signal, or signals were crossed, and the clarinets come in on the next section, and there never was a Tenor solo!

When Hadley was at the end of his life, Galen Green, a fantastic young tenor player, was seeing Hadley and saying goodbye. Hadley said, "well, we should practice," and they played exercise # 4 out of the Taffanell flute book on their saxes. That is a great exercise, by the way. It goes thru all the keys, major and minor, and goes all the way to high B on the sax, which is higher than the standard range from most books. The last time I saw Hadley was about a week before he died. Travis Ranney, who, in addition to being one of the best sax players around, is also a great repairman. I was at his shop and just leaving when a big Cadillac pulled up, and a very puffy, swollen Hadley got out. Travis quickly ran over to help Hadley. Hadley had brought his horn in to get it repaired. This was only a week or two before the end. He is a hero to me. One last story of Hadley concerns his memorial. At Hadley's memorial, his horn was on display. The mouthpiece on the horn was loaned to Hadley by my friend Stuart MacDonald. Stuart looked over at this mouthpiece wistfully. I have not checked with Stuart about this. But I love the story, and this book is all about stories.

Bill (Rams) is still around (but retired from the band), but we lost Hadley, Floyd, Buddy, and Don.

Now after 25 years in the band, I'm an "old-timer." Hmmmm.... Yes, I think I am the oldest member now.

CHAPTER SIXTY-FOUR

Centrum Jazz Week, Bud Shank and Conti Condoli

A t age 50, in 1999, I discovered I had Hep C. Very depressing, but other areas in my life were going pretty well.

One positive was the Port Townsend Jazz Camp, where I took over for Don Lanphere. Don had a class for beginning applicants that had them playing along with Jamey Abersold play-a-longs.

I had been vocal in the jazz community about what I thought about the Abersold aids. I once said that it was like making love to a blow-up doll; it would never kiss you back or something to that effect. We are in a hazardous environment now for a statement like that. If some kid decided that they had been "damaged" by that horrible statement, jobs could easily be lost.

Don't get me wrong, for people that can already play, some Abersold play-a-longs work well. One can play in time and learn tunes or brush up on songs seldom played. But for a methodology, I think there are better approaches. They asked me, "Do you have anything against using those tools?" Of course, I wanted to get on, so I said, "no." But in the back of my mind, I had other plans. It turns out I never had to use

Abersold material. I had beginning combos but had fun with them, and they would get better after a week of the Jay boot camp. Time, time, time, and simple vocabulary.

+++++

I was teaching and playing at the camp, maybe my second or third year, when saxophonist Bill Perkins, who was also teaching there, had to suddenly return to LA because his grandson had been shot and killed.

Bud Shank was planning on recording his band, Silver Storm, at the end of the camp the following week. The other members of the band were Conte Condoli[121], who was one of my childhood idols, my friend, pianist Bill Mays, Bob Magnusson on bass, and Joe La Barbara, from the Bill Evans trio fame, on drums. I was asked to come to a rehearsal on tenor. I fit in nicely, so I played the show on the festival main stage with that band with just one rehearsal. And the following week, I stayed in Port Townsend to record with that band.

The music was fun and called for reading and blending and all the skills I had accumulated over a lifetime, but the real treat was the band members. Getting to know Conte was special. Conte told me stories, and we had a ton of laughs. He was a very funny guy. One time he said to me, "you sound like," and then he pretended like he was really racking his brains; "you sound like," he repeated after a pause, "You sound like you!"

He was fucking with me. I laughed.

During the recording, we recorded a Benny Carter song that goes all over the place called "Summer Serenade". Conte was not happy with his solo and said to me in a quiet voice, "Man, I wish I could play that one again." We were using Pro Tools, and even though these guys were all super session men, they had not been doing many recordings since Pro Tools showed up. I said to Conte, "you can." So, I suggested we back up to before Conte's solo and let Conte cut another one, which they could float in later. That way, it was not overdubbing, which most jazz people hate. It was just an insert for later.

I was pushing the limits with Bud! Later on, in the session with Bud, several other occasions came up with editing options. However, Bud was pretty set in his ways, and finally, at one point, he said to me, "shut the fuck up!" That was a pretty common phrase with Bud! Both Conte and I cracked up after he said that. Perhaps not the response Bud was expecting.

Conte always left his trumpet on the stand, out of the case, and that way, it always beckoned him. So, he would pick it up, on and off pretty much all the time, or so he told me. When he was a kid, he said his father worked in the steel mills, and his mother said to him once, don't knock it; it's a good job, and it enabled your father to provide and raise you kids, etc. His dad overheard this exchange and vehemently said he did not want his boys working in a steel mill. It was very hard, back-breaking labor.

Conte's brother, Pete, was older and already a star trumpeter on big bands and was endorsed by instrument companies and was given horns for his endorsements. Pete gave Conte one of those trumpets, and Conte said he was so proud of that trumpet but said he could not play it very well at first.

Even so, Conte became a prodigy on the trumpet and was on recordings while still in his teens. My dad turned me on to a Woody Herman recording where Conti played a great solo on the tune, "Put That Ring on My Finger". He was just 16. Conte told the story when, years later, he and Pete were on the Stan Kenton band, and his elderly parents were in LA visiting. At that time, a young Maynard Ferguson was in the band. After checking the band out, Conte's dad was a little worried-looking and said in a small voice, referring to Maynard, "He might be able to play higher than Pete!" Immediately his mother piped up, "bullshit."

We did some gigs that summer after the recording, and it was a fun association. Later that year, I started treatment for Hep C. In those days, it was only Interferon, and they added another drug called Ribavirin. This little cocktail kicked my ass and made me crabbier than usual. I have been having a hard time keeping track of this period, but I know exactly what I did from that reference point while taking this treatment.

When I become friends with Conte, he told me he also had Hep C. Anyway, shortly after that, Conte said to some people back in LA on a gig one night, "I'm not feeling so good," or something to that effect. Conte went in for tests, and he had cancer that was far along; he died within a short time. I'm not sure, but he might not have even returned home from the hospital. I do know it was very quick.

In the movie Mulholland Drive, the iconic film from 2001, there is a scene where out of the blue, Conte Condoli comes out from behind a curtain and plays a note on his trumpet. Conte was not only a monster player but also film friendly. There is a great little episode of Adventures in Paradise with Conte. Adventures in Paradise was a familiar theme in the Sixties. In this case, instead of a couple of guys driving along Route 66 and helping a damsel in distress, it was a big sailing ship that sailed into a strange port every week. The boat and crew would find themselves caught up in some problem for the handsome captain to solve before literally sailing off in the sunset.

In one episode, a jazz band is stranded in Borneo. It has great footage of Conte Condoli, Richie Kamuca, Pete Jolly, and Shelly Manne playing. You can get a sense that the whole "West Coast" thing was mislabeling for many musicians. Some East Coast writers mistakenly had labeled West Coast Jazz as somehow not as hardcore or swingin' or funky as East Coast Jazz. West Coast jazz, of course, did have some surfer covers. But Hampton Hawes, Conte Condoli and Roger Kellaway, and countless others lived in LA because of the work and the weather and did not have a coast-attached label. I know Bud Shank was particularly incensed over this labeling. When we did the Germany tour, the band was labeled *West Coast Jazz All-Stars*, and Bud hated that.

Bud contacted me to replace Conte on a tour in Europe. It was to be very short, a few concerts in Germany, and ending in Amsterdam. Becca came along, and it could have been more fun, but unfortunately, this was during the time I had started my treatments for Hep C. The Hep C treatment was kicking my ass and making me very cranky.

The band was: Bud Shank - alto saxophone, Plas Johnson[122] - tenor saxophone, Jay Thomas - trumpet, tenor saxophone, flugelhorn, Pete Jolly – piano, Chuck Berghofer – bass, Joe LaBarbera - drums

(*There is a 1½ hour video on YouTube; West Coast All-Stars Internationale Jazzwoche Burghausen, Wackerhalle, Germany, April 18th, 1001) I'm not particularly happy with my playing, but at least I started and stopped in the right places*!)

CHAPTER SIXTY-FIVE

Cruise Ship Musicians

Today, many musicians have gigs on cruise ships. Places like Vegas and similar sources of gigs have dried up, but for those musicians who are adaptable and can play, cruise ship gigs are a way to play your instrument and get paid. Even though the pay is low, it is possible to live for free and spend little money on the ship.

During this same period, when I was doing the Hep C treatment, I got a call to do a repositioning cruise. That is a short cruise where they put the boat on a different route. Since it was short-term, I said yes. I think it was for three weeks. The ship had been plying the waters from Seattle to Alaska during the summer and was going to reposition to the Caribbean.

I was going to play baritone in the cruise ship big band. There were also a couple of other opportunities to play, a jazz night like a jam session. I knew the band leader, Shane Trout, a drummer from Seattle. Shane was pals with Jon Wikan and had graduated from Central Washington University.

287

I went down to NW Winds and got a Bari from Brad. It was a great sounding horn and went like a Son of a Gun. I borrowed some Berg Larsen mouthpieces, and I was in business!

These ships are gigantic, virtually floating cities. One of the things about this cruise was, I had a passenger status. That was good for meals etc. What I did not realize was I had a roommate in a tiny cabin. That immediately put me in a funk. The guy I roomed with was a good player but a little bit of a right-wing Christian. He was a nice guy, but I had to steer clear of Politics and Religion.

I had been spending a lot of time trying to get deeper into the flute. I took a couple of lessons from Rick Brightstein, an excellent flute player and teacher, so I started practicing. My roommate, Tony Rondalone, was a particularly good flute player. So, we played some duets, and he talked about how he had learned a lot of Rampal's stuff just the way we do Charlie Parker. He learned by copying and listening carefully. Rampal was a famous French flute player. Rampal was the James Galway of the previous generation.

The boat was so big I could walk and quickly put in miles. I was trying to stay on top of the Hep C treatment. It was interesting; I got off in the ports, did some tourist things, and played the big band show every night. I remember taking a swim in Acapulco and doing body surfing. However, we were going into hurricane weather, and the waves were so big that one deposited me on my head in the sand. A good way to break one's neck, I suppose. One of the things I hated about the ship was the constant announcement about events taking place. We could not get it turned off in our cabin. I would be relaxing, and suddenly, I would get an urgent announcement for skeet shooting out on deck five!

We sailed thru the Panama Canal, and the next thing, we were in the Caribbean. We went to Columbia and saw the old stuff in the harbor, etc. Then we were in Puerto Rico. We caught a plane from there to Newark, and then home to Seattle. When we were in Newark, they informed us that the plane was overbooked. They asked for volunteers to take the next flight, which was about an hour or an hour and a half later. The perk was we would get a free ticket anywhere in the U.S. or Caribbean. I immediately said, "yes." Tony Rondalone said, "no way, I wanna get back as soon as possible." He was always very impatient. I waited for a little over an hour for the next plane. When I arrived in Seattle, Tony was still at the airport, all hot and bothered because his bags were on my aircraft. He had to wait anyway, with no bonus at the end of the tunnel!

For those with self-discipline, a cruise ship can be financially attractive, but many fall into despair and start drinking. The grind of playing music where the goal of making gray-haired, retired people happy is not that rewarding.

CHAPTER SIXTY-SIX

Wenatchee Teaching

About this time, I got hooked up for a gig with Joe LaBarbera, Bruce Paulson, and Tom Petersen. Tom and Bruce were LA musicians who were successful in studios and various big bands etc. Bruce played on the Tonight Show band for 17 years. Joe, I knew from Port Townsend and the Bud Shank band. We used Kristen Korb on bass. Kristen was briefly heading up the Central University jazz program. We were hired to go to Wenatchee and help kids learn jazz. It paid well, so I decided to bow out of a recording James Knapp was currently doing. Sometimes money is the most important! The Hep C treatment made me really crabby, and I'm glad I warned everyone about my possible symptoms.

The money spent on this program probably could have been used better, getting these kids better instruments and private lessons. The next thing would have been to work with the directors and teachers. That is where it all starts. If the directors are clueless, it does not bode well for student jazz programs.

Tom and Bruce were funny guys and played music together as friends going back to middle school in Minnesota. It was fun to get to know and play with them. For a minute, I thought maybe LA would be the right place for me. Then I thought, maybe I'm fine where I am. But it felt good when they told me they thought I would do well in LA. I like the Northwest fine, plus the only place these days that is a real launching pad for jazz would be New York.

We were doing clinics and working with bands nonstop for five days straight. One day the Central Washington University band came and performed in a rehearsal setting, and we were asked to make comments. They sounded so good we all had reservations about saying anything critical. No comments were forthcoming from the instructors; I hesitated for about a second, then dove into the fray. I realize that there is no situation so great that can't be made better; unfortunately, it goes the other way too! They did one song with close harmonies throughout the band that reminded me of a Brookmeyer or Gil Evans' arrangement. From hanging with Chuck Israels, I knew about bass amps. Chuck was adamant that the bass could put a real damper on how the acoustic instruments sounded if the amp is too present. Too much amplified bass acts like a blanket or sort of white noise, and even some old-timers are unaware of this phenomenon. So, I had the bass player turn his amp way down and told him he had to pull the strings hard. I told him that as an experiment, I wanted space between the notes.

I told the drummer that he had to line up with the bass player, so his attack notes were identical and, on the forward side of the beat. I also told the drummer to feather the bass drum. Ray Brown once drew a line on the floor and said, "Now get up to the line and lean forward over the line without falling; that is where the swing is."

Then I turned to the band and asked them to play again, softly. They started, and I immediately stopped them and said, "half that volume." I had to do this several times, and their sound started to go from good to "magic." Unfortunately, most bands gravitate to a much more testosterone-driven sound left to their own devices and bad habits. Trumpets wanna play high if they can; saxes want fast, intricate solis, drummers like it loud, and bass players turn amps up, so essentially, there is not one moment of space. There is always a blanket over everything.

I sometimes say, "space makes Jay play, (pause for effect), and I don't mean space as the final frontier... I mean the absence of sound." From a practical standpoint, what that means is when there is no pitch or sound, you can play anything! The imagination comes into play more readily. Rhythm sections must realize that. This is especially true for piano players when comping.

I once saw Terence Blanchard play at the Earshot Jazz Festival when a young Aaron Parks was also on the band. They played their material and delivered a strong set. Then, for an encore, they just called a standard, as I remember it was, "I Thought About You". Of course, we know there are many ways to play the changes. And an infinite amount when you get into re-harmonizing and substitutions. Anyway, the band started, and there were real suspense and tension along with the beauty of the playing. There was so much space, and they were collectively re-harmonizing the song in real-time on the spot. For that to happen, everyone had to be open and not assume what would be played. To just play "correct" changes or licks was not going to work in this situation. For the musicians in the room, this was a real lesson in open playing. There was so much space, but energy also. The audience knew something special had happened and went wild with their response. What had happened was music on a tightrope with no net underneath. Music performed this way with masters can be so exciting. Of course, Miles' bands were at the forefront of that kind of playing 35 years earlier.

Concerning Wenatchee, I felt sorry for these kids trying to play jazz with inadequate instruments needing repair and trying to play material that they did not have the technical skill to tackle. Another negative was students were being taught by band directors that did not have a good idea of what makes a big band swing or feel good *in the time.* I used to do more adjudicating. Often, I could get the lay of the land in one phrase. If they did not have a swing feel based on the basic polyrhythm of one against three or were not in the triplet, I would just check that box and did not need to go much further.

CHAPTER SIXTY-SEVEN

CUG Recording

I remember events clearly at this time because of the effect the Hep C treatment was having on me. CUG was scheduled to do another CD, and they hired Paul Wycliff from New York as the engineer. Paul was the engineer for the Jim Knapp recording at Bear Creek. Kohama was also using my friend and engineer, Masa Fukudome from Triad Studios in Bellevue. Triad is where I recorded with Cedar on the *Easy Does It* CD. Masa was having visa problems, so he was in Japan. Masa and Paul also served as the "outsiders" who acted as quasi producers so that no bad tuning and slop was allowed. Kohama, to his credit, wanted this to happen.

At first, Kohama had sounded me to get Dick Oats to play lead alto. Dick would have been a great choice, but when considering the cost and the many travel details, and the fact that I don't know him that well, I said, "why not Mark Taylor?" In New York, Mark had studied from Dick and had substituted several times for Dick on the Monday Night Vanguard Orchestra. Kohama agreed with that idea.

The studio was within sight of Mt. Fuji and was the most beautiful studio I had ever seen. It was a large space, and everywhere you looked was beautiful woodwork. Immediately Paul got into it with the studio over the piano tuning. The piano was not up to Paul's standards. We also had a situation where I had an extra guy on my part. The guy was a relatively weak player, but he had to be involved because he did many things for the band. (this has all changed, and now CUG is tip top and no dead weight in any section).

Also, the drum chair was from the original band, and while he had a good set of hands, he refused to take any suggestions from me. I wanted less cymbals and more drum-drum and even some feathering of the bass drum ala Higgins and virtually everyone I dug on drums. Tain, all the cats, do it, but it is subtle, and for some reason, many drummers hate to do that. And he would not set up figures. Because of the lack of grounded drum-drum, it most often sped up rather than steady and swingin'. I used to say, "instead of the rub-a-dub dub that is the full groove...It would be Rub-a-dub and a half dub!"

Personally, even though I was also kind of weak from the treatments, I managed to hang in there. After that recording, CUG was way more consistent with tuning and blending. Now the band is completely changed. We have an excellent bone section headed up by a player from Sapporo, Hiro Sakemoto. The saxes are very good all through the section. The trumpets are great. Yoshiro Okazaki is a fine player who plays with Makoto Ozone's band, and Miiki Hirose was added to the trumpet section. Miiki used to play around New York for many years and played with Tatum Greenblatt, a Seattleite who has made quite a name in New York. Tatum and Miiki both played on George G's swing band together in New York. We still have Tsutomu Watanabe on lead trumpet. Tsutomu is a fantastic, strong player and has no limit to his range and endurance.

At the end of that tour and recording, we did our annual springtime gig at the little Kabuki theater in Osu, a shopping area in Nagoya with miles of covered shopping stalls. Crowds of shoppers and the smell from food-stands are everywhere. At the Osu gig, Kohama had many volunteers, literally herding people into the theater. Bullhorns were announcing the gig, bringing it to the people. The audience was a wide-eyed group, people of all ages. Some band members are real comedians, and for that gig, we played special music the people liked. Some Disney stuff, sometimes a high note thing like Maynard's theme from Rocky, as well as our arrangements. I love that theater. It is very musty and old, and there might have been a cat that made it his or her home. It's a real part of Japan that is off the grid for most foreigners. Mark and Paul were both all smiles and shiny faced after this gig. It was a magic zone, and we had slipped into a unique space where current events held no sway whatsoever.

Kind of an oasis in a time where normal, everyday problems do not intrude.

CHAPTER SIXTY-EIGHT

East-West Alliance and More About Japan

On one of my Japan tours, I went to Sapporo with Kohama and Daisuke. After a few gigs in Sapporo, I had a gig in Tokyo with Akira Mori, an alto player who had spent a lot of time in New York and had played with the Machito band. Akira also recorded with Michael Brecker and others on the last Charlie Mingus album. He's also a 49er! Born the same year as me.

After the trip to Sapporo and back in Tokyo, I met alto player Atsushi Ikeda once again. This time Atsushi was very friendly and completely different than the icy, scary guy I met at Swing a few years earlier. I asked Atsushi why he had changed so much. He said, "Kohama changed my life."

The sextet gigs with Atsushi turned out to be great. It was a frontline of Kohama and Atsushi and me; Goh Shimada on bass, Daisuke Kurata on drums, and either Kogi Goto or Shuhei Mizuno on piano.

A little about Goh Shimada. Goh is a very strong bass player with a beat and attack reminiscent of Paul Chambers or even Wilbur Ware. His sound is organic and woody; he knows a ton of tunes, can thump with the best and has some modern odd time signature gears so that he can do a lot of stuff. I met and played with Goh when I first contacted Ko-hama earlier. When the C.U.G. Big Band was in Seattle, I made sure he met Buddy Catlett. I took Goh to the New Orle-ans restaurant where Buddy was playing. Goh had big eyes for Buddy. Goh had done his homework and knew exactly who Buddy was. Goh also played that evening, and Buddy said, "OP !!" Meaning Oscar Pettiford. It was a love fest that night.

Anyway, that first tour we played with Kohama, Atsushi and me as a front line was great fun, and we had a special bond and chemistry. When we played, the music went more profound than just notes into actually the meaning of the word "humanity." This group became the basis for the East/West Jazz Alliance.

Atsushi had a funky place in Tokyo where I stayed on a fu-ton in his studio upstairs. I was looking around the room and noticed little music manuscript books. I looked in them, and they were filled with transcriptions—Trane, Bird Sonny Rol-lins, etc.

This new musical configuration soon became one of the primary groups I play with when I am in Japan. Later, I brought them to Seattle for an Earshot Jazz Festival. I ap-proached John Gilbreath about having the band play in Seat-tle, and he was amenable to the idea. Earshot is a festival that tries to focus on more contemporary and lesser-known groups and is always bringing bands from other parts of the world.

The band made quite a splash starting with a high-profile gig at City Hall with various dignitaries on hand. They vide-otaped us and used multiple cameras, so it was a rare musical experience preserved in time. Usually, they are gone into thin air after the performance, but these videos are still on YouTube.

Atsushi has chops to spare and musically traverses territory reminiscent of Lee Konitz, Jackie McLean, and Charlie Parker. But he also has his original take on jazz, and that is pure Atsushi. Atsushi has been at the top of the scene for several years. He comes from Tokyo, where his mother is a famous Haiku poet. Atsushi is a true artist, and I call him the "soul" of the band.

When the band came to Seattle, we used Phil Sparks on bass and John Hansen on piano. It was equal parts West and equal parts East. Even though a little more East considering that Phil is Japanese and African American. Phil is like many with that background in that he speaks no Nihongo. You would think that would be a big problem in the band, but not so. The Japanese are well educated, and one of their schools' requirements is that they study English. Though they often can read and write better than they speak. I have found that if I say something in English but pronounce it the way they would, they usually understand better.

Their language is very consistent in pronunciation; in Romanji, which is anglicized Japanese.

 I is always pronounced ee

E is always like eh.... A is always Ah

O is always like the letter name O .... U is always OO etc.

So, if I want to say "sorry" so they would understand, I say "soery."

When they came to Seattle, we recorded a CD at Triad Studios, the same studio I recorded *Easy Does It* with CedarWalton. Jim Knapp gave us some charts, and some arrangements were from the band as well. Atsushi wrote a tune that had a Latin straight eights Latin feel, and it was untitled. At the same time, we were thinking of recording George Cables tune "I Told You So" arranged by Jim Knapp. My dad Marvin said, "I like that one better," referring to the Atsushi tune I just mentioned. The title became "Marvin Likes It," and we recorded it.

One of the things different about the Japanese musicians is their ability or, dare I say it, "need" to reach a consensus. One other thing is, when we play gigs in Japan, we hang at the club for a long time after the gig. The club will often supply little pizzas and pasta and various snacks and sometimes out and out feasts. I started to see there was a very firm but unwritten code of mutual obligations in that society. One is, you don't cut and run after the gig. For the club, the responsibility is hospitality to musicians doing everything humanly possible to provide the best music and presentation possible.

One time we played a gig at *Body and Soul* in the Roppongi district of Tokyo. After the gig, we were going to travel by car to Nigata, about six hours north thru the Japanese Alps, where they had the winter Olympics one year. So, not only was it a long drive at night, but it was through snow and mountainous regions. Well, I was hoping, in this case, we would be packing and out of the club shortly after the last note! No such luck. We dinked around and had little snacks and hung out for at least an hour and a half. It was close to midnight when we got on the road. We drove for about three hours and were in the middle of the journey, and there was snow everywhere, and it was freezing. All of a sudden, Kohama said, "I'm hungry."

We looked out the window, and there are some lights in a field, and it looks like a brightly lit restaurant. Sure enough, it was a Ramen place run by young people with various shades of bright-colored hair. The Ramen was delicious. Then Kohama says, "let's take a bath." So, we took off to a close-by Onsen or hot spring.

We parked, went inside, disrobed, got a locker for clothes and shoes, grabbed some slippers, and went to the bathing area. First, you sit on these little plastic stools. There are many small stations. You have a hose where you can control water pressure and heat. They have shaving utensils and many different body and hair soaps and conditioners. So, the deal is, you get squeaky clean, then you hit the various hot tubs of natural spring water.

And you soak. We ended outside under the stars in freezing weather in a very hot pool of water. After soaking, we went to an area where there were mats and a little fence around each station. When we cashed out in the morning, only a total cost of $15. It was an experience I will always remember.

I was having a hard time with the Japanese term for left and right. Right is Migi, and left is Hidari, so I finally got it by the Hi part of the word for left, Hidari. I use a mnemonic device to remember, "he hangs to the left," referring, of course, to the fact that every tailor asks, "do you hang to the left or right?" me, left. I was so proud of myself, and I communicated this to Daisuke, pronounced dice-kay. Anyway, Daisuke said, "I hang right; I'm left-handed." He showed me when we were sitting in the pool outside in the boiling mineral spring water out under the stars surrounded by snow.

I asked myself, "how did I get here?"

CHAPTER SIXTY-NINE

Elvin and Steve

Some of my favorite people in Seattle are from other parts of the country or even other countries. Seattle has many perks, including the natural beauty of the mountains and lakes and Puget Sound. The weather is relatively mild and temperate, with long summers. Seattle also has many companies such as Microsoft, Starbucks, and Amazon that got their start here. Seattle has been a hub of innovation in the tech world for a while now. So, I can safely say Seattle is not hurting for creative, brainy people!

One such brainy individual, who I have been friends with for 25 years now, is Steve Griggs, saxophone player, and all-around creative entrepreneurial cat! I first met Steve at a Jim Knapp rehearsal back in the mid-nineties. Steve was playing tenor. Steve's main ax is tenor, but he plays soprano and alto and flute as well. Steve lived in New York, and it turns out he was only a block away from where Milo Peterson resided in New York. In addition to being a creative musician, Steve was also involved in a tech company based in Seattle called Immunex

In the 90s, Steve, Milo Petersen, Phil Sparks, and I played in different venues around Seattle. Then in 1998, Steve wrote music for a recording session with legendary drummer Elvin Jones. In the pantheon of jazz Elvin has earned a sacred spot. Elvin was the engine that propelled the John Coltrane Quartet. Elvin's drumming is deep and primordial. Elvin and Art Blakey are both in this exalted category. They both have the most direct ancestral African drum connection all the way to the highly urban present-day of modern American jazz.

I think Elvin had played a gig at the Jazz Alley, and then he recorded with us. The recording was done at Bear Creek Studios in a scenic rural enclave of Seattle called Woodinville. We recorded for four or five days. Steve had catered food brought in, and because the sun was shining and it was warm, we would sit out on the porch in the sun on a break with Elvin and chat about everything. Elvin was friendly and loved to talk and tell stories. I asked him about Jimmy Garrison, for instance. He said, "I didn't know he was so sick. He came by and borrowed a hundred dollars from me right before he died."

As I talked to Elvin, it turns out we had a love of Science Fiction in common! Elvin loved the Berzerker sci-fi books. The *Berserker* stories (published as novels and short stories) depict the fight between Berserkers and the sentient species of the Milky Way Galaxy. *Homo sapiens* (referred to as "Earth-descended" or "ED" humans, or as "Solarians") is the only sentient species aggressive enough to counter Berserker.

During the recording, we quickly adapted to Elvin. Steve had written certain things for the drums, but if Elvin played it differently several times, hey, let's go with Elvin! It was thrilling to be playing and recognize things Elvin would play that we remembered from records like *A Love Supreme* or Wayne Shorter's "JuJu".

We recorded with earphones, all in the same room. At one point in the recording, I took off my earphones to hear what it sounded like in the room. Oh my god, he was strong and loud! There were crosscurrents and poly-rhythms in his playing, and it was pure ecstasy and a little overwhelming. I quickly put my phones back on. His playing was a force of nature, like a volcano or hurricane. Like those forces of nature, they were also a little dangerous; one could get sucked into the vortex. He could also turn way down and play brushes on a ballad with tenderness and grace. I will never forget that week. We recorded enough for two albums, and they were titled: *"Jones for Elvin Vol I "and "Jones for Elvin, Vol II."*

Lately, Steve has been getting performance and composition grants for various projects connected to socially relevant causes. Steve composed music related to a historical site in Seattle and was inspired by the novel *"On the Corner of Bitter And Sweet."* The story was about a love affair between a young Chinese boy and a Japanese girl. The site was the Panama Hotel in Old Nihon Machi or Japan Town, now called the Chinatown International District but, in the old days, called just, Chinatown. The music had scenes in mind relating to the Internment Camps, where the Japanese American Citizens were sent during WWII. The hotel has a glass floor in the coffee room where you can look down into the basement and see all the baggage left by the Japanese Americans who were whisked off to camps. It was a compelling and moving mixed media experience. We had many people from that period come to the performances. From my standpoint, the music was jazz, and we got to play together. We did that for two years.

Thanks to Steve, we did several other projects also. One for an African American sculptor. Another was for legendary saxophonist Joe Brazil, from Detroit who relocated to Seattle called *Cup of Joe*. We also did a very moving tribute to an Indian Totem Pole carver named John T. Williams, who was shot by a policeman. This music highlighted the plight of Indians and shone a light on the careless use of lethal force by police in today's world.

CHAPTER SEVENTY

Cantaloupes and the Ship Canal Grill

After getting my head handed to me on more than one occasion in Japan regarding bebop and playing fast and many other things, I upped the level of my transcribing and remedial bebop study. When I first started playing, it was not a bebop scene, so I did not get deep into it. Now I'm slowly working my way backward in time and trying to keep going forward, listening, and developing new stuff. I do a lot of transcribing songs I want to play. I have always been a doubting Thomas, and that dovetails with my research into songs I like. I will listen to different versions. If it is a standard, I will listen to various jazz renditions. I will also go to the vocal performances that were the original tracks that people heard. Often the vocal cuts will have very accurate melodies. I'm continually learning new stuff by delving into the music. I like transcribing the songs and changes by ear, and occasionally I'll peel a solo as well. Music is great because there is no end to learning.

I started putting together afternoon sessions with bassist Chuck Kistler. Chuck quit music for years but was getting started again in a big way. Chuck has a gifted ear. Chuck can do copies of Bob Mintzer charts by just listening to one note at a time. He hears the whole chord and horn voicings up and down and writes them out without a piano.

Chuck was after it in a big way. He had a practice schedule in his studio, where he had his daily practice sessions with various tasks for 8 hours a day! Chuck is also a bebop nut, and we started getting together once a week. John Hansen was on board, and we added a young drummer, Adam Kessler. It soon became a workshop, and we would figure out our arrangements on standards and originals.

This band got a few gigs, including one at SAM, AKA the Seattle Art Museum, where we recorded a CD specializing in Boogaloo. Our direction was what I affectionately refer to as "junkie music," Jackie McLean and Freddie Redd at the top of that category. I always loved the album *Shades of Red* by Freddie Redd that featured Jackie and Tina Brooks and Philly Joe and Paul Chambers, an all-junkie band. I also loved to play boogaloo music, but slightly changed. We did the standard tunes, but with altered chords and other time signatures, so it became Neo-Boogaloo. Boogaloo is a combination of Latin and Soul jazz and songs like; "Gregory is Here", "Jody Grind", and "We're Right in There". I wrote an arrangement on Cantaloupe Island with mixed meters and added different changes.

+++++

Around this time, my old friend Norma Leith called me. Norma was Marty Tuttle's "ex." Marty is the son of the foremost jazz trombonist in Seattle, Dave Tuttle. Marty played drums in the Playboys Swing band long ago. Norma was part-owner in a restaurant club that was near to my house, called the Ship Canal Grill. I got a gig there with the same band we were rehearsing with at Kistler's. It was a Wednesday night gig, not a lot of money, but it was super fun because we opened it up for a jam session after our first set. It made us all feel good. It hooked us individually to other opportunities to play, which is how these things work sometimes.

My old friend and former student, trumpeter Mike Van Bebber, and Dan Marcus bone player started showing also. Those guys are more well employed than me and were doing it for the fun and love. Those sessions were great because the quality was at a high level, and we got a lot of young high school and college players from Roosevelt, Garfield, and Cornish. The two big jazz high schools in Seattle are Roosevelt and Garfield. They are so good it's sick! Many of their soloists are already top-flight pro-level players while still in high school. Cornish College of the Arts has some good young players as well. We had a lot of fun moments down there. Also, young players studying in New York would come in when they were home for Christmas or during the summer. Alas, after a year and a half, it stopped. I really miss that scene.

During that time, after we added Marcus and VanBebber, we started putting together a cool sextet book. I named the band the Cantaloupes because of the three songs we played with Cantaloupes in the title. At first, I thought that was an awful and bizarre name, but now it seems normal.

I had and still have a great time with that band.

CHAPTER SEVENTY-ONE

Willie and Oliver and the "Newnet"

At the same time I did the recording for Willie's book, I also played in a band recording Oliver Groenewald's charts. Oliver had been doing post-graduate work from Germany with Chuck Israels. Chuck is an excellent arranger, and Oliver became a teaching assistant at the school when he studied under Chuck. I played at Oliver's graduation recital also. When Oliver first got to Bellingham, he shared a house with Willie Thomas. Ollie ended up marrying Willie's daughter, Wendy. After graduation, Ollie returned to Germany and taught at a university for many years. Ollie arranged music for European and US classical and jazz groups, including a Mark Murphy project. He was an integral part of the German jazz scene, and he became close with ex-pat Art Farmer.

In 2013 Ollie returned to the Northwest to live on Orcas Island, located in the San Juan Islands. At that time, Ollie and I reconnected. We got to talking, and it turned out he wanted me to round up some musicians to play some of his music. I called lead trumpeter Brad Allison, my old cohort from the

Ramsay/ Kleeb days, and Dan Marcus trombone and Travis Ranney tenor. At that time, I had a band with a regular Wednesday gig /jam session at the Ship Canal Grill, and I used that rhythm section. John Hansen, piano, Adam Kessler, drums, and Chuck Kistler, bass. Alex Dugdale was our first Bari player, but he had schedule conflicts, so it ended up with Pete Galio on Bari.

The first rehearsal was a revelation. The music was unique, and like Jim Knapp's music, it was breaking some new ground. I heard voicings for the horns that I had never encountered before. That does not happen often. An essential factor in forming any band is chemistry when we are all in a room and learning together. We had a deep rapport that included lots of laughter and a willingness to buckle down and learn the material and take direction from Oliver.

I love the fact that I get to play alto, flute, and soprano sax in the band. Playing 1st alto in a larger ensemble is particularly fun because it occasionally allows me to play the lead in the ensemble. In contrast, on trumpet, the lead part is not in my wheelhouse.

Ollie wrote a feature for me on "You Don't Know What Love Is", and I thought it was beautiful, fun, and challenging. This got me thinking of a more ambitious project featuring the various horns I play backed by Ollie's orchestrations. I approached Ollie with my idea, and we collaborated on material for over a year. Ollie and I have a ball hanging out, and we laugh easily together, so it was a fun project to put together. Most of the selections were songs I had learned from recordings, and Ollie had a few originals as well. After Christmas in January of 2018, we went into a studio and recorded for two days. The CD is on the Origin label and had radio play across the US and Europe. I play trumpet/flugelhorn on five tunes, tenor on four, alto on two, and soprano on one, so it is a good showcase for what I do.

These days it's not about making money from CD's so much as having a presence, and it is still a good calling card and helps with name recognition. Whenever I do something creative, it is its own reward, just the doing of it. In today's world, making a CD is a career investment that pays off over time. The CD is called *I Always Knew* from a song Ollie wrote. We changed the song title because before, it had a German name that translated to Nude. However, in German, the concept of naked or vulnerable sounded great, but it was hard to come up with a suitable English translation.

I find it interesting that, through jazz music, I am best friends with a musician from Germany and several musicians from Japan. I am a baby boomer, and the US had just finished fighting with Japan and Germany when I was born.

Hooray for jazz, and peace and love is all I can say to that!

CHAPTER SEVENTY-TWO

Wrapping This Up

I'm now in Japan for the 44th time playing with my friends here, and I am looking forward to the upcoming recording session.

The band CUG has changed over the years, with some new blood and quite a few younger members.

In addition to the recording, we will do a gig at the biggest Noh theater in Japan, located in Nagoya across the street from the Warlord Castle. That castle was originally built in the first Shoguns reign and rebuilt after the war. The Nagoya Castle was also the site of my first gig in Japan back in 1986.

I admire the group spirit in Japan. Can it hurt that the bonds are tightly wound with mutual respect and myriads of responsibilities? I'm starting to become one of the "guys," and they are now giving me little tasks. Last night they gave me a stack of fliers to hand out everywhere I go. It goes against my nature, but I have fallen under their spell and guess I will do it for the common good. I am 69 years old as I write this and feel truly fortunate that jazz is kind to age. There are still many great older players going all the way up to Roy Haynes, who just hit 94 and still plays great. James Moody is another example of an older jazz musician who never stopped developing. He never gave up practicing and trying to better himself. There is a story about James Moody doing a concert with some young jazz saxophonists. The story goes that the young cats were playing in a mainstream style reminiscent of the 1950s. Moody, on the other hand, came out with all kinds of new sounds. Moody asked the young cats, "what are you doing?"

Jimmy Heath is in his 90's and can still play great. Pablo Casals, who many consider the greatest cello player ever, was once interviewed way into his 90's. When Pablo mentioned his practice schedule, the interviewer was incredulous and asked him why he would practice so many hours a day? Pablo replied, "it's working."

My dad is 90 and has a big band where they play Basie as well as other stuff. His guitar player retired at 97. Ha, I should double-check that.

Back in Japan, I love the mentoring process here. Yuki Hirate and many of the younger guys start as general helpers and subs. As their skill set rises, they slowly become full-fledged members of the group. The other thing I find refreshing here is that just having musical skills is not the whole picture. There is also the idea of being an artist and what that might mean. What you are trying to do and why you are playing is as important as just the II V I nuts and bolts of the craft.

CHAPTER SEVENTY-THREE

CENTRUM, July 2019

I'm getting ready to head to Port Townsend, along with a contingent of Japanese students to attend the camp. It's getting to be a "thing" now. Enough students have come to Centrum from Japan that it is gaining momentum since many former students are doing well as working jazz musicians in Japan.

At the end of the camp, I'm doing a gig at Tula's with Matt Wilson[123] and Gary Smulyan[124] and the great George Cables[125] on piano and young bassist, and Buddy Catlett protege, Michael Glynn.

I first met George one afternoon in 1968 at Slugs Saloon, a former jazz club on the lower east side of Manhattan. Slugs is infamous because Lee Morgan met his untimely end there at the hands of his common-law wife. Many are familiar with the recent movie, "I Called Him Morgan," about the life and tragic death of Lee Morgan. I got to Slug's a little early on a sunny summer afternoon and waited around for the musicians to arrive. The first couple of guys had tubas. (It was almost like the joke about the bass players who were hired by Joe Ventuti to all show up on one street corner in Hollywood.)

314

Eventually, there were four tubas!! And an excellent rhythm section composed of George Cables on piano, plus bass and drums. It turns out it was no joke because when they started playing, it was four-part writing covering an incredible range. It was Howard Johnson's tuba band.

A little over a decade later, I got to work with George at Parnell's right after his CD, *Cable Vision* was released. *Cable Vision* got a lot of play and put George on the map as a composer. One catchy tune has become a standard called "I Told You So". Later, in 1989, I recorded with George on a Chuck Metcalf record called *Elsie Street*. I always love seeing George; besides being one of the greats, he is warm and just lights up a room.

I first became aware of Matt Wilson after seeing a New York performance with a great band that included Joel Frahm, Andrew D'Angelo, and Yosuke Inoue. They were playing adventurous music that was also humorous and had theater and showbiz thrown in. On a tune called, Schoolyard Bully they wore little tin foil helmets, and in some parts of the song, they shouted in unison and got to act menacing and leap about on stage! The band was able to carry it off because of their credentials as serious players. Not that anybody needs credentials to be creative and entertaining. Later, I met Matt at a jazz camp and have had the pleasure of performing with him many times.

Gary Smulyan is a complete character and bebop brother and fellow Kenny Dorham fanatic. I say this because on one of our first encounters, the tune, "Straight Ahead" was called. Straight Ahead is a "Rhythm" tune always played in A flat with a modified bridge section ala "Eternal Triangle". As the piano player was soloing, Gary and I started to sing Kenny's solo in unison from the recording. Gary is deep.

The thing I always tell young players is, "play with people better than you." This gig at Tula's is me taking my own advice! Regarding taking my own advice, I have to say that it is a rare occurrence. Many times, when things go left, I ask my-self why didn't I follow my advice?

It is a constant task and desire to stay up to my fellow trav-elers' ever-increasing demands and expectations. I am not sure what place jazz will have in society in the future, but I know for a fact it has been the primary vehicle for my life. Jazz will not solve the world's ills but is a celebration of some-thing fleeting and hard to grasp and beautiful. Being a musi-cian can be its reward above and beyond the obvious need to figure out how to survive and still do what we want and need to do. To some, music and the arts are irrelevant. I can see their point; if they are starving, a cheese sandwich is worth more than a Picasso painting. But, by being completely di-vorced from the usual tit-for-tat world of "important things," I actually see it as the most important thing, with a double emphasis on most. For me, jazz has more to do with the "soul" of being alive and finding meaning in existence.

Now, my biggest issue today is finding a reed or two, warming up my flute and brass chops, and memorizing a song I will be play-ing soon.

Jay Thomas
Seattle 2019

Ps. The gig at Tula's with George, Gary, Matt, and Michael went great.

The club was Sold Out!

The next day I recorded with Matt Wilson and friends. CD out soon. Watch for: **High Crimes and Misdemeanors.**

APPENDIX

---

[1] **Rolf Thorstein Smedvig** (September 23, 1952 – April 27, 2015) was an American classical trumpeter. He was the founder of the Empire Brass Quintet. He is renowned for his velvet pure tone and accurate intonation."

[2] **Fletch Wiley** graduated from Shoreline High School; in (1964-1966) played with The Dynamics in Seattle as a trumpet player. He studied music at the University of North Texas at Denton, where he obtained his Bachelor of Music and at Yale. For more than 30 years he worked as a Grammy Award Winner, composer, arranger, producer and instrumentalist in the United States.

[3] **Ralph Mutchler** in 1960 became the conductor and director of the wind orchestras at the Olympic College in Bremerton. He was also a teacher at the Stan Kenton Jazz Camps and from 1960 to 1975 he organized the Olympic College Jazz Festivals every year.

[4] **Floyd Standifer** (1929- 2007) American jazz musician (trumpet , saxophone vocals),and music educator. Studied at the University of Washington. Was part of a circle of musicians including Quincy Jones, Ray Charles, Ernestine Anderson and Buddy Catlett. In 1959, Standifer became a member of the Quincy Jones Big Band, which toured Europe for nine months. After returning to Seattle. he taught at Cornish College of the Arts , the University of Washington, Olympic College, Bremerton, and Northwest School. In addition, he was a member of the Seattle Repertory Jazz Orchestra. The city of Seattle honored Standifer in 1996 and 2000 with a Floyd Standifer Day.

[5] **Freddie Greenwell** (1924-1994) Sax Virtuoso
Greenwell, who died at 70 of diabetes, in a career spanning half a century had played with Benny Goodman, Woody Herman, Buddy Morrow, Artie Shaw and many others. Jazz historian Paul de Barros, calls Mr. Greenwell "among the top 10 musicians to come out of the area."

317

⁶ **William Orval Crow** (born December 27, 1927) an American jazz bassist. In 1950, Crow moved to New York City. Within two years of starting to play the double bass. He was part of Gerry Mulligan's groups as a bassist during the 1950s and 1960s. He wrote two books, *Jazz Anecdotes* and his autobiography, *From Birdland to Broadway*.

⁷ **Hampton Barnett Hawes Jr.** pianist (1928-1977) By his teens Hawes was playing with leading jazz musicians Dexter Gordon, Wardell Gray, Art Pepper and Shorty Rogers. At 19, he was playing with the Howard McGhee Quintet with Charlie Parker. Hawes was arrested on heroin charges on his 30th birthday and sentenced to ten years in a federal prison hospital. After serving three years, in 1961 Hawes was pardoned in the final year of Kennedy's presidency. After his release from prison, Hawes resumed playing and recording.

⁸ Saxophonist **Ulysses "Jabo" Ward** was a highly revered and beloved figure on the Northwest jazz scene for over 60 years. He was a central figure in Seattle's legendary Jackson Street music scene. Mr. Ward's music never sounded dated because he had a rare ability to play the most modern of jazz styles while retaining his Kansas City blues roots.

⁹ Another coffeehouse, The **Queequeg**, was set up from the start with entertainment in mind. it had a sizeable stage, not just a riser.

¹⁰ The **Llahngaelhyn** a legendary coffee house that hosted jazz from 1965 to 1968. Mr. Heldman was the proprietor and also a performer. The Llahngaelhyn was known for all-night jam sessions, where touring musicians such as pianists McCoy Tyner and Chick Corea and saxophonist Roland Kirk dropped by, and local players such as David Friesen, Larry Coryell, Jay Thomas, Carlos Ward and Ralph Towner cut their teeth.

¹¹ **The Penthouse** was a jazz club in Seattle, most remembered for John Coltrane's performance there in September 1965. The Penthouse opened in 1962 in Seattle's Pioneer Square, founded by Charlie Puzzo. Over the next seven years, Puzzo presented such artists as Miles Davis, Bill Evans, The Montgomery Brothers, Stan Getz, Anita O'Day, Bill Cosby, Little Richard and Aretha Franklin. The Penthouse closed in 1968.

¹² **Mike Mandel**, US keyboardist Mike Mandel grew up in rural Yakama, Washington less than 50 miles from his childhood friend Larry Coryell. They formed the band the Checkers in 1960. Mandel joined The Eleventh House in 1974 lending a funky, synthesizer-driven style to many tracks. Mandel recorded in the late 1970s with some of the hottest musicians in New York. He is currently music director to the Ellen DeGeneris show.

¹³ **Larry Coryell** 1943-2017) was an American jazz guitarist known as the "Godfather of Fusion". In 1965, Coryell replaced guitarist Gábor Szabó

in Chico Hamilton's quintet. In 1967–68, he recorded with Gary Burton. During the mid-1960s he played with the Free Spirits, his first recorded band. His music during the late-1960s and early-1970s combined rock, jazz, and Eastern music.

[14]**Joseph Brazil** (1927- 2008) Co-founded the Black Music curriculum at the University of Washington and founded the Black Academy of Music in Seattle. He taught at the University of Washington from 1969 to 1976 but was denied tenure. He appeared on the albums Om by John Coltrane and Ubiquity by Roy Ayers.

[15] **Leonard Geoffrey Feather** (1914- 1994) was a British-born jazz pianist, composer, and producer who was best known for his music journalism and other writing. Feather was born in London, but settled in New York City in 1939, where he lived until moving to Los Angeles in 1960. Feather was co-editor of Metronome magazine and served as chief jazz critic for the Wall Street Journal and Los Angeles Times.

[16] **DownBeat** is an American magazine devoted to "jazz, blues and beyond", The publication was established in 1934 in Chicago, Illinois. Down Beat publishes results of annual surveys in a variety of categories. The Down Beat Jazz Hall of Fame includes winners from both the readers' and critics' poll. DownBeat was named Jazz Publication of the Year in 2016 and 2017 by the Jazz Journalists Association

[17] **Milton Mesirow** (1899-1972), better known as Mezz Mezzrow, was an American jazz clarinetist and saxophonist from Chicago, Illinois. He organized and financed historic recording sessions with Sidney Bechet. He briefly acted as manager for Louis Armstrong. Mezzrow is equally well remembered as a colorful character, as portrayed in his autobiography, Really the Blues.

[18] **Berklee College of Music**, located in Boston, Massachusetts, United States, is the largest independent college of contemporary music in the world. Known for the study of jazz and modern American music, it also offers college-level courses in a wide range of contemporary and historic styles.

[19] **David Berger** (born March 30, 1949) is an American jazz composer, arranger, conductor, bandleader, educator, author, and trumpet player. A leading authority on the music of Duke Ellington and Billy Strayhorn), having transcribed more than 500 complete scores by them. Between 1988 and 1994, Berger served as the conductor and arranger for the Lincoln Center Jazz Orchestra. Berger conducts his big band, the Sultans of Swing.

[20] **A Love Supreme** is an album by American jazz saxophonist John Coltrane. He recorded it in one session on December 9, 1964, at Van Gelder Studio in Englewood Cliffs, New Jersey, leading a quartet featuring pi-

anist McCoy Tyner, bassist Jimmy Garrison, and drummer Elvin Jones. A Love Supreme was released by Impulse! Records in January 1965. It was one of Coltrane's bestselling albums and some critics consider it his masterpiece, as well as one of the greatest albums ever recorded.

[21] **THE JIMMY HANNA BAND** was formed in 1965 after Jimmy Hanna left as vocalist of The Dynamics. They were active from 1965-68. The band performed a mix of R&B, jazz and rock styles, in a unique big band configuration. They performed solo and backed touring groups of the 60's, and their music had roots in James Brown's Band and Bobby Blue Bland's Band.

[22] **Motown Records** is an American record label originally founded by Berry Gordy Jr. as Tamla Records in 1959 and was incorporated as Motown Record Corporation on April 14, 1960. Motown played an important role in the racial integration of popular music as an African American-owned label that achieved significant cross-over success in the 1960s.

[23] **Jackson Street After Dark**, Paul de Barros, In Jackson Street After Hours, Paul de Barros takes a meticulous, affectionate look at the jazz scene that thrived in Seattle during the 1940s and 1950s with legends like Ray Charles, Quincy Jones or Ernestine Anderson, scrapping for a gig.

[24] **Randal Edward Brecker** (born November 27, 1945) is an American trumpeter and composer. He is a sought-after player, equally accomplished in playing jazz, rock, and R&B. He has also worked as a studio player for many famous musicians. He has performed or recorded with numerous   pop   and   jazz   groups.
.

[25] The **Black & Tan Club** was a Seattle music club that ran from 1932 to 1966 and was equally accessible for the white and African American population. Already in 1932 it was considered "Seattle's most esteemed and longest-lived nightclub" (de Barros). Not only a venue for top black entertainers such as: Ernestine Anderson, George Benson, Gladys Knight, Ivie Anderson , Jimmy McGriff ,Little Willie John , Phil Upchurch, Guitar Shorty , Etta James , Sarah Vaughan, Ray Charles and in 1962, a young Jimmy Hendrix.. In the 1950s / 60s, the Black and Tan was the center of the soul scene in Seattle.

[26] "**Jerome Gray** is reputed by musicians to be the best pianist who ever played in Seattle" quoted from Jackson Street After Hours" by Paul de Barros. Gray's students have included such well-known performers as guitarist Larry Coryell, vocalist Diane Schuur, and pianist Michael Wolff. Gray has been an educator of professionals for over 40 years.

[27] **Callen Radcliffe "Cal" Tjader, Jr** (1925 –1982) was an American Latin jazz musician, known as the most successful non-Latino Latin musician.

He explored other jazz idioms, even as he continued to perform the music of Cuba, the Caribbean, and Latin America for the rest of his life. Tjader played the vibraphone primarily He is often linked to the development of Latin rock and acid jazz. His Grammy award in 1980 for his album La On-da   Va   Bien   capped   off   his   career.
.

[28] **Henry Grimes** (born November 3, 1935) is a jazz bassist, violinist, and poet. After more than a decade of performance, notably as a leading bassist in free jazz, Grimes completely disappeared from the music scene by 1970. Grimes was often presumed dead, but he was rediscovered in 2002 and returned to performing.

[29] **Slugs' Saloon** was a jazz club at 242 East 3rd Street, in Manhattan's East Village, operating from the mid-1960s to 1972. In 1964, it opened as a club called "Slugs' Saloon. In the mid-1960s it started attracting regular jazz performances, developing a reputation as a musician's bar.

[30] **George Braith** (born 1939) is a soul-jazz saxophonist from New York. Braith is known for playing multiple horns at once. Of his album, Musart, AllMusic wrote, "Musart is his masterpiece; it is one of the most diverse yet refined albums to come out of the '60s and has few peers.

[31] **Lynn Oliver Studios** Mr. Oliver, a trombonist whose big band performed in the New York metropolitan area, operated a studio for more than 30 years on the Manhattan. The studio was the site of many rehearsals for recordings and concerts by musicians like Duke Ellington, Quincy Jones and Gerry Mulligan. He persuaded many band leaders who rented his studio to donate arrangements for his students to use and he built a large library of big-band music. Mr. Oliver's alumni have performed with Buddy Rich, Art Blakey, Blood, Sweat & Tears and many others.

[32] **Carmine Caruso** was a teaching genius. Not just a brass teaching genius, a flat-out brilliant teacher. Carmine and the power of his approach to practice convinced players that they could make a career playing the trumpet.

[33] **Machito** (1908–1984) was a Latin jazz musician who helped refine Afro-Cuban jazz and create both Cubop and salsa music. He was raised in Havana. In New York City, Machito formed the band the Afro-Cubans in 1940, and with Mario Bauzá as musical director, brought together Cuban rhythms and big band arrangements in one group.

[34] **Warren Fitzgerald** The 1955 album co-lead by Warren Fitzgerald, trumpet with Bob Dorough, is a cult classic in Japan, and it's easy to see why. This session is vintage West Coast cool, with sleek harmonies, lithe grooves and optimistically lyrical soloing.

[35] **Mario Bauzá** (1911– 1993) was an Afro-Cuban jazz musician. He was one of the first to bring Cuban music to the New York City jazz scene. In 1941, Bauzá became musical director of Machito and his Afro-Cubans. The band produced its first recording for Decca in 1941, and in 1942 Bauzá brought in a young timbalero named Tito Puente.

[36] **Woodstock** was a music festival held on a dairy farm in the Catskill Mountains, between August 15–18, 1969, which attracted an audience of more than 400,000. Billed as " 3 Days of Peace & Music", it was held at Max Yasgur's 600-acre dairy farm 43 miles southwest of Woodstock. Over the sometimes-rainy weekend, 32 acts performed outdoors. It is widely regarded as a pivotal moment in popular music history, as well as the definitive nexus for the larger counterculture generation. Rolling Stone listed it as one of the 50 Moments That Changed the History of Rock and Roll.

.

[37] **Wilbur Bernard Ware**. (1923-1979) was an American jazz double-bassist known for his creative use of time and space, and his angular, unorthodox solos. He was a staff bassist at Riverside Records in the 1950s, playing on many of the label's sessions, including LPs with J.R. Monterose, Toots Thielemans, Tina Brooks, Zoot Sims, and Grant Green.

[38] **J.C. Moses** (1936 – 1977)) was an American jazz drummer. He was born in Pittsburgh, Pa and first began playing around Pittsburgh in the 1950s with Stanley Turrentine. In the 1960s he worked with Clifford Jordan, Kenny Dorham and Eric Dolphy. In 1963, he performed and recorded with the New York Contemporary Five.

[39] **Frederick Dewayne Hubbard, (Freddy Hubbard)** (1938- 2008) was an American jazz trumpeter. He was known primarily for playing bebop and hard bop styles from the early 1960s onwards. His unmistakable and influential tone contributed to new perspectives for modern jazz and bebop. In the 1960s Hubbard played as a sideman on some of the most important albums from that era. Hubbard was described as "the most brilliant trumpeter of a generation."

[40] **Albert Preston Dailey** (1939-1984) was an American jazz pianist. Dailey was born in Baltimore, Maryland. He played with Dexter Gordon, Roy Haynes, Sarah Vaughan, Charles Mingus, Freddie Hubbard and intermittently with Art Blakey's Jazz Messengers. In the 1970s Dailey played with Sonny Rollins, Stan Getz, Elvin Jones, and Archie Shepp. In the 1980s he did concerts at Carnegie Hall and was a member of the Upper Manhattan Jazz Society. He died of pneumonia in 1984, aged 46.

[41] **James Emory Garrison** (March 3, 1934 – April 7, 1976) was an American jazz double-bassist. He is best remembered for his association with John Coltrane from 1961 to 1967.

[42] The **Albert Hotel** for decades, the hotel occupied a vibrant, iconic place in the cultural life of New York's Greenwich Village. From its opening in 1887, the Albert was home, hotel and hang-out for generations of artists, activists, writers, poets and musicians. By the 1960s A.P. Herbert described the hotel as cheap, God-forsaken and miserable. It was then the Albert became a haven to musicians, both on the way up and the way down. By the mid-1970s, the sex and drugs and rock'n'roll had taken their irredeemable   toll.

[43] **Howard Pyle Wyeth** (1944 –1996), also known as Howie Wyeth, was an American drummer and pianist. Wyeth is remembered for work with the saxophonist James Moody, The Albert band, and the rhythm and blues singer Don Covay. Best known as a drummer for Bob Dylan, he was a member of the Wyeth family of American artists.

[44] **Michael Gibson** (1944-2005) a musician, trombonist and orchestrator, nominated twice for the Tony Award for Best Orchestrations. He won the Drama Desk Award for Outstanding Orchestrations for My One and Only in 1983. Gibson began his career as a studio musician in New York City, often working with James Brown. In 1972 become an orchestrator. Best known for his work on the original motion picture version of Grease (1978) and the Broadway musicals Steel Pier (1997) and Cabaret (revival, 1998)

[45] **Roy Owen Haynes** (born March 13,1925) is an American jazz drummer and group leader. Haynes is among the most recorded drummers in jazz, and in a career lasting over 70 years has played in a wide range of styles ranging from swing and bebop to jazz fusion and avant-garde jazz. He has a highly expressive, personal style,"Snap Crackle" was a nickname given him in the 1950s.

[46] **Solomon Burke** (1940 – 2010) was an American preacher and singer who shaped the sound of rhythm and blues as one of the founding fathers of soul music in the 1960s. He has been called "a key transitional figure bridging R&B and soul" and was known for his "prodigious output".

[47] **Don Covay** (1936 -2015),), was an American R&B, rock and roll, soul singer and songwriter most active from the 1950s to the 1970s. His most successful recordings include "Mercy, Mercy" (1964), "See-Saw" (1965), and "It's Better to Have and Don't Need" (1974). He also wrote "Pony Time", a US number 1 hit for Chubby Checker, and "Chain of Fools", a Grammy-winning song for Aretha Franklin.

[48] **James Moody** (1925 – 2010) was an American jazz saxophone and flute player and very occasional vocalist, playing predominantly in the bebop and hard bop styles. Long associated with Dizzy Gillespie, Moody

had an unexpected hit with "Moody's Mood for Love," a 1952 song written by Eddie Jefferson that used as its melody an improvised solo that was played by Moody.

[49] **The Albert** CD(s). And the award for most confusing discography goes to...**The Albert!** Two albums, both self-titled, the first LP was released in 1970, the second in 1971, and on the same label. Yea, that makes it easy to research. The Albert CDs definitely fall on the soul-jazz/pop side of the horn rock equation. But there's some really fine horn charts, hard guitar and organ that separate this one from the pack. Also check out the **well-done sax and trumpet solo**s. I think fans of the genre will definitely want to hear this. Horns n horns, more horns n horns. are still a mystery to me *red telephone 66* has taught me to stick with it and allow myself to go with the flow. After Track ONE to FOUR.this is a stone-cold jazz psyche classic. The Albert sound like a band that played for themselves and to hell with the audience thinking that the audience would be bound to get it, however, the recordings on show here are very complex and classical. this is serious head music not for the type-cast dance floor? I sure would have liked to see the cool cats grooving to this! The depth and wealth of creativity on show here is astounding, a lot of which does not stir me or make emotional contact. This is the music of streets I have not walked; this is music to be appreciated by those living 8 Days a Week.

[50] **Billy Tillman,** Dallas , Texas , (1947 -2012) was a saxophonist , flutist and entrepreneur American , known for being member of the jazz rock Blood, Sweat & Tears. In 1965 he began to develop his professional career as a musician, playing with various bands. In 1974 he entered Blood, Sweat & Tears, replacing Lou Marini , staying with the band until 1978.

[51] **Sal Marques** It`s a long way from El Paso, Texas, to the band of "The Tonight Show.By the time he was in high school, Marquez could play everything from classical music to mariachi. Semesters at Texas A&M University and a stint in the Army, Marquez began building his career in earnest. He remains in demand for session work with top artists. But "The Tonight Show" gig takes up much of his time.

[52] **Methadone** is an opioid used for opioid maintenance therapy in opioid dependence, and for pain. Detoxification using methadone can either be done relatively rapidly in less than a month or gradually over as long as six months. While a single dose has a rapid effect, maximum effect can take five days of use. The pain-relieving effects last about six hours after a single dose, similar to morphine's.

[53] **David Eugene Lewis** (1938 – 1998) was an African American rock and rhythm & blues keyboardist, organist, and vocalist based in Seattle, Washington. The Dave Lewis Combo was "Seattle's first significant Afri-

can American 1950s rock and roll band" and Lewis himself as "the singularly most significant figure on the Pacific Northwest's nascent rhythm & blues scene in the 1950s and 1960s."

54 **Chuck Sher**. Creator of Educational Jazz Publications including The New Real Book Series The founder of Sher shares his perspectives about music and business Chuck Sher: "In the late '70s, I had an extended period of tendonitis which prevented me from playing for about a year, so I gathered the notes I had kept from teaching bass and created my first book, "The Improvisor's Bass Method." So, my becoming an author and publisher was an accident in a way, but my ability to organize a lot of material came in handy in writing and publishing books."

55 **Mark Levine** (born 1938).) is an American jazz pianist, trombonist, composer, author and educator. He has played with Dizzy Gillespie, Woody Shaw, Freddie Hubbard, Joe Henderson, Tito Puente, Mongo Santamaría, Cal Tjader, Willie Bobo, Bobby Hutcherson, and many others. He has written three popular books: *The Jazz Piano Book*, *The Jazz Theory Book*, and *The Drop 2 Book*. He was nominated for a Grammy for Best Latin Jazz Recording in 2003 for his CD *Isla*, with his band Mark Levine & The Latin Tinge. He was nominated for a Latin Grammy award in 2010 for his CD; Off & On, the Music of Moacir Santos." He produces the BAJA (Bay Area Jazz Archives) series of archival CDs for Jazz School Records.

56 **Chuck Metcalf** (1931- 2012) was an American jazz double-bassist. He taught at Garfield High School's Magnet Program with saxophonist Joe Brazil in 1968. In 1980 he toured with Dexter Gordon. His first studio album named Elsie Street was released in 1989 and Help Is Coming (1992)

57 **Jessica Jennifer Williams** was born in Baltimore, Maryland on March 17, 1948. She started playing the piano piano at age four, began music lessons with a private teacher at five, and at age seven was enrolled into the Peabody Preparatory. She studied classical music and ear training with Richard Aitken and George Bellows at the Peabody Conservatory of Music. Williams also had the ability to play anything she heard. At age twelve she was listening to Dave Brubeck, Miles Davis, and Charles Mingus. She knew she was destined to become a jazz pianist. She began performing jazz in her teens, playing with Richie Cole, Buck Hill, and Mickey Fields. In a rare radio interview with Marian McPartland on NPR's Piano Jazz, she states that her main influences were not pianists, but horn players, most notably Miles Davis and John Coltrane.

.

58 **Henry "Jack" Schroer** (1944-1995) was a saxophonist, pianist and arranger best known for his work with Van Morrison in the 1970s as a member of his band The Caledonia Soul Orchestra.

---

[59] **Johnny Coppola** began playing professionally when he was 13. He played with Charlie Barnet, Charlie Haden and Woody Herman's big band, and was the lead trumpet for Stan Kenton. Jerry Dodgion, the noted saxophonist said, "He was a great lead trumpet player, a teacher and a mentor to me. He always shared what he knew. He was a special person."

[60] **The Synanon** organization, initially a drug rehabilitation program, was founded by Charles E. "Chuck" Dederich, Sr., (1913–1997) in 1958 in Santa Monica, California. By the early 1960s, Synanon had also become an alternative community, attracting people with its emphasis on living a self-examined life.

[61] **Cathryn Casamo** http://www.cathryncasamo.com/ and http://www.cathryncasamo.com/themagicbus1.htm

[62] **Merry Pranksters** When the publication of his second novel, *Sometimes a Great Notion* in 1964, required his presence in New York, Kesey, Neal Cassady, and a group of friends called the Merry Pranksters took a cross-country trip in a school bus nicknamed Further. This trip was the group's attempt to create art out of everyday life, and to experience roadway America while high on LSD. In an interview after arriving in New York, Kesey is quoted as saying, " If people could just understand it is possible to be different without being a threat." A huge amount of footage was filmed on 16mm cameras during the trip, which remained largely unseen until the release of Alex Gibney's Magic Tripin' 2011.

[63] **Norm Bobrow**, (1917-2008) Jazz was his life, not just a living. Bobrow was a mainstay on the Seattle jazz scene in the 1940s and 1950s and founded the Colony, a defunct downtown Seattle supper club. He also worked as an actor, producer and broadcaster, gracing the airwaves for KOMO/4, KING/5 and other stations.

[64] **Red Kelly** the list of the name bands that he worked with is incredible. It included those of Ted Fio Rito, Randy Brooks, Sam Donahue, Chubby Jackson, Herbie Fields, Charlie Barnet, Claude Thornhill, Jimmy Dorsey, Stan Kenton, Maynard Ferguson, Les Brown and Harry James. When Kelly retired, he and his wife Donna ran a restaurant and night-club in Tacoma, Washington. In 1976 Kelly mounted a tongue-in-cheek campaign for the seat of Washington's state governor, forming the Owl ("Out with Logic, On With Lunacy") party. (He came in third in the voting.) He was inducted into the Seattle Jazz Hall of Fame in 2000 and died June 9, 2004.

[65] **Barney McClure** is one of the most respected jazz musicians in the Pacific Northwest. A successful jazz pianist long before he got involved in politics, McClure, 40, said he sees a correlation between the two jobs. McClure's work as a jazz musician had led him to live in New York, Chi-

cago and Frankfurt, Germany, as well as Los Angeles. Despite the demands of politics, McClure finds plenty of time for playing jazz. He is a backup pianist for many of the big-name jazz artists that stop in Seattle and other Northwest cities.

66 **George James Catlett** (1933-2014), known professionally as Buddy Catlett, was an American jazz bassist. A childhood friend of Quincy Jones, he joined Jones's band for a European tour. He worked with Louis Armstrong, Bill Coleman, Curtis Fuller, Freddie Hubbard, Coleman Hawkins, Junior Mance, Chico Hamilton, Johnny Griffin and Eddie Lockjaw Davis.

67 **Big Mama Thornton**, the Blues legend, was born in Ariton, Alabama in 1926. Known for her powerful voice and sexually explicit lyrics, Thornton was the original performer of the hit song "Hound Dog," commonly associated with Elvis Presley, and "Ball and Chain," covered by Janis Joplin. She died of a heart attack in Los Angeles, California, on July 25, 1980

68 **Parnell's**. Seating 125, the club had brick walls, large cushions and Tiffany-style lamps suspended over the tables. Airbrushed portraits of jazz adorned the walls. " Recalled Seattle's Jim Wilke, radio host of "Jazz After Hours": "I don't know if there ever was a more comfortable jazz club. It was always like a party in Roy's living room." The long list of musicians who played Parnell's over the years included Bill Evans, Chet Baker, Art Pepper, Earl "Fatha" Hines, Blue Mitchell, Eddie "Lockjaw" Davis, Anita O'Day, Joe Williams, Harold Land, Milt Jackson, Bob Dorough, Ray Brown, Dave Frishberg, Ernestine Anderson, Phil Woods, Charlie Byrd, Sonny Stitt, Cal Tjader and many more. Many name players in the '70s hired local rhythm sections, a boon for Seattle players. In 1980 Parnell sold the club to Marv Thomas, a former big-band trumpet player whose son, trumpeter and saxophonist Jay Thomas, is a fixture on the local jazz scene. Thomas in turn sold the venue 3 ½ years later to a group of four investors that included Seattle singer Ernestine Anderson.

69 **Arthur Edward Pepper Jr.** (1925-1982) was an American alto saxophonist and very occasional tenor saxophonist and clarinetist. A longtime figure in West Coast jazz, Pepper came to prominence in Stan Kenton's big band. In 1952, he began a long series of incarcerations for violations of drug laws. He served time for the Feds and for the State of California (San Quentin). He prided himself on being "a stand-up guy," a good criminal. Art Pepper died June 15, 1982, of a cerebral hemorrhage. But the 1979 publication of Straight Life revived Art's career. He spent the last years of his life touring worldwide with his own bands, recording over a hundred albums, writing songs, winning polls, respect, and adulation.

[70] **Harold Land** is an underrated tenor saxophonist He grew up in San Diego and started playing tenor when he was 16. Land had his first high-profile gig in 1954 when he joined the Clifford Brown/Max Roach Quintet. Land performed and recorded with the group until late 1955. He recorded a pair of memorable albums for Contemporary (1958-1959), led his own groups in the 1960s, and co-led groups with Bobby Hutcherson (1967-1971) and Blue Mitchell (1975-1978). Harold Land continued freelancing around Los Angeles up until his death in 2001.

[71] **Chesney Henry Baker Jr.** (1929-1988) was an American jazz trumpeter and vocalist. Baker earned much attention and critical praise in the 1950s, particularly for albums featuring his vocals. Jazz historian Dave Gelly described the promise of Baker's early career as "James Dean, Sinatra, and Bix, rolled into one." His well-publicized drug habit also drove his notoriety and fame. Baker was in and out of jail before enjoying a career resurgence in the late 1970s.

[72] **John Haley "Zoot" Sims** (1925-1985) was an American jazz saxophonist, playing mainly tenor but also alto and alto saxophone. He first gained attention in the "Four Brothers" sax section of Woody Herman's big band, afterward enjoying a long solo career, often in partnership with fellow saxmen Gerry Mulligan and Al Cohn and trombonist Bob Brookmeyer.

[73] **William George Ramsay ("Bill" or "Rams"**); born January 12, 1929, in Centralia, Washington) is an American jazz saxophonist, band leader and arranger based in Seattle. In 1997, he was inducted into the Seattle Jazz Hall of Fame. Ramsay performs on all the primary saxophones – soprano, alto, tenor, and baritone – as well as clarinet. Currently Ramsay has been a member of the Seattle Repertory Jazz Orchestra since its founding in 1995. He is the co-leader, with Milt Kleeb of a ten-piece jazz band based in Seattle. Ramsay played Bari sax in the Count Basie Orchestra for two years; Ramsay was hired in April 1984, three weeks before Basie died. Also performed with the bands of Thad Jones, Mel Lewis, Gene Harris, Les Brown, Grover Mitchell, Maynard Ferguson, Buddy Morrow, Benny Goodman Octet and Quincy Jones In the 1980s, Ramsay led his own big band that performed at festivals and clubs in the NW. Ernestine Anderson's recording, "You Made Your Move Too Soon" featured arrangements by Ramsay.

[74] **Bulee "Slim" Gaillard** (1911- 1991), was an American jazz singer and songwriter who played piano, guitar and vibes. Gaillard was noted for his comedic vocalese singing and word play in his own constructed language called "Vout-o-Reenee", for which he wrote a dictionary. He rose to prominence in the late 1930s with hits such as "Flat Foot Floogie" and "Cement Mixer" after forming Slim and Slam with "Slam" Stewart. During World War II, Gaillard served as a bomber pilot in the Pacific. In 1944, he re-

sumed his music career and performed with notable jazz musicians such as Charlie Parker, Dizzy Gillespie. In the 1960s and 1970s, he acted in films—sometimes as himself, and also appeared in bit parts in television series such as Roots. In the 1980s, Gaillard resumed touring the circuit of European jazz festivals and, in 1983, settled in London, where he died on 26 February 1991, after a long career in music, film and television, spanning nearly six decades.

[75] **William Allen Mays** (1944), best known as Bill Mays, is an American jazz pianist from Sacramento, California. From 1969 to the early 1980s Mays worked as a studio session musician in Los Angeles. He has been an accompanist to singers Al Jarreau, Peggy Lee, Anita O'Day, Frank Sinatra, Sarah Vaughan and Dionne Warwick. In 1984, he moved to New York City and began to do more work as a bandleader, composer, and arranger. He has recorded over two dozen albums under his own name and has been heard on hundreds more by others.

[76] **Cedar Anthony Walton, Jr** (1934- 2013) was an American hard bop jazz pianist. He came to prominence as a member of drummer Art Blakey's band before establishing a long career as a bandleader and composer. Several of his compositions have become jazz standards, including "Mosaic", "Bolivia", "Holy Land", In the early 1960s, Walton joined Art Blakey's Jazz Messengers as a pianist-arranger for three years. He left the Messengers in 1964 and by the late 1960s was part of the house rhythm section at Prestige Records, where in addition to releasing his own recordings, he recorded with Sonny Criss, Pat Martino, Eric Kloss, Jay Thomas and Charles McPherson. For a year, he served as Abbey Lincoln's accompanist, and recorded with Lee Morgan from 1966 to 1968. During the mid-1970s, he led the funk group *Mobius*. Walton arranged and recorded for Etta James helping her win a Grammy Award for Best Jazz Vocal Album for Mystery Lady: Songs of Billie Holiday.

[77] **Charles McPherson** (born 1939) is an American jazz alto saxophonist born in Joplin, Missouri, and raised in Detroit, Michigan, who worked intermittently with Charles Mingus from 1960 to 1974, and as a performer leading his own groups. McPherson also was commissioned to help record ensemble renditions of pieces from Charlie Parker on the 1988 soundtrack for the film Bird.

[78] **Mark Solomon**, Solomon Arts & Entertainment was founded in 1984 by Mark Solomon as a Seattle entertainment agency focusing on private party entertainment. Over the past 30 years he has booked well over 8,000 jobs for a multitude of clients.

[79] **The Heath Brothers** is an American jazz group, formed in 1975 in Philadelphia, by the brothers Jimmy (tenor saxophone), Percy (bass), and

Albert "Tootie" Heath (drums); and pianist Stanley Cowell. Tony Purrone (guitar) and Jimmy's son Mtume (percussion) joined the group later. Tootie left in 1978 and was replaced by Akira Tana for a short period before returning in 1982. They also added other sidemen for some of their recording dates.

[80] **Red Rodney**. Born in Philadelphia, Pennsylvania, he became a professional musician at 15, working in the mid-1940s for the big bands of Jerry Wald, Jimmy Dorsey, Georgie Auld, Elliot Lawrence, Benny Goodman, and Les Brown. He was inspired by hearing Dizzy Gillespie and Charlie Parker to change his style to bebop, moving on to play with Claude Thornhill, Gene Krupa, and Woody Herman. He was part of the Charlie Parker Quintet from 1949–1951. As the only white member of the group, he was billed as "Albino Red" when playing in the southern United States. During the 1950s, he worked as a bandleader in Philadelphia and recorded with Ira Sullivan. He became addicted to heroin and started a pattern of dropping in and out of jazz. During 1969, Rodney played in Las Vegas with fellow Woody Herman colleague, trombonist Bill Harris through 1972. He returned to jazz but in 1975 he was incarcerated in Sandstone, Minnesota for drug offenses He reunited with Ira Sullivan and from 1980 to 1982, Rodney made five albums with Sullivan. On these albums he started to play post-bop jazz.

[81] **Ira Sullivan** Plays both trumpet and saxophone and in the 50s in Chicago with such seminal figures as Charlie Parker, Lester Young, Wardell Gray and Roy Eldridge, garnering a reputation as a fearsome bebop soloist. After playing briefly with Art Blakey (1956), Sullivan moved south to Florida but continued to play in the Miami area, often in schools and churches. Contact with local younger players, notably Jaco Pastorius and Pat Metheny led to teaching and to a broadening of his own musical roots. Sullivan moved to New York and in 1980 formed a quintet with bop trumpeter Red Rodney to produce some fresh and stimulating music.

[82] **Salvatore Nistico** (1941-1991) was an American jazz tenor saxophonist. Associated for many years with Woody Herman, Nistico played in the 1962–65 group, considered one of Herman's best bands, with Bill Chase, Jake Hanna, Nat Pierce, and Phil Wilson. From 1959 to 1961, he played with the Jazz Brothers band (Chuck Mangione and Gap Mangione). In 1965, he joined Count Basie but returned on many occasions to play with Herman.

[83] **George Cables** was born in New York City on November 14, 1944. He was initially taught piano by his mother, then studied at the High School of Performing Arts and later at Mannes College (1963–65). Cables' early influences on piano were Thelonious Monk and Herbie Hancock.

Cables has played with Art Blakey, Sonny Rollins, Dexter Gordon, Art Pepper, Joe Henderson, and many other well-established jazz musicians. His own records include the 1980 Cables' Vision with Freddie Hubbard. From 1983 Cables worked in the project Bebop & Beyond. He left later in the 1980s but returned for two early 1990s albums, before rejoining in 1998

[84] **Benny Green** was born in New York City. He grew up in Berkeley, California, and studied classical piano from the age of seven. He also had an interest in jazz from an early point, as his father was a jazz tenor saxophone player. Benny Green, while still in his teens worked in a quintet led by Eddie Henderson. After high school he spent time in San Francisco but became more successful on his return to New York. Green joined Betty Carter's band in 1983, and since 1991 he has led his own trio. Green frequently teaches in jazz workshops such as Jazz Camp West in California, and Centrum/Jazz Port Townsend in Washington. He currently tours globally with the world-famous Benny Green Trio.

[85] **Jimmy Ryan's** was a jazz club in New York City, USA, located at 53 West 52nd Street from 1934 to 1962 and 154 West 54th Street from 1962–1983.[1] It was a popular venue for Dixieland jazz.

[86] **Ernie Garside** is a man who has been involved with jazz for over 60 years. A trumpeter with a passion for jazz, Ernie started a jazz club in early 1960 in Manchester, U.K. called the "Club 42." An appearance at the club by a young Maynard Ferguson led to Ernie being his manager for ten years. Garside would go on to also work as a manager promoting jazz artists that included Chet Baker, Dizzy Gillespie, Arturo Sandoval, Diana Krall, and others.

[87] **Hep Records** was founded in 1974 by its present owner, Alastair Robertson, whose aim was to issue albums of well-known jazz musicians and bands of the mid 1940s drawn from radio acetates and transcriptions.

[88] **James Columbus "Jay" McShann** (January 12, 1916 – December 7, 2006) was a jazz pianist and bandleader. He led bands in Kansas City, Missouri, that included Charlie Parker, Bernard Anderson, Ben Webster, and Walter Brown.

[89] **George Holmes "Buddy" Tate** (February 22, 1913 – February 10, 2001) was a jazz saxophonist and clarinetist. Tate was born in Sherman, Texas, and began performing on alto saxophone. Tate quickly switched to tenor saxophone making a name for himself in bands such as Andy Kirk. He joined Count Basie in 1939 and stayed with him until 1948. After his time Basie ended, he found success on his own, starting in 1953 in Harlem. His group worked at the "Celebrity Club" from 1953 to 1974. In the late 1970s, he co-led a band with Paul Quinichette and worked with Benny

Goodman. The 1990s saw him slow down, but he remained active playing with Lionel Hampton among others.

⁹⁰ **Jakk Corsaw** The Seattle Post-Intelligencer's landmark sign since 1948, the globe is 30 feet in diameter, weighs 13.5 tons and stood for years atop the newspaper's former location at Sixth Avenue and Wall Street. The globe was designed by Jakk Corsaw, who was a University of Washington art student when he beat out 350 other entrants in a design competition. Jakk had an art gallery in Pike Place Market in the 1960s. His real name was Jack, but he went by Jakk.

⁹¹ **Jack Brownlow** (1923-2007) was an American jazz piano player. Brownlow was born in Spokane, Washington, and after serving in the Navy in World War II he lived in Los Angeles from 1945–46, playing with Boyd Raeburn among others. He returned to Wenatchee after that to work in the family business. In the mid-1960s he returned to playing music full-time. Jack Brownlow was the most respected jazz pianist working in Seattle from the late 1960s until his death on 27 October 2007 of kidney failure. He was 84 when he died.

⁹² **David Friesen** (born May 6, 1942) is an American jazz bassist born in Tacoma, Washington. He plays double bass and electric upright bass. Friesen picked up bass while serving in the U.S. Army in Germany. He played with John Handy and Marian McPartland and following this, with Joe Henderson; in 1975, he toured in Europe with Billy Harper. His first album as a session leader appeared that year. In 1976, he began collaborating with guitarist John Stowell; the pair would work together often. He appeared with Ted Curson at the Monterey Jazz Festival in 1977. Following this, he worked with Ricky Ford, Duke Jordan, Mal Waldron, and Paul Horn. His 1989 album Other Times, Other Places reached No. 11 on the U.S. Billboard Top Jazz Albums chart. He has also played with Chick Corea, Michael Brecker, Stan Getz, Dexter Gordon, Kenny Garrett, Dizzy Gillespie, and Mal Waldron.

⁹³ **John Stowell**, who plays electric and acoustic guitar, was born in New York and raised in Connecticut. After he met bassist David Friesen in New York City, Stowell took a trip to Portland, Oregon, where Friesen lives, and decided to stay. The two formed a duo in 1976 that recorded and toured prolifically for seven years, with performances in the United States, Canada, Europe and Australia. The duo continues to perform thirty years after their first meeting. In 1983, Stowell and David Friesen joined flutist Paul Horn for a tour of the Soviet Union. In 1977 Stowell recorded his debut album Golden Delicious; his sidemen were Jim McNeely, Mike Richmond, and Billy Hart. In 2005 he published Jazz Guitar Mastery.

[94] **Diane Joan Schuur** (born December 10, 1953), nicknamed "Deedles", is an American jazz singer and pianist. Schuur has been blind from birth but has been gifted with absolute pitch memory and a clear vocal tone. As of 2015, Schuur had released 23 albums, and had extended her jazz repertoire to include essences of Latin, gospel, pop and country music. Her most successful album is Diane Schuur & the Count Basie Orchestra, which remained number one on the Billboard Jazz Charts for 33 weeks. She won Grammy Awards for best female jazz vocal performance in both 1986 and 1987 and has had three other Grammy nominations. Schuur has performed in venues such as Carnegie Hall, The Kennedy Center, and the White House, and has performed with many artists including Ray Charles, Frank Sinatra, Quincy Jones, and Stevie Wonder. Co-performers on Schuur's albums have included Barry Manilow, José Feliciano, Maynard Ferguson, Stan Getz, Vince Gill, Alison Krause, and B.B. King. Her album with B.B. King was number one on the Billboard Jazz Charts. She was on Johnny Carson's Tonight Show 11 times, and in 1996, she was a guest performer on Sesame Street.

95Vocalist **Becca Duran** is a Los Angeles native, but she found her jazz wings in the Pacific Northwest. She is an accomplished jazz singer who, if you ask the top-flight jazz instrumentalists she has worked with, is known for the beauty of her sound, excellent time feel and beautiful phrasing. Her singing matches flexibility and purity of tone with intelligence, wit and sensuality. From Brazilian jazz to the blues, Becca shines. Here is a singer who does not confuse vocal acrobatics or avante garde meandering with jazz artistry. She can tell a story and create an ambiance in the best tradition of the art form. This is a vocalist who swings with the best of them and who consistently delivers emotionally honest phrasing true to the lyrics and melodies of a wide variety of re-examined standards.

Becca has toured Japan performing at major Tokyo clubs. She opened the new Four Seasons Hotel in Maui and has been a popular headliner at Bumbershoot, Centrum, Bellevue, Earshot and the Pike Place Market Jazz Festivals in Seattle. She was selected to represent Seattle as a jazz artist in a cultural exchange with sister city, Kobe, Japan.

[96] **Nagoya Castle** (名古屋城 Nagoya-jō) is a Japanese castle located in Nagoya, central Japan. During the Edo period, Nagoya Castle was the heart of one of the most important castle towns in Japan, Nagoya-juku, which was a post station on the Minojiroad linking two of five important trade routes, the Tōkaidō and the Nakasendō. This name is used for many city institutions, such as Meijō Park, the metro's Meijō Line and Meijo University, reflecting the cultural influence of this historic structure.

[97] **Cedar Anthony Walton, Jr** (1934- 2013) was an American hard bop jazz pianist. He came to prominence as a member of drummer Art Blakey's band before establishing a long career as a bandleader and composer. Several of his compositions have become jazz standards, including "Mosaic", "Bolivia", "Holy Land", In the early 1960s, Walton joined Art Blakey's Jazz Messengers as a pianist-arranger for three years. He left the Messengers in 1964 and by the late 1960s was part of the house rhythm section at Prestige Records, where in addition to releasing his own recordings, he recorded with Sonny Criss, Pat Martino, Eric Kloss, Jay Thomas and Charles McPherson. For a year, he served as Abbey Lincoln's accompanist, and recorded with Lee Morgan from 1966 to 1968. During the mid-1970s, he led the funk group Mobius. Walton arranged and recorded for Etta James helping her win a Grammy Award for Best Jazz Vocal Album for Mystery Lady: Songs of Billie Holiday

[98]. **Billy Higgins** was born in Los Angeles.[2] Higgins played on Ornette Coleman's first records, beginning in 1958. He then freelanced extensively with hard bop and other post-bop players, including Donald Byrd, Dexter Gordon, Grant Green, Herbie Hancock, Joe Henderson, Don Cherry, Paul Horn, Milt Jackson, Jackie McLean, Pat Metheny, Hank Mobley, Thelonious Monk, Lee Morgan, David Murray, Art Pepper, Sonny Rollins, Mal Waldron, and Cedar Walton. He was one of the house drummers for Blue Note Records and played on dozens of Blue Note albums of the 1960s. In his career, he played on over 700 recordings, including recordings of rock and funk. Billy Higgins died of kidney and liver failure on May 3, 2001.

[99] **Hidehiko "Sleepy" Matsumoto** (松本英彦) (1926 - 2000) was a Japanese jazz saxophonist and bandleader. Matsumoto played bebop in Japan in the late 1940s with the group CB Nine, then joined The Six Josés and The Big Four. In 1959 he became a member of Hideo Shiraki's small ensemble and played with Gerald Wilson at the 1963 Monterey Jazz Festival and Toshiko Akiyoshi in 1964. Starting in 1964 he led his own ensembles. On July 22 and 24, 1966, he played with the John Coltrane quintet in Tokyo while the group was touring Japan.

[100]**Discovery Records** was founded in 1948 by jazz fan and promoter Albert Marx. The record label eventually would record jazz notables such as Dizzy Gillespie, Georgie Auld, Red Norvo, Art Pepper and Charles Mingus for issue on his Discovery label headquartered in Hollywood, California. He also started the Trend AM-PM label in the 1980s to document and promote talented educational and college level jazz ensembles. His estate sold the Discovery, Trend and Musicraft jazz labels in 1991 to Jac

Holzman, which he refashioned into a contemporary label. In 1993, Discovery Records was acquired by Warner Music Group and was absorbed by Sire Records in 1996

[101] **Herb Ellis,** Born in Farmersville, Texas and raised in the suburbs of Dallas, Ellis first heard the electric guitar on a radio program and was proficient on the instrument by the time he entered North Texas State University. In 1943, he joined Glen Gray and the Casa Loma Orchestra and then Ellis joined the Jimmy Dorsey band where he played some of his first recorded solos. Ellis remained with Dorsey through 1947. Then joined John Frigo and Lou Carter to form the Three Winds. Frigo, Lou Carter and Ellis wrote the classic jazz standard *"Detour Ahead"*. Ellis became prominent after performing with the Oscar Peterson Trio from 1953 to 1958 along with pianist Peterson and bassist Ray Brown. In addition to their great live and recorded work as the Oscar Peterson Trio, this unit usually with the addition of a drummer, served as the virtual "house rhythm section" for Norman Granz's Verve Records. The trio were one of the mainstays of Granz's Jazz at the Philharmonic concerts, almost constantly touring the United States and Europe. The years of 1957 through 1960 found Ellis touring with Ella Fitzgerald. In 1994 he joined the Arkansas Jazz Hall of Fame. On November 15, 1997 he received an Honorary Doctorate from the University of North Texas College of Music. Ellis died of Alzheimer's disease at his Los Angeles home at the age of 88.

[102] . **Chuck Israels** Born in New York City, Chuck Israels was raised in a musical family. In 1948, the appearance of Louis Armstrong's All Stars in a concert series produced by his parents gave him an opportunity to meet and hear jazz musicians. His first professional job after college was working with pianist Bud Powell in Paris. His first professional recording was Coltrane Time with John Coltrane, Cecil Taylor, Kenny Dorham, and Louis Hayes. The recording showcased Israels as a composer with his composition "Double Clutching". Israels is best known for his work with the Bill Evans Trio from 1961 through 1966 and as Director of the National Jazz Ensemble from 1973 to 1981. He was the Director of Jazz Studies at Western Washington University in Bellingham, Washington until 2010. In 2011, he created the Chuck Israels Jazz Orchestra and recorded Second Wind: A Tribute to the Music of Bill Evans.

[103] **Willie Thomas** was raised in Orlando, Florida and started playing the trumpet around the age of 10. In the 1950s, Willie was a member of the Third Army Band, where he met and played with pianist Wynton Kelly, which became his first real break into the New York jazz scene. In his 45 years as a jazz trumpeter, Thomas has performed or recorded with many jazz greats including the MJT+3, the Slide Hampton Octet with Freddie

Hubbard and George Coleman, the Woody Herman Orchestra, the Al Belletto Sextet, and singer Peggy Lee. Thomas created the series of jazz educational books Jazz Anyone? the International Association of Jazz Educators' Jazz Education Hall of Fame in 1994.

[104] **Randy Jones, Tenor Madness** carries one of the largest selections of Selmer Mark VI's as well as modern horns such as P Mauriat, Yamaha, Yanagisawa, Selmer, Keilwerth, etc. In addition to their great selection of horns, Tenor Madness owner Randy Jones has been praised by many players as one of the He was also an active member of the International Association for Jazz Education and was inducted into best saxophone repairman in the business. If you are looking to try out some of the best horns on the market or get your current horn setup up professionally by Randy Jones, definitely check out his shop.

[105] **Travis Shook** (born March 10, 1969, in Oroville, CA) is a jazz pianist who grew up in Olympia, WA, moved to New York City in the mid-1990s and currently resides in Woodstock, NY. Shook made his Columbia Records debut in a quartet that included Tony Williams and Bunky Green. He received much critical acclaim for this first effort but failed to hold on to the contract when Sony purged a large percentage of the Columbia jazz roster upon acquiring the label in 1993. After spending some time as a member of the Betty Carter Trio, he dropped out of the public eye for a number of years. In 1993, Shook and his wife, jazz singer Veronica Nunn, started the record label, Dead Horse Records, and has released four recordings to date.

[106] **Yasuhiro Kohama** Kohama told me he was at the Village Vanguard on a Monday evening listening to the Mel Lewis band when he had an epiphany, and the heavens parted for him when sitting in front of the Vanguard Orchestra. He heard the history, the soul, the skill, the continuity of the band. Plus, all the musicians playing together without exhibiting their egos, but each soloist celebrated their individuality and unique expression. He told me he could not stop crying. Kohama had an almost religious experience and vowed to create a similar band in Japan. **He had found his life's calling.**

[107] **CUG** -Big Band jazz is alive and thriving with the Continued in the Underground Jazz Orchestra. Whether they are caressing a ballad, reinventing a jazz standard, swinging the blues, or careening through an Ornette Coleman piece with joyful abandon and stop-on-a-dime precision, this band is a compelling and exciting presence. In addition to astounding technical skills, *Continued in the Underground* has tons of heart, soul, and passion. With their obious reverence for the jazz tradition, an enthusiastic

creative spirit, and chops to burn, these guys have the prescription to keep jazz healthy long into the future. This band can make magic!

[108] **Jim Wilke** grew up in New London, Iowa and graduated from the University of Iowa in 1959. At school he played saxophone in a jazz band. He moved to Seattle and started at KING-FM in 1961. In 1962 The Penthouse jazz club opened with a phone line from the club to KING-FM. Wilke set up a mixing board near the piano and four microphones on stage. Ernestine Anderson was the first singer to be broadcast. Wilke taught jazz history at Cornish College of the Arts from 1975–2002. He taught radio broadcasting at Bellevue Community College on their station KBCS-FM from 1977–1983. From 1978–1993, he worked for the Bellevue Parks and Community Service, coordinating music festivals and outdoor concerts. During 1981–2001 he worked at KUOW-FM. In 1985 he started the recording studio Hatchcover, the production company responsible for Jazz Northwest. He records at the Seattle Art Museum for the Earshot Jazz Art of Jazz program. Wilke has worked with jazz record labels to release recordings he made in the early 1960s. These include music by Johnny Griffin, Eddie "Lockjaw" Davis, Wes Montgomery, Cannonball Adderley

[109] **Billy Wallace** Jazz Pianist Billy Wallace: 1929–2017Jazz pianist Billy Wallace passed away on December 9, 2017, in Denver, Colorado. Wallace got his start performing with Buddy Ryland, Max Roach, Clifford Brown, and Charlie Parker, and played as an accompanist for Billie Holiday, Carmen McRae, Anita O'Day, and many others. As for his impact on the Seattle jazz scene, he performed with Floyd Standifer, and recorded Soulful Delight (1994) with Phil Sparks and Clarence Acox. In his later years, Wallace became a steadfast member of the Denver jazz scene, performing regularly until his passing. He will be missed by many in the music communities of Chicago, Seattle, and Denver.

[110] **Jim Knapp** studied trumpet and composition at the University of Illinois. In 1995 he formed the Jim Knapp Orchestra. This band, which performed at clubs and festivals in the region and has recorded 3 CDs, drew its repertoire largely from Knapp's original compositions and arrangements. Knapp has also written music for theatre and dance companies. He is a skilled trumpeter although the chief focus of his talent is in his work as a composer and orchestrator of music of great lyrical beauty.

[111] **Tula's Jazz Club**, one of the top 20 jazz clubs in the US, Tula's opened 1993 and closed September 2019. While jazz greats like Wynton Marsalis and the late Roy Hargrove have graced its stage, Tula's has been committed to showcasing local and regional talent, its calendar speckled with Seattle heavy hitters like Jay Thomas, Greta Matassa, Thomas Marriott and Jovino Santos-Neto.

[112] **Clifford Everett "Bud" Shank Jr.** (May 27, 1926 – April 2, 2009) was an American alto saxophonist and flautist. He rose to prominence in the early 1950s playing lead alto and flute in Stan Kenton's Innovations in Modern Music Orchestra and throughout the decade worked in various small jazz combos. He spent the 1960s as a first-call studio musician in Hollywood. In the 1970s and 1980s, he performed regularly with the L. A. Four. Shank ultimately abandoned the flute to focus exclusively on playing jazz on the alto saxophone. He also recorded on tenor and baritone sax. His most famous recording is probably the version of Harlem Nocturne used as the theme song in Mickey Spillane's Mike Hammer.[1] He is also well known for the alto flute solo on the song "California Dreamin'" recorded by The Mamas & the Papas in 1965.

[113] **Centrum Jazz Camp Port Townsend** is the perfect opportunity to experience excellent musicians, soak up a weekend of jazz in a seaside paradise and participate in a wide array of mainstage and nightclub performances. Artistic Director John Clayton inspires a true sense of family during this special week of events that showcases internationally known performers in new and unexpected pairings. Jazz Port Townsend has emerged as one of the leading jazz festivals in the nation.

Festival mainstage performances take place in Fort Worden State Park's 1200-seat McCurdy Pavilion. Jazz Port Townsend also features the popular "Jazz in the Clubs" series, throughout Fort Worden, come alive with the sounds of jazz.

[114] **Roy Anthony Hargrove** (1969 – 2018) was an American jazz trumpeter. He won worldwide notice after winning two Grammy Awards for differing types of music in 1997 and in 2002. Hargrove primarily played in the hard bop style for the majority of his albums, especially performing jazz standards on his 1990s albums. A briskly assertive soloist with a tone that could evoke either burnished steel or a soft, golden glow, Hargrove was a galvanizing presence in jazz over the last 30 years.

[115] **SRJO**: A Seattle Institution. SRJO is the Northwest's premier big band jazz ensemble. Founded in 1995, the 17-piece big band is made up of the most prominent jazz soloists and band leaders in the greater Seattle area.

The SRJO is co-directed by drummer Clarence Acox, nationally recognized director of bands at Seattle's Garfield High School, and saxophonist/arranger Michael Brockman, long-time faculty member at the University of Washington School of Music. The SRJO's extensive and growing repertoire is drawn from the 100-year history of jazz, from turn-of-the-20th century ragtime to turn-of-the-21st century avant-garde. This includes works by America's most famous jazz composers, among them Fletcher

Henderson, Charles Mingus, Gil Evans, Thelonious Monk, Dizzy Gillespie, Gerry Mulligan, Thad Jones, and of course, Count Basie and Duke Ellington. In addition, the SRJO's repertoire grows each year as the ensemble adds previously unpublished works to its library.

Recovering jazz classics for performance by the ensemble is accomplished by co-director Michael Brockman, our region's outstanding practitioner of the art of transcribing lost-to-print composition and arrangement, note for note, from vintage recordings.

[116] **Donald Gale Lanphere** (June 26, 1928 – October 9, 2003) was an American jazz tenor and soprano saxophonist born in Wenatchee, Washington, known for his 1940s and 1950s work and recordings with Fats Navarro (in 1948), Woody Herman (1949), Claude Thornhill, Sonny Dunham, Billy May, and Charlie Barnet. Lanphere briefly studied music at Northwestern University in the 1940s but moved to New York City as a member of Johnny Bothwell's group to become part of the bebop jazz scene. In New York, Lanphere was in a relationship with Chan Richardson, who later married Charlie Parker and then Phil Woods. In 1951, Lanphere was arrested and charged with heroin possession in New York City. After his release from jail, he worked in his family's music store in Wenatchee, where he met Midge Hess. They married in 1953. In the late 1950s and early 1960s Lanphere performed with Herb Pomeroy and with Woody Herman. Lanphere was mostly inactive musically throughout most of the 1960s but began performing in the Seattle area after becoming a born-again Christian in 1969, at which time he also stopped using drugs and alcohol. In the 1980s Lanphere began recording again and started releasing albums, doing tours in New York City and Kansas City in 1983 and a European tour in 1985.

In his later years, Lanphere was a jazz educator in the Pacific Northwest, giving lessons out of his home in Kirkland, Washington. He instructed clinics and small groups, as well as performed, at the Bud Shank Jazz Workshop, an annual, week-long summer camp in Port Townsend, Washington for jazz students of all ages. The Bud Shank Jazz Workshop coincided with the annual Port Townsend Jazz Festival. He died in Redmond of hepatitis C at the age of 75.

[117] **William George Ramsay** ("Bill" or "Rams"); born January 12, 1929, in Centralia, Washington) is an American jazz saxophonist, band leader and arranger based in Seattle. In 1997, he was inducted into the Seattle Jazz Hall of Fame. Ramsay performs on all the primary saxophones – soprano, alto, tenor, and baritone – as well as clarinet. Currently Ramsay has been a member of the Seattle Repertory Jazz Orchestra since its

founding in 1995. He is the co-leader, with Milt Kleeb of a ten-piece jazz band based in Seattle. Ramsay played Bari sax in the Count Basie Orchestra for two years; Ramsay was hired in April 1984, three weeks before Basie died. Also performed with the bands of Thad Jones, Mel Lewis, Gene Harris, Les Brown, Grover Mitchell, Maynard Ferguson, Buddy Morrow, Benny Goodman Octet and Quincy Jones In the 1980s, Ramsay led his own big band that performed at festivals and clubs in the NW. Ernestine Anderson's recording, *You Made Your Move Too Soon* featured arrangements by Ramsay.

[118] **Floyd Standifer** (1929- 2007) American jazz musician (trumpet , saxophone vocals),and music educator. Studied at the University of Washington. Was part of a circle of musicians including Quincy Jones , Ray Charles , Ernestine Anderson and Buddy Catlett. In 1959, Standifer became a member of the Quincy Jones Big Band, which toured Europe for nine months. After returning to Seattle. He taught at Cornish College of the Arts , the University of Washington, Olympic College, Bremerton, and Northwest School. In addition, he was a member of the *Seattle Repertory Jazz Orchestra*. The city of Seattle honored Standifer in 1996 and 2000 with a *Floyd Standifer Day*.

[119] **George James Catlett** (1933-2014), known professionally as **Buddy Catlett,** was an American jazz bassist. A childhood friend of Quincy Jones, he joined Jones's band for a European tour. He worked with Louis Armstrong, Bill Coleman, Curtis Fuller, Freddie Hubbard, Coleman Hawkins, Junior Mance, Chico Hamilton, Johnny Griffin and Eddie Lockjaw Davis.

[120] **Hadley Caliman** Raised by his mother in rural Idabel, Oklahoma until the age of ten, he moved to Los Angeles with his father and studied at Jefferson High School, the same school as saxophonist Dexter Gordon. One of his teachers was trumpeter Art Farmer. He worked with Earl Hines, Carlos Santana, the Grateful Dead, Joe Henderson, Freddie Hubbard, Jon Hendricks, Earl Anderza, In the late 1960s, he was a member of a jazz-rock fusion group led by Ray Draper.

He recorded his first solo album in 1971 before moving to Cathlamet, Washington with his third wife to raise a family. Throughout the 1990s and 2000s, he led quartet and quintet in Seattle. He was on the music faculty at Cornish College of the Arts until his retirement in 2003 and taught private lessons to area musicians. He moved to Seattle, where he lived with his fourth wife and recorded three solo albums after being diagnosed with liver cancer in 2008. He died in September 2010 at the age of 78.

[121] **Conti Condoli (Secondo (Conte) Candoli)** was born on July 12, 1927, in Mishawaka, Indiana to Italian immigrant parents who had settled in the United States after World War I. Conte's father, a rubber plant factory worker, also played in a band at a local Italian club. It was through his encouragement that Conte and his older brother Pete began to play music at a young age.

Upon a recommendation from Pete, Conte joined Woody Herman's First Herd at the age of 16, filling in during his high school summer vacation. Pete was already part of the band when Conte joined. Conte then joined the band full-time after his high school graduation in 1945. The military draft cut Conte's time with the band short and he served in the United States Army from September 1945 to November 1946. After his discharge, he joined fellow Herman band alum Chubby Jackson's Fifth Dimensional Jazz Group, which toured Scandinavia.

Following his time with Jackson's group, Conte worked with Stan Kenton (1948), Charlie Ventura (1949), rejoined Woody Herman (1949-1950), Charlie Barnet (1951) and Stan Kenton again (1951-1953). Conte led his own group in Chicago in 1954 before moving to California to take session jobs and join Howard Rumsey's Lighthouse All Stars. From the late 1950's to the early 1960's, Conte worked regularly with vibraphone player Terry Gibbs, toured Europe with saxophonist Gerry Mulligan's Concert Jazz Band, and worked again with Woody Herman, Shelly Manne and Stan Kenton. During his career, Conte appeared with Woody Herman at the Monterey Jazz Festival and participated in reunions with Herman in 1976 and 1986. Conte also performed as a member of Supersax from 1972 through the 1980's and beyond, emulating the style of Dizzy Gillespie in the group's re-creations of Charlie Parker's music. Beginning in 1968, Conte made occasional appearances with Johnny Carson's Tonight Show Band led by Doc Severinsen. He became a permanent Tonight Show Band member in 1972 when Carson relocated the show from New York to Burbank, California. Conte retired from the Tonight Show, along with the rest of Severinsen's band, when Carson retired in 1992. After his Tonight Show Band retirement, Conte toured with the Doc Severinsen Band on occasion and was also in constant demand as a teacher at trumpet clinics and jazz festivals, touring extensively throughout the 1990's.

Conte collaborated frequently with his older brother Pete, leading a band with him in Monterey in 1973 and then continuing to perform together throughout the 1980's and 90's. Conte and Pete were inducted into the International Jazz Hall of Fame in 1997.

Before cancer slowed his activities, Conte continued performing at clubs, playing festivals, doing session work, and recorded 18 months prior to his death, completing Candoli Live during this time. His complete discography lists some 770 separate tracks and 123 albums on which he played. Conte Candoli died on December 14, 2001, at Monterey Palms Convalescent Home in Palm Desert, California.

122 **Plas Johnson** (born July 21, 1931) is an American soul-jazz and hard bop tenor saxophonist. In the late 1950s and early 1960s he was a regular member of Henry Mancini's studio orchestra and in 1963 he recorded the Pink Panther theme, written by Mancini with Johnson in mind. Johnson joined the studio band for the Merv Griffin Show in 1970, and also played with a number of jazz and swing bands of the period. He later recorded for the Concord label, worked with the Capp-Pierce Juggernaut, and toured in 1990 with the Gene Harris Superband.[4] He continues to record and perform, particularly at jazz festivals.

123 **Matt Wilson** New York based drummer and Grammy nominee Matt Wilson is one of todays most celebrated jazz artists. He is universally recognized for his musical and melodic drumming style as well as being a gifted composer, bandleader, producer, and teaching artist., Wilson's dedication to jazz has helped establish him as a beloved world ambassador for the music, on and off the bandstand.

Matt performed at the White House as part of an all-star jazz group for a State Dinner concert hosted by President Obama. In 2010, Wilson conducted over 250 outreach programs promoting jazz including an acclaimed Jazz for Young Peoples concert at Jazz at Lincoln Center.

Wilson has appeared on 250 CDs as a sideman and has released 9 as a leader for Palmetto Records as well as co-leading 5 additional releases. Matt was featured on the covers of both Downbeat and JazzTimes magazines in November 2009 and was for 5 consecutive years voted #1 Rising Star Drummer in the Downbeat Critic's Poll. The readers of JazzTimes recently chose him as one of the top 4 drummers in the 2010 Readers Poll. In 2003, he was voted Drummer of the Year by the Jazz Journalists Association.

Matt resides in Baldwin, NY with his wife Felicia, daughter Audrey and triplet sons, Henry, Max and Ethan.

124 **Gary Smulyan** Baritone saxophonist Gary Smulyan was born April 4, 1956, in Bethpage, New York. The gifted multi-instrumentalist started his career by first learning alto during his teenage years on Long Island. Today he is critically acclaimed across-the-board and recognized as the major voice on the baritone saxophone. His playing is marked by an aggressive rhythmic sense, an intelligent and creative harmonic approach — and perhaps most importantly — a strong and incisive wit.

[125] **George Cables George Cables** was born in New York City on November 14, 1944. He was initially taught piano by his mother, then studied at the High School of Performing Arts and later at Mannes College (1963–65). Cables has played with Art Blakey, Sonny Rollins, Dexter Gordon, Art Pepper, Joe Henderson, and many other well-established jazz musicians. His own records include the 1980 Cables' Vision with Freddie Hubbard. From 1983 Cables worked in the project Bebop & Beyond. He left later in the 1980s but returned for two early 1990s albums, before rejoining in 1998.

MUSICIANS AT PARNELL'S, THOMAS OWNERSHIP

Abbey Lincoln	Ernestine Anderson	Jon Hendricks
Anita O'Day	Etta Jones	Julian Priester
Archie Shepp	Freddie Hubbard	Les McCann
Art Lande	Geo Coleman	Kenny Werner
Art Pepper	Geo Shearing	Mark Murphy
Barney Kessel	George Cables	Max Roach
Barry Harris	Hank Crawford	Mingus Dynasty
Bill Mays	Harold Land	Mongo Santamaria
Bill Ramsay	Heath Brothers	Mose Allison
Blossom Dearie	Herb Ellis	Ornette Coleman
Bob Dorough	Houston Person	Red Kelly
Bobby Shew	Howard Roberts	Red Rodney
Carmen McRae	Ira Sullivan	Red Holloway
Charlie Shoemake	Jack McDuff	Red Norvo
Chas MacPherson	Jackie McClean	Phil Woods
Chas Tolliver	Jeff Lorber	Sal Nistico
Chet Baker	Jim Hall	Shelia Jordan
Cleanhead Vincent	Jimmy Smith	Slim Gaillard
Clifford Jordan	JimmyWitherspoon	Sonny Stitt
David Friesen	Joe Farrell	Steve Turre
Diane Schuur	Joe Henderson	Teddy Wilson
Dizzy Gillespie	Joe Williams	Tenor Dynasty
Eddie Harris	John Stowell	Woody Shaw
		Zoot Sims

JAY THOMAS DISCOGRAPHY

CDs as LEADER

Easy Does It	1989	Studio (with Cedar Walton Trio)
Blues for McVouty	1993	Studio (with Cedar Walton Trio)
Rapture	1994	Studio
360 Degrees	1995	Studio
Boy, What a Night	1998	Wilke, Live recording
Live at Tula's	1998 (1999)	Wilke, Live recording
12th and Jackson Blues	1999	Wilke, Live recording
Live at Tula's, II	2001	Wilke, Live recording
The Underdog	2001	Wilke, From previous live
Blues for JW	2002	Wilke, Live recording
Accidentally Yours	2004	Studio (with Geoff Keezer Trio)
Streams of Consciousness	2007	Studio (with John Stowell)
The Jay Bird	2010	Live recording
The Cats	2012	Studio
Art of Jazz	2015	Wilke live recording
Low Down Hoe Down	2015	Studio (with Gary Smulyan)
Bop Live Bop	2018	Wilke live recording
I Always Knew	2018	Studio(with NewNet Orchestra)
The Promise	2018	Studio (with Yuki Hirate)
High Crimes and Misdemeanors	2019	Studio (with Matt Wilson)
UPSIDE	1007/2020	Wilke live recording

SIDEMAN WITH SMALLER GROUPS

Aaron Parks	The Wizard
Alan Jones	Spirits
Barney McClure	Not a Day Goes By

Barney McClure...Tidings of Comfort and Joy
Brian Kinsella... Omen
Brian Owen .... Unme i
Bud Shank Silver Storm   On the Trail **with Conti Condoli, Bill Mays**
Buddy Catlett..Here Comes Buddy
Chris Ameniya...Jazz Coalescence
Christopher Boscole..Natural Instincts
Chuck Metcalf...Elsie Street **with George Cables**
Chuck Metcalf... Help is Coming
Dan Greenblatt ....Stretch
David Friesen... Tomorrow's Dream
Don Lanphere .... The Jazz Alley Tapes
Doug Miller.. Regeneration
Herb Ellis.............................. Roll Call **with Jake Hanna, Mel Ryne**
James Moody .... The Teachers
Jason Bodlovich .... Blues For Dexter **with Ray Brown**
Jessica Williams .... Jessica's Blues
Jessica Williams ....Joy
Jimmy the Scuffer.. d-Bop
Keith Henson ....Our Delight
Michael Powers ....Full Circle
Mike Strickland ....Starry Night
Milo Peterson..Visiting Dignitaries
Norm Bellas...Out of the Norm
Oliver Johnson ....Slide and Joy
Origin Arts Compilation .... The Piano, Seattle's Finest
Phil Sheeran ....It's a Good Thing
Randy Halberstadt.. Open Heart
Seattle Horns... Frankie's Dream
Slim Gaillard, Anytime, Anyplace **with Jay McShann and Buddy Tate**
Sonando .... La Rumba esta Buena
Sonando ....Sonando
Steve Griggs .... Jones for Elvin **with Elvin Jones**
Steve Griggs ....Jones For Elvin, II **with Elvin Jones**
Steve Messick............................... Transmissions from Planet Bass
The Albert...The Albert Band (1970)
The Lubag/Wikan Trio .... Lubag/Wikan Jazz Trio
Tatum Greenblatt ....Tatum
Tony Gable .... Seven Hills
Various Artists.....................................The 15th Anniversary Stash Sampler
Victor Noriega ....Fenceless

Wataru Hamasaki.. Live at Tula's
With Origin Records
https://originarts.com/artists/artist.php?Artist_ID=148

WITH SINGERS

Becca Duran..If You Could See Me Now
Becca Duran...In Love Again
Becca Duran.. Song For Rita
Greta Matassa..Got a Song That I Sing
Jan Stentz .... Forever
Jan Stentz .... Profile
Janis Mann..Lost In His Arms
Katie King..Jazz Figures
Katie King..Mostly Ballads
Kelly Harland..12 Times Romance
Lincoln Briney..5
Valerie Joyce..Reverie

SIDEMAN ... SOLOIST... ... ...BIG BANDS

Seattle Repertory Jazz Orchestra.."SRJO LIVE"
Seattle Repertory Jazz Orchestra..............Benny Carter's Kansas City Suite
Seattle Repertory Jazz Orchestra .... Jimmy Heath, The Endless Search
Seattle Repertory Jazz Orchestra................Sacred Music of Duke Ellington
Ramsay/Kleeb Band.. Red Kelly's Heroes
Milt Kleeb Orchestra.. Something if Nothing Else
Phil Kelly's NW Prevailing Winds ....Convergence Zone
Phil Kelly's NW Prevailing Winds .... Ballet of the Bouncing Beagles
Teo Macero Production .... New Brew
Charlie May All Star Big Band .... Arrangements of Gaylord Jones
Jim Knapp Orchestra.. Things For Now
Jim Knapp Orchestra..On Going Home

JAY WITH JAPANESE BANDS

Continued in the Underground Jazz Orchestra or C.U.G.
Continued in the Underground .... June 1999
Use Us .... April 2002
On the Road .... December 2004
Going On the Road .... December 2004
Takin' the Road... September 2007
Road to a Better Planet .... April 2010
HOPE .... March 2012
Flame of Peace .... October 2013
Twenty-five and Counting.. March 2014
NOW .... March 2016

East-West Alliance Sextet
East West Alliance.. October 2006
Band of Brothers.. March 2012
Flame of Peace .... October 2018

Yoshiro Okazaki & Jay Thomas Quintet
Soul Summit.. October 2013

About the Author

Jay Thomas is a versatile multi-instrumentalist (trumpet, flugelhorn, alto, tenor, soprano, and flutes). His music is eclectic, drawing on all musical situations in his life. His music could be described as lyrical without losing touch with the blues.

A professional musician for over 55 years, Jay has performed with major jazz artists in clubs andfestivals throughout the United States, Canada, Great Britain, and Japan. In Japan, Jay is currently a member of one of the top big bands and joins them 2 to 3 times a year, playing concerts and teaching clinics. Jay can be heard on over 100 CDs, including ten as leader. His distinctive sound is on many commercials and a few film scores. Reviews and articles on Jay have appeared in many jazz magazines and newspapers in the US, Great Britain, and Japan.

Jay's musical voice is a very personable and recognizable sound, characterized by warmth, lyricism, and rhythmic authority.

Jay makes his home in Seattle, WA with his wife, singer, artist, Becca Duran, and their two Chihuahuas, Louie and Lala. At age 71, he still continuous a daily practice schedule on all horns. With teaching and a member or co-leader of several bands, Jay still has much to say musically.